Ms. Duffy,

Even though I spent many hours struggling to complete the many assignments you gave us, you have been one of the best teachers I have ever had. While other students may complain about the amount of homework we had, I am glad you gave us a lot, because I am smarter and a much better student because of it. Thank you for preparing me for high school. I hope this book on Presidents will help you and your future students (if you choose to lend this book out) learn more about a subject you already know so much about. Thanks you again.

Sincerely,

David
Reed

Presidential Inaugurations

PRESIDENTIAL
INAUGURATIONS

PAUL F. BOLLER, JR.

HARCOURT, INC.

NEW YORK ★ SAN DIEGO ★ LONDON

www.harcourt.com

Library of Congress Cataloging-in-Publication Data
Boller, Paul F.
Presidential inaugurations/Paul F. Boller, Jr.–1st ed.
p.   cm.
Includes index.
ISBN 0-15-100546-X
1. Presidents–United States–Inauguration–History. 2. Presidents–United States–History. 3. Washington (D.C.)–Social life and customs. 4. Inauguration Day–History.   I. Title.

F196 .B65 2001
973'.09'9–dc21   00-049893

Text set in Baskerville Book
Designed by Joy Chu

First edition
K J I H G F E D C B A

Printed in the United States of America

for
JIM and KATHY
PETE and MEG

CONTENTS

★ *v i i* ★

PREFACE

Books on presidential inaugurations have been few and far between; the first appeared in 1893 and the sixth and most recent in 1971.[1] Most have taken a chronological approach, presenting brief accounts of each of America's quadrennial celebrations beginning with George Washington's in 1789 and ending with the inauguration just before the book's date of publication. It is time, I think, to take another look at the nation's inaugurations from the point of view of Americans living at the beginning of the twenty-first century, with special emphasis on the great changes that have taken place since Washington's day.

The present book is almost purely topical. Except for including an initial chapter on Washington's first inauguration, a momentous precedent setter, I have concentrated on the major features of the inaugural celebrations since Washington's first: problems with the day chosen for the ceremony; the triumphal trips of our early presidents to Washington for their swearing in; the effects of weather on the inaugural festivities; the state of mind of the presidents on the eve of their induction into office; the morning processions between the White House and the Capitol; the installation of the vice president in office; the president's oath-taking ceremony, with all its religious accompaniments; the inaugural address; and the receptions, afternoon parades, and inaugural balls that complete the inauguration day's activities. Throughout, I have kept in mind Franklin Roosevelt's famous admonition to an economist who was citing statistics—"People aren't cattle, you know!"—and I have tried to emphasize the personal side of the president's inaugural experience.

The first inauguration held in the twenty-first century, January 20, 2001, was enormously different from George Washington's in 1789. It was far more elaborate and took longer, for one thing, and, for another, the issues discussed by the new president in his inaugural address and the festivities surrounding his induction into office would have been unthinkable in Washington's time. Still, the simple oath, prescribed by the U.S. Constitution, was exactly the same for both, and its recital will doubtless continue to be the crucial event of all the inaugurations in the years to come.

My sources have been newspapers, journals, and magazines covering the inaugurations through the years as well as the autobiographies of the presidents and their wives; the memoirs of their relatives, friends, and associates; and the reports of other observers who were there on the great day.

PAUL F. BOLLER, JR.
Texas Christian University
Fort Worth, Texas

*I would like to thank Barbara Lane
for permission to quote from the song,
"The White House Polka," which she wrote
for the 1997 inauguration. And I want to
give my warm thanks to literary agent
Gerry McCauley for all the help and encouragement
he has given me on this and other
presidential projects through the years.*

INTRODUCTION

PRESIDENTIAL INAUGURATIONS ARE ALMOST PURELY EXTRA-constitutional. The U.S. Constitution describes in great detail how presidents are to be chosen by an electoral college, but when it comes to installing a president in office, the Constitution is breathtakingly laconic. Article II, Section 1, simply states: "Before he enter on the Execution of his Office, he shall take the following Oath or Affirmation:—'I do solemnly swear (or affirm) that I will faithfully execute the Office of President of the United States, and will to the best of my Ability, preserve, protect and defend the Constitution of the United States.'"

Who administers the oath? In whose presence? Where does the oath-taking take place? When? The Constitution saith not. So far as the Constitution-makers were concerned, once the electoral college makes its choice, the president-elect takes the thirty-five-word oath (presumably before a properly accredited law officer), and then embarks on the executive duties outlined in the Constitution. If he objects to taking oaths, as some religious people do ("swear not at all"), then he can simply affirm loyalty to the Constitution. It's as easy as that.

But such minimalism was hardly conceivable in 1789 when the electoral college unanimously voted to make George Washington the new nation's first president. The Founding Fathers certainly didn't want a British-style coronation, with its pomp, pageantry, and religious rites, but they didn't want to be casual about their first president's inauguration, either. They were convinced that the launching of their experiment in self-government was a historic event, and they wanted the world to know they took it seriously.

They were eager to honor Washington, too, and to show their respect, esteem, and affection for him as he took his oath. After all, he was the great Citizen Soldier: the man who had led his people to victory in the War for Independence, showed his respect for civilian authority throughout the war, presided over the Constitutional Convention afterward, and then, spurred by his deep sense of public duty, had reluctantly abandoned his private life at Mount Vernon to serve his country again as president. A few senators in the first Congress wanted to confer on him what the great comedian W. C. Fields would later call "a euphonious appellation"—"His Excellency," "His Serene Highness," "His Elective Highness," "His Highness, the President of the United States and Protector of the Rights of the Same"—but fortunately they eventually came to their senses and settled for addressing him simply as "Mr. President."[1]

Soon after the first Congress convened in the temporary capital in New York in early April 1789, the newly installed members appointed a committee to plan the inauguration; they picked the time and place to induct Washington into office, selected an official to administer the oath, and made other arrangements they deemed desirable.

But when April 30, the very morning of the inauguration arrived, the lawmakers weren't exactly sure how to behave when Washington made his appearance in the Senate to take his oath and deliver his address. Should they stand or sit during the ceremony? The Senate debated the question. Richard Henry Lee told his colleagues that the House of Lords sat during the king's addresses, while the House of Commons remained standing; but when Ralph Izard pointed out that the Commons stood because there were no seats for them in the House of Lords, Charles Carroll suggested that it didn't matter to the United States how things were done in Britain.

At this juncture, members of the lower house arrived for the inaugural ceremony and began scrambling for seats in the Senate chamber. When the "confusion" (as one senator called it) ended, three senators went out to meet President-elect Washington and escort him to the joint session of the two houses. In the end, everyone remained standing during Washington's inaugural address. No one planned it that way; it just seemed the right thing to do at the time.[2]

The vice presidential oath, specified by a congressional statute passed on June 6, 1789, was the same as that taken by members of Congress and executive officers of the United

States, and turned out to be longer than the presidential oath. The vice president pledged that he would "support and defend the Constitution of the United States against all enemies, foreign and domestic; that I will bear true faith and allegiance to the same; that I take this obligation freely, without any mental reservation or purpose of evasion, and that I will well and faithfully discharge the duties of the office on which I am about to enter." From the beginning, members of Congress were wordier than the framers of the Constitution.

Washington's first inauguration set precedents for the future: cannon salutes and bell ringing on inauguration morning; the ceremonial trip of the president-elect to Congress for installation in office; the use of a Bible for the swearing in and the addition of the words "So help me God" to the constitutional oath; the delivery of an inaugural address; and a fireworks display on the night of the inauguration.

After Washington, additional inaugural activities developed, and although some presidents insisted on what Thomas Jefferson called "Republican simplicity," the trend over the next two centuries was toward increasingly elaborate celebrations.

By the end of the twentieth century, the supplements to the Constitution's meager instructions—stately processions to the Capitol on inauguration morning, lengthy afternoon parades, multifaith prayers at the oath taking, poetry readings, musical presentations, multiple inaugural balls, starstudded preinaugural galas and variety shows—had become so lavish that Washington's inauguration came to seem parsimonious by comparison.

From time to time strict constructionists complained about the extravagance, and a few presidents here and there tried, without much success, to return to Jeffersonian austerity. Most Americans, though, appeared to be loose constructionists when it came to inducting presidents into office. "Furbelows and frosting, if you please," exclaimed a *New York Times* writer on the occasion of Lyndon B. Johnson's inauguration in 1965. "Yet the inauguration is and ought to be more than a simple swearing in, equally befitting the President of the United States or some deputy water commisioner."[3]

In 1901, when critics complained about the extravagance of William McKinley's second inauguration, Earl W. Mayo, writing for *Harper's Weekly,* leaped to the defense. "It is natural enough," he declared, "that as the United States has expanded and grown greater and stronger, as population and wealth have increased, and as the facilities for travel have improved, the ceremonial side of the inauguration has grown more elaborate. But it is reassuring to those who fear that the example of monarchical governments in the matter of form and ceremonial may undermine the principles on which the founders of our government intended it to be carried out that in its essentials the inaugural has not changed from its first observance to the present time."

Mayo acknowledged that McKinley was cheered on his way to the Capitol by more people than had attended any previous inauguration, but at the same time, he pointed out, "the administering of the oath of office was as simple and solemn" as it had been for Washington and Jefferson. The "power conveyed into his hands," moreover, was constitutionally "no whit greater than that which they enjoyed." And while there were thousands in the inaugural parade in 1901, where once there had been only hundreds, there was "no element of adulation of the man in the ceremony, but only a desire to do high honor to the office which was conferred upon him as the first citizen of the republic."[4]

A PRESIDENTIAL inauguration, like the presidential campaign preceding it, is both serious and silly. It is important in the nation's life as a public demonstration of the peaceful transfer of power from one president to another, regardless of political views and party affiliations, and as an occasion to celebrate the basic values that unite the American people—despite differences in race, class, ethnic background, and politics—and continue to shape the nation's life. But a presidential inauguration is a carnival, circus, pageant, and big show, as well as an occasion for solemnity, and, compared to a royal coronation, it is, as someone once observed, "kitsch."[5] But Americans loved the kitsch. And in the late twentieth century, as the pre-inaugural activities—parties, receptions, concerts, and star-studded variety shows—came to be extensive, people began flocking to Washington to celebrate inauguration week as well as inauguration day.

Some observers deplored the funmaking. In 1961, the *New Republic*'s anonymous columnist, T.R.B., wrote despondently about the forthcoming inauguration of John F. Kennedy. "Our culture has a genius for demeaning greatness," he lamented. "The inauguration of a new President should be a moment of solemnity and of consecration—we have produced a ceremony that is incongruous, tawdry, ignoble. Bands and balls and silly floats—they have tried to make a Mardi Gras out of it!" He conceded that the "vulgarity" didn't spoil the "mighty" oath-taking ceremony completely, but he deplored the showy accoutrements accompanying it. But somewhat to his own surprise, he returned from the JFK inauguration exhilarated by the folderol as well as by the fanfare. "It was an inaugural we'll never forget," he exclaimed in his next column. He couldn't help repeating himself. "The inaugural was fun. We shall never forget it."[6]

Presidential Inaugurations

1789—The First Inauguration

George Washington's inauguration as first president of the United States on April 30, 1789, was a momentous event. In a world ruled largely by kings, queens, czars, emperors, shoguns, and sultans, the American people were trying something different: a representative government based on the freely given consent of the governed. There was no certainty of success. Many, perhaps most, Europeans looked skeptically upon the American experiment in self-government. America's bête noire—King George III—was convinced that Washington would become a dictator after the American Revolution and that the American people would soon long for a return to royal rule. When he learned that the hero of the American Revolution planned to resign his commission as commander of the Continental Army, he was astonished. "If he does that, sir," the king exclaimed, "he will be the greatest man in the world!"[1] And so it happened: Washington did resign his commission at the end of the war and many Americans came to regard him as the greatest man in the world. There was little hankering for monarchy in the newly independent nation.

Still, there were some Americans—intelligent ones at that—who had serious doubts about the Constitution drawn up by the Founding Fathers in 1787. Alexander Hamilton called it a "frail fabric," Patrick Henry worried about the power entrusted to the new Federal Government, and even the usually hopeful Benjamin Franklin feared that the republican system provided for by the Constitution might end in despotism. But Franklin was sure of one thing: "the first man put at the helm"—he was, of course, thinking of Washington—"will be a good one." Like everyone else, Franklin regarded the former Revolutionary commander, with his enormous prestige, as indispensable for getting the new framework of government off to a good start. Thomas Jefferson felt the same way. Washington, he said, was "the only man in the United States who possessed the confidence of the whole."[2]

Washington himself was painfully aware of what he was getting into when he agreed to serve as the new nation's first chief executive. The problems were enormous: the centripetal tug of provincial loyalties; the huge Revolutionary debt; foreign hostility; the task of making viable specificities out of constitutional generalities. Before leaving Mount Vernon for New York, the temporary capital of the new government, on April 16, Washington wrote his old Revolutionary friend, General Henry Knox, to tell him "in confidence... that my movements to the chair of government will be accompanied by feelings not unlike those of a culprit who is going to the place of execution; so unwilling am I, in the evening of a life nearly consumed in public cares, to quit a peaceful abode for an ocean of difficulties, without that competency of political skills, abilities and inclination which is necessary to manage the helm."[3] Washington had turned fifty-seven in February and would have preferred spending the rest of his life at Mount Vernon.

Despite his misgivings about returning to public life, Washington made conscientious preparations for his inauguration in New York. Soon after the electoral college voted unanimously to make him the nation's first chief executive, he wrote a seventy-three-page draft of an inaugural address, with the help of David Humphreys, his friend and former aide-de-camp during the Revolutionary War, who dabbled in poetry. But he was not satisfied with his handiwork. The speech was too lengthy, he realized, and it was overloaded with details about the difficulties Americans had encountered during the War for Independence, about the economic problems facing the country after the war, and about the various ways in which the new Constitution might put the young nation on the yellow-brick road to peace and prosperity.

Far worse, though, than the tiresome historical details was the clumsy personal note that Washington injected into his first try at an inaugural address. For one thing, he insisted he had planned to return to private life after the Revolution and that it was his strong sense of public duty, not personal ambition, that had drawn him back into public life. For another, he went out of his way to assure the American people that since he had no children there was simply no way he could transform the presidency into a hereditary monarchy, even if he wanted to. It "will be recollected," he explained, "that the Divine providence hath not seen fit that my blood should be transmitted or my name perpetuated by the endearing though sometimes seducing, channel of personal offspring. I have no child for whom I could wish to make provision—no family to build in greatness upon my country's ruins."[4]

Filled with doubts about the manuscript, Washington sent it to his friend James Madison for comments. Madison, who had just been elected to the lower house of the first Congress meeting under the new Constitution, looked it over, suggested another try at an inaugural address, and went on to draft a new speech himself, utilizing some of the material appearing in the Washington-Humphreys manuscript. Washington liked what Madison had written and decided to use it as the basis for his inaugural instead of the speech he and Humphreys had drafted. He went over it carefully, editing and revising and adding material of his own, and when he finished, the speech contained all the ideas he wanted to convey to the American people at the outset of his administration: his reluctance to become president, his ardent love for his country, the dependence of the young republic on the "Almighty Being who rules the universe," and his awareness of the significance of the venture in liberty and self-government that the American people were launching in April 1789. The new address fortunately omitted the first draft's awkward reference to his childlessness.

March 4 was the day picked for the inauguration by the Continental Congress before it went out of existence, partly, according to legend, because Franklin calculated there were fewer Sundays occurring on that date in the years to come. Unfortunately, there weren't enough members of the new Congress assembled in New York by then to form a quorum, so the ceremony was postponed until April 30. This gave Washington plenty of time to make preparations for moving from Mount Vernon to New York City for the inauguration. It was too late, though, to change the date on the inaugural souvenirs. They turned up in New York on inauguration day inscribed with the original date, March 4.

Washington's journey from Mount Vernon to New York to take his oath as the first president of the United States unexpectedly turned into an important event in itself. After borrowing money for travel expenses, Washington left his home on April 18, accompanied by David Humphreys, his aide, and Tobias Lear, his secretary, as well as by Charles Thomson, the secretary of Congress (who went to Virginia to notify Washington of his election as president). The president-elect and his entourage reached New York on April 23, after passing through Maryland, Delaware, Pennsylvania, and New Jersey on a 280-mile trip. Everywhere Washington went—Alexandria, New Brunswick, Baltimore, Philadelphia, Trenton—he was wined, dined, toasted, acclaimed, saluted, lauded, honored, eulogized, and even serenaded. Reports of his journey sparkled with extravagant appellations: "the great and illustrious Citizen of America"; "the Most Illustrious President of the United States"; "Fabius"; "his Excellency the President General"; "The Father of the People"; "our beloved Washington"; "his Excellency the President."[5] Time and again, processions of local militiamen, city and state officials, and ordinary citizens took form outside towns and cities to escort him to his lodgings for the night. One such procession was deemed "greater than any triumphant Rome ever beheld."[6]

Washington's request, at the outset, for "a quiet entry" into New York, "devoid of ceremony," was jubilantly ignored.[7] Reaching Baltimore, "This great man," the *Pennsylvania Packet* reported, "was met some miles from Town, by a large body of respectable citizens on horseback; and conducted, under a discharge of cannon, to Mr. Grant's tavern through crowds of admiring spectators."[8] There he was entertained at supper and presented with a flowery congratulatory address, to which he graciously responded. Having retired a little after ten o'clock, he was up early the next morning, boarded his carriage after breakfast, "under discharge of cannon, and attended, as he left, by a body of citizens on horseback." At Philadelphia, he was welcomed by the highest officials of both the city and the state and rode into town on horseback at the head of an honorary procession. "The number of spectators who filled the doors, windows, and streets, which he passed," according to the *Pennsylvania Gazette,* "was greater than on any occasion we ever remember.... The joy of the whole city upon this august spectacle cannot easily be described. Every countenance seemed to say, Long, long live George Washington, THE FATHER OF THE PEOPLE!"[9]

When Washington crossed the Schuylkill River, the *Gazette* reported, he found the bridge contained "magnificent arches" at each end, "composed of laurel, emblematic of the ancient triumphal arches used by the Romans, and on each side of the bridge a laurel shrubbery, which seemed to challenge even Nature herself for simplicity, ease, and elegance. And as our beloved WASHINGTON passed the bridge, a lad, beautifully ornamented with sprigs of laurel, assisted by certain machinery, let drop, above the Hero's head, unperceived by him, a civic crown of laurel."

The next day, as Washington got ready to leave, it started raining, and the Philadelphians offered him a carriage, but he turned them down, saying he would ride horseback in the open just as the men provided as his escort were doing. Exclaimed one observer: "How different is power when derived from its own just source, viz., the PEOPLE, from that which is derived from conquest or hereditary succession! The first magistrates of the nations of Europe assume the titles of gods and treat their subjects like an inferior race of animals. Our beloved magistrate delights to show, upon all occasions, that he is a man and, instead of assuming the pomp of master, acts as if he considered himself the FATHER—the FRIEND—and the SERVANT of the PEOPLE!"[10] This was a constant theme of the preinaugural celebrations: you can treat Washington royally because he has no kingly ambitions.

Trenton was Washington's next stop, and the people there centered their reception on his famous victory in the area during the American Revolution. Lining the Jersey bank of the Delaware River to celebrate his arrival were a troop of horses commanded by a captain, a company of infantry in uniform, and a large number of people from Trenton and neighboring towns. "As soon as he set foot on shore," reported the *Pennsylvania Packet,* "he was welcomed with three huzzas, which made the shores re-echo the chearful [*sic*] sounds." The militiamen and citizens formed an escort for Washington, and when they reached the bridge over the Assunpink Creek, there was a triumphal arch awaiting him, about twenty feet high, supported by thirteen columns covered with masses of evergreen and wreaths of laurel. In front of the arch, in large gilt letters, appeared the words: THE DEFENDER OF THE MOTHERS WILL ALSO BE THE PROTECTOR OF THE DAUGHTERS. Above the inscription was a dome of artificial flowers and evergreens encircling the date of the Battle of Trenton, inscribed in large gilt letters. On top of the dome was a huge sunflower, which, "always pointing to the sun, was designed to express this sentiment or motto— *'To you alone'*—as emblematic of the affections and hopes of the PEOPLE being directed to him, in the united suffrage of the millions of America." Standing by the arch was a crowd of women with their daughters, "thus to thank their Defender and Protector." As Washington passed under the arch, some of the young women, dressed in white and decked with wreaths and holding baskets of flowers, solemnly sang a sonata for the president-elect, composed by Major Richard Howell, who later became governor of New Jersey, and set to music by one of his associates:

> *WELCOME, mighty Chief! once more,*
> *Welcome to this grateful shore:*
> *Now no mercenary foe*
> *Aims again the fatal blow—*
> *Aims at thee the fatal blow,*
> *Virgins fair, and Matrons grave,*

Those thy conquering arms did save,
Build for thee triumphal bowers
Strew, ye fair, his way with flowers,
Strew your Hero's way with flowers.

As they sang, the young women scattered flowers in front of Washington, and when they finished, he thanked them politely, and was escorted to his lodgings for the night.[11]

At Elizabeth Town, Washington boarded a forty-seven-foot barge, manned by thirteen pilots, for the last stage of his journey, fifteen miles across the bay to New York. Accompanying him were members of a joint congressional reception committee and a number of New York state and city officials. As the barge got under way, it was joined by scores of boats carrying hundreds of Washington's admirers, and when the flotilla neared Bedloe's Island, a large sloop came alongside and about twenty men and women on it sang an ode to Washington, composed in his honor, to the tune (ironically) of "God Save the King." When the singers finished their ode, "a school of porpoises appeared in the midst of the little fleet," according to one report, "bobbing up and down as though inquiring as to the reason there was so much commotion and rejoicing."[12]

Washington's reception in New York City was, of course, lavish. A thirteen-gun salute was fired as his barge passed the Battery and it was repeated when he landed at Murray's Wharf, on the East River at the foot of Wall Street, and walked up the crimson-carpeted steps to the street. New York governor George Clinton was there with many of his associates to greet the president-elect and escort him to Franklin House, the fine mansion on Cherry Street that was to be the executive mansion during the time that New York City was the temporary capital of the new nation. Soon after Washington met Clinton, an army officer stepped up, saluted, and announced that he commanded the guard assigned to the president-elect and that he awaited orders. "As to the present arrangement," said Washington politely, "I shall proceed as is directed, but after this is over, I hope you will give yourself no further trouble, as the affection of my fellow-citizens is all the guard I want."[13]

That evening, it was reported, "the city was elegantly illuminated. The joy and satisfaction universally expressed on the safe arrival of this illustrious Personage clearly evince, that patriotism and magnanimity are still held in respect and veneration among our citizens."[14] The following day, members of the House and Senate called to congratulate Washington on his safe arrival in New York, and the day after that the Chamber of Commerce presented him with a grandiloquent welcoming address to which he responded briefly but graciously. In the days remaining before his inauguration, Washington made conscientious efforts to get to know some of the members of Congress with whom he would be working when he became president. One of his calls was on Pennsylvania's democratic-minded senator, William Maclay. Wrote Maclay in his diary afterward: "the greatest man in the world paid me a visit."[15] Like his colleagues, he had great expectations.

VICE president–elect John Adams had reached New York on April 20, a few days before Washington. He had received a nice send-off when he left Boston and experienced some of the same kind of adulation that Washington did when he passed through the towns and villages of New England en route to the capital. But his induction into office was without ceremony. The day after his arrival in New York, Adams was ushered into the Senate chamber and greeted by New Hampshire senator John Langdon, president pro tem of the Senate. "Sir," announced Langdon, "I have it in charge from the Senate to introduce you to the chair of this house; and also to congratulate you on your appointment to the office of Vice President of the United States of America." Adams then took the chair of the presiding officer and made a little speech—which Senator Maclay found tiresome—promising to do his best. But Adams was not sworn in until the following June, after Congress passed a bill that contained an oath of office for vice presidents, members of Congress, and executive officers of the government to take.[16]

WHEN inauguration day, April 30, arrived, New York was crowded with people—perhaps ten thousand—ready to celebrate the great event. At sunrise, thirteen guns sounded at the southern end of Manhattan, and shortly afterward Washington began preparing for the day's festivities. He had his hair powdered, donned a brown suit (made in America) with buttons decorated with spread-winged eagles, and put on white silk stockings and shoes with silver buckles. He also got out his dress sword. By the time he had eaten breakfast, church bells were ringing and people were gathering in front of his house.

A few minutes after noon, a congressional delegation arrived at Franklin House to escort the president-elect to

Federal Hall (formerly the city hall), the meeting place set aside for Congress at the intersection of Wall and Broad Streets. Washington greeted the delegates with a bow, shook hands with them, and then boarded an elegant coach, drawn by four handsome horses, and, at 12:30, started off amid cheering crowds of people. When he reached Federal Hall, he got out of the carriage, walked through the ranks of militiamen lined up outside, entered the building, and was escorted to the Senate chamber, where the senators, representatives, foreign diplomats, and an array of government officials awaited him. Chancellor Robert R. Livingston, presiding judge of New York State's highest court, was also on hand. Since Congress had not yet provided for legislation creating the Supreme Court contemplated by the Constitution, the inaugural planners had picked Livingston to induct Washington into office.

When Washington appeared in the Senate chamber, Vice President Adams gave him a formal welcome and then announced: "Sir, the Senate and the House of Representatives are ready to attend you to take the oath required by the Constitution. It will be administered by the Chancellor of the State of New York." "I am ready to proceed," responded Washington. Adams bowed, and then led him out to a small half-enclosed portico overlooking Broad and Wall Streets, in the front of which was a small table, draped in red, containing a large Bible resting on a crimson velvet cushion. The Bible was a last-minute acquisition. When the congressional committee arranging the inauguration (four senators and four representatives) decided to include a Bible in the ceremony that morning, they couldn't find one in Federal Hall, and had to send a messenger posthaste to the nearest Masonic lodge—St. John's—to borrow one. By the time Washington was ready to take his oath, the streets in front of Federal Hall were so crowded with spectators, according to one observer, that "one might literally walk on the heads of the people." The windows and rooftops of all the adjoining buildings were also packed with spectators.[17]

When Washington appeared on the portico, a great shout went up from the crowd below, and he put his hand on his heart and bowed several times before taking his seat in the armchair placed next to the table with the Bible on it. He waited until the applause died down, then arose, moved to the railing where the people below could see him, and, as Chancellor Livingston came forward, he put his hand on the Bible held for him by the secretary of the Senate and prepared to take his oath of office.

"Do you solemnly swear," intoned Livingston, "that you will faithfully execute the office of President of the United States and will, to the best of your ability, preserve, protect, and defend the Constitution of the United States?"

"I solemnly swear," responded Washington, repeating the presidential oath prescribed in the Constitution. When he finished, he added words of his own, "So help me God," and, in another improvisation, bent forward to kiss the Bible.

"It is done," announced Livingston, and, turning to the crowd below, he shouted: "Long live George Washington, President of the United States!" His words were later criticized as too monarchistic ("Long live the king!") to be suitable for the American republic, and these words were never uttered again at an inauguration, but at the time they produced no objections. The crowd took up the cry, in fact, as the flag went up on the cupola of Federal Hall, thirteen guns sounded on the Battery, and church bells began tolling.

Washington bowed several times to acknowledge the ovation and then returned to the Senate chamber, took his seat on the dais, and waited for people to resume their places. A little later, when he rose to read his inaugural address, everybody in the Senate chamber got up, too, and remained standing until he came to the end of the address.[18]

Washington began his address on a personal note. He confessed to feelings of anxiety upon being notified of his choice as president by the electoral college, and acknowledged that he had hoped for a quiet life in retirement at Mount Vernon after the Revolution. But "I was summoned by my country," he went on, "whose voice I can never hear but with veneration and love," and, while conscious of his lack of experience in "the duties of civil administration," he was deeply moved by "this transcendent proof of the confidence of my fellow-citizens" in his ability to serve as the nation's first chief magistrate.

He then turned religious. A member of the Episcopal Church, he went on to ground America's destiny in a providential ordering of events. It would be "peculiarly improper," he said, "to omit . . . my fervent supplications to that Almighty Being who rules over the universe, who presides in the councils of nations, and whose providential aids can supply every human defect, that His benediction may consecrate to the liberties and happiness of the people of the United States a Government instituted by themselves for these essential purposes." No people, he went on to say, were more bound to "acknowledge and adore the Invisible Hand which conducts the affairs of men" than Americans, for every step of the way toward national independence had been "distinguished by some token of providential agency." He called for "pious gratitude" for the blessings that "the Great Author of every public and private good" had bestowed on the American people, and "an humble anticipation of the future blessings which the past seem to presage."

When it came to his responsibilities as president under the new Constitution, Washington decided not to recommend specific measures to Congress on this occasion, but, instead, to call attention to "the talents, the rectitude, and the patriotism" characterizing members of the House and Senate, and to urge them to put aside local prejudices and party animosities and lay "the foundation of our national policy" in "the pure and immutable principles of private morality." There was, Washington insisted, "an indissoluble union between virtue and happiness; between duty and advantage; between the genuine maxims of an honest and magnanimous policy and the solid rewards of public prosperity and felicity." The "propitious smiles of Heaven," he said, "can never be expected on a nation that disregards the eternal rules of order and right which Heaven itself has ordained."

Then came the most quoted passage in the inaugural: "the preservation of the sacred fire of liberty and the destiny of the republican model of government are justly considered, perhaps, as *deeply,* as *finally,* staked on the experiment intrusted to the hands of the American people."

The new president went on to say something about the amendments to the Constitution then being considered, and though not referring directly to what came to be called the "Bill of Rights," he urged members of Congress to preserve "a reverence for the characteristic rights of freemen and a regard for the public harmony" in any action they might take.

Toward the end of his address, Washington turned personal again, announcing his intention of declining "every pecuniary compensation" and accepting remuneration only for expenses in his service as chief magistrate. He turned religious again, too, in the last part of his address. "I shall take my present leave," he said, "but not without resorting once more to the benign Parent of the Human Race in humble supplication that, since He has been pleased to favor the American people with opportunities for deliberating in perfect tranquillity, and dispositions for deciding with unparalleled unanimity on a form of government for the security of their union and the advancement of their happiness, so His divine blessing may be equally *conspicuous* in the enlarged views, the temperate consultations, and the wise measures on which the success of this Government must depend."[19]

Washington's audience in Federal Hall was deeply moved, some people to tears, by his performance that day. It was "a very touching scene, and quite of the solemn kind," wrote Massachusetts senator Fisher Ames, who was himself to become known for his oratory. "His aspect grave, almost to sadness; his modesty, actually shaking; his voice, deep, a little tremulous, and so low as to call for close attention; added to the series of objects presented to the mind, and overwhelming it, produced emotions of the most affecting kind upon the members. I, Pilgarlic, sat entranced."

New Hampshire senator John Langdon was similarly impressed. "His Installation was Truly Solemn and Magnificent," he told a friend later. "He Delivered his Speech to

Both Houses with a Majesty, Dignity and propriety that almost exceeded himself. All his movements are Truly Natural and he appears in the Cabinet, as in the Field, a
Washington."[20]

Like Langdon, Senator Maclay was impressed by Washington's high seriousness, but he was also surprised and
a bit dismayed by his nervousness. "This great man," he
wrote in his diary, "was agitated and embarrassed more
than ever he was by the leveled cannon or pointed musket.
He trembled, and several times could scarce make out to
read." While he was speaking, Maclay added, Washington
moved the manuscript of his address awkwardly from one
hand to the other, and "when he came to the words *all the
world,* he made a flourish with his right hand, which left a
rather ungainly impression." Maclay thought that Washington tried too hard to read the manuscript effectively. "I sincerely, for my part," he reflected, "wished all set ceremony
in the hands of dancing-masters, and that this first of men
had read off his address in the plainest manner, without
ever taking his eyes from the paper, for I felt hurt that he
was not the first in everything."[21]

But most people were deeply impressed by the twenty-
minute address. "It seemed to me," Senator Ames told a
friend, "an allegory in which virtue was personified, and addressing those whom she would make her votaries. Her
power over the heart was never greater, and the illustration
of her doctrine by her own example, was never more perfect." To another acquaintance he reiterated this allegorical
vision of Washington as virtue personified, and then added:
"The crowd was great, but not a stupid one—each express-
ing as much admiration and joy as a painter would have on

his canvas. The modesty, benevolence, and dignity of the President cannot be described."[22]

Washington's address set the style for his successors. Subsequent inaugural addresses generally included an expression of gratitude for being elevated to high office, an avowal of modesty about his abilities, a promise to do the best he could by his country, and appeals to the Almighty for help in his and the nation's endeavors. The emphasis on religion was especially notable, since Washington, like Jefferson, was basically deistic, rather than evangelical, in his outlook. After 1789, all the inaugural addresses, including those of presidents who were not church members, contained references to Almighty God (although none of them to Jesus), ranging from the deeply heartfelt to the merely conventional. Until Abraham Lincoln's second inaugural address in 1865, however, no inaugural address devoted so much space to religion as Washington's (though Lincoln's views were far more somber). Like Jefferson, Washington certainly favored separation of church and state, for the Constitution he helped devise was a purely secular document, but at the same time, there is no question that he considered religion of vital importance to the health of the new nation.

When the inaugural ceremony ended, Washington was scheduled to attend services at St. Paul's Chapel, performed by Samuel Provoost, Episcopal bishop of New York, recently chosen as chaplain of the Senate. The new president couldn't ride there, however, because his carriage had been parked some distance from Federal Hall during the ceremony, and the streets were too crowded to get it back in time for the service. When Washington suggested walking, he got a lukewarm response, for the chapel was seven blocks away, but he started off anyway, with a large number of Congressmen and other public officials tagging along after him. Some of them didn't get there until the service was over and Washington was boarding his carriage (now on hand for his use) to return to his lodgings. During the service, Senator Ames sat in the same pew with Washington and was struck by his appearance. "Time has made havoc upon his face," he noted. "That, and many other circumstances not to be reasoned about, conspire to keep up the awe which I brought with me."[23]

That night Washington dined with some of his friends at Franklin House, and then joined Chancellor Livingston in the latter's home to watch the fireworks. "The Spanish ambassador's house was illuminated" that evening, Colonel John May wrote his wife, "so as to represent Wisdom, Justice, Fortitude, Sun, Moon, Stars and Spanish Arms, etc. The French Ambassador also illuminated handsomely. Federal Hall presented a fine appearance. The likeness of our Hero, illuminated, was presented in a window of a house at a little distance (in Broad Street). The best likeness I have yet seen of him, so much like him that one could hardly distinguish it from life, excepting for the situation, over a beer house, a place he never frequents. The best of all was a picture of the United States; the President a full length the central figure; on his right, Justice; over his head, Fortitude; on his left, Wisdom; high over his head were two female figures in gay colors and supporting on their arms the American eagle. The fireworks were brilliant and greeted with tremendous applause." Around ten that evening Washington returned home on foot, with "the throng of people being so great as not to permit a carriage."[24]

There was no inaugural ball that night, but inaugural souvenirs continued to be hawked in stores and on the streets after the inaugural ceremonies: people bought buttons, watch fobs, plates, medals, brooches, and tankards with Washington's face on them, along with the words, THE GREATEST MAN ON EARTH. A week after the inauguration, Comte de Moustier, the French minister, threw a grand ball at which the new president, who liked to dance, took to the floor for the minuet and the cotillion with the wives of some of his associates, charming the guests with his "impressive dignity and courtliness."[25] Martha Washington, unable to get away from Mount Vernon in time for the inauguration, arrived in New York six weeks later, and soon joined her husband in setting precedents for their successors in the President's House. "I greatly fear," sighed Washington, when the inaugural festivities were over, "that my countrymen will expect too much from me."[26]

JAMES Madison, who had helped out with the inaugural address, performed another inaugural service for the president after the oath-taking ceremony on April 30. He drafted the response of the House of Representatives to Washington's speech, and then, at Washington's request, helped draft the president's response to the House's statement. In the Senate, Vice President Adams suggested a senatorial response to the president's "most gracious speech" on April 30, but Senator Maclay was on his feet at once. The words, "most gracious speech," he protested, were precisely the words Parliament used in responding to the British king's speeches, and were certainly not acceptable in a republic like the United States. He reminded Adams that "we lately had a hard struggle for our liberty against kingly authority," and that to use the words Adams proposed would "give offense" to most Americans. "I consider them improper," he exclaimed. "I therefore move that they be struck out." The Senate voted to delete them, without muting its respect and admiration for the new president in its message. In drafting his reply to the Senate, Washington again turned to Madison for assistance.[27]

The nation's first inauguration gave the *Maryland Gazette*–and most Americans–enormous pleasure. "Every honest man," wrote the editors, "must feel a singular felicity in contemplating this day–good government, the best of blessings, now commences under favorable auspices. We beg leave to congratulate our readers on the great event."[28] A little later the French minister to the new nation reported to Paris that "never has sovereign reigned more completely in the hearts of his subjects than did Washington in those of his fellow-citizens.... He has the soul, looks, and figure of a hero united in him."[28]

PICKING THE DAY

AMERICA'S FIRST INAUGURATION TOOK place on the wrong day. But March 4 was the date picked by the last Congress under the Articles of Confederation as the young nation's inauguration day, and March 4 it would be for many years. In later years there were people who regretted that April 30, the date of Washington's first inauguration, didn't become permanent; the weather was more likely to be salubrious in late April than in early March.

In 1792, Congress passed legislation making March 4 official; and the Twelfth Amendment (ratified in 1804) put March 4 into the Constitution. And so it remained until 1933, when the Twentieth Amendment, ratified that year, moved inauguration day from March 4 to January 20.

Weather had nothing to do with the shift; frigid temperatures hit Washington in January as well as in March. The change was made to shorten the interval between the election of the president and his installation in office. In any case, in 1793, Washington dutifully took his second oath on March 4, and so did most of his successors until 1937, when Franklin D. Roosevelt, on the occasion of his second inauguration, became the first president to be sworn in on January 20.

In 1821 came a bit of a crisis. For the first time, March 4 fell on a Sunday, and James Monroe, ready to be inaugurated for a second term, doubted the propriety of scheduling the ceremony for his second inauguration on the Sabbath Day. After consulting Chief Justice John Marshall and the other Supreme Court justices, he decided to postpone his swearing in until the following day. But this opened up a problem. Monroe's first term as president officially ended at noon on Sunday, the fourth, and postponing the oath-taking meant that the country, strictly speaking, was without a president until he took his oath on Monday, the fifth. There was "a sort of interregnum," as Secretary of State John Quincy Adams put it in his diary, "during which there was no person qualified to act as President."[1]

According to the law passed by Congress in 1792, if the offices of president and vice president became vacant, the responsibilities of the chief executive passed to the president pro tempore of the Senate, and then, if that office was vacant, to the Speaker of the House. In 1821, the president of the Senate happened to be South Carolina's John Gaillard, and there were those who believed that during the "interregnum" Gaillard was actually president for a day. But

Adams didn't look at it that way. He called the "interregnum" an "event of no importance," though he admitted it "might be far otherwise under supposable circumstances." Most people shared his equanimity at changing the inaugural date to March 5. Sabbatarianism—keeping the Sabbath day holy—was powerful in those days, and no one argued for holding the inaugural ceremony on Sunday.[2]

The Sabbatarianism continued. In 1849, when March 4 fell on a Sunday again, the planners of Zachary Taylor's inauguration postponed the swearing in until Monday. But this led Missouri senator David R. Atchison, president pro tempore of the Senate, to claim later on that he had been "President for a Single Day"—from noon, March 4, when James K. Polk's term expired, until noon, March 5, when Taylor took his oath of office. A few people took Atchison seriously, but he really didn't have a case. The Thirtieth Congress, in which he had been chosen president pro tem of the Senate, came to a close on Saturday, March 3, and this meant that he was actually out of office himself until he was qualified as a member of the Thirty-first Congress (to which he had been reelected in 1848) at its first session on Monday, March 5. Was the United States, then, without a president for a day, as in 1821? Strictly speaking it was. But there seems no reason to doubt that in 1849, as in 1821, if a crisis had developed requiring prompt action, Taylor would have been quickly sworn in as president in a private ceremony so that he could have acted at once. And this was exactly what happened in 1877.

In 1877, when March 4 fell on a Sunday again, there was, for the first time, a real crisis in Washington. The returns from the election of 1876 (Rutherford B. Hayes vs.

Samuel J. Tilden) had been bitterly contested, and, to settle the dispute, Congress set up an electoral commission shortly after the election to look into the matter. After several weeks of investigation, the commission (made up of eight Republicans and seven Democrats) finally announced its choice on March 2: Hayes over Tilden by a vote of eight to seven. There was an inevitable cry of outrage among the Democrats at the partisan decision, and even some talk of blocking Hayes's inauguration. The *New York Sun* featured a picture of Hayes with the word *Fraud* on his forehead, and other papers began referring to him as "His Fraudulency" and "RutherFRAUD B. Hayes." One man, who turned up in Washington to announce that he had been "directed by God" to do away with Hayes, was carted off to an asylum by the police.[3]

Only a few extremists, in fact, talked of disrupting Hayes's inauguration; Tilden himself urged peaceful acceptance of the electoral commission's decision, even though he was convinced he had been cheated out of victory. But the Republicans were naturally anxious to install Hayes in office as soon as possible, and they proposed a private ceremony on Sunday, March 4. Hayes was a devout Methodist, however, and he absolutely refused to desecrate the Sabbath by taking his oath on the fourth. In the end, not only did the Republicans postpone the public inauguration until Monday, as in 1821 and 1849, they also, with the consent of the president, Ulysses S. Grant, arranged a private ceremony in the White House to swear Hayes in on Saturday, March 3. For once, the United States seems to have had two presidents for a day. "I did not altogether approve," Hayes admitted, but "acquiesced."[4]

The ceremony went off nicely. Saturday evening, President Grant held a state dinner at the White House in honor of Hayes, and as the guests, about thirty-six, began assembling at 7:30, President Grant, President-elect Hayes, Chief Justice Morrison R. Waite, and Secretary of State Hamilton Fish slipped off into the Red Room to make Hayes president. The proceedings were brief and to the point. Hayes raised his hand, repeated the oath after Chief Justice Waite, signed a document testifying to the oath-taking, with Grant and Fish as witnesses, and then entrusted it to the secretary of state. None of the participants in the little ceremony said anything about it when they joined the other guests for dinner, but to quell rumors floating around Washington, they released the news the following day. Sunday, March 4, passed uneventfully, though about two hundred people gathered at the Capitol, expecting an inauguration, and on Monday, March 5, Hayes's second oath-taking, this time in public, took place, although many Democrats boycotted it out of principle. "The day was bright and beautiful," reported the *New York Herald,* "and nothing marred the splendor of the ceremony."[5]

In 1917, for a fourth time, inauguration day fell on Sunday, and the inauguration—Woodrow Wilson's second—was postponed until the following day. Like his three predecessors, Wilson approved the change, and like Hayes, he agreed to a private ceremony beforehand. Unlike Hayes, though, he did not balk at the idea of taking his first oath on Sunday, even though he was just as devout as the Ohioan. "This simple ceremony," Wilson's wife, Edith, wrote in her memoirs, "was more to our taste than the formal Inauguration which followed on Monday, March 5th."[6] Mrs. Wilson was proud of the fact that she was the only woman present at her husband's oath-taking. The private ceremony was set for noon on Sunday, the exact time when both the Sixty-fourth Congress and Wilson's first term came to an end. Unlike Hayes, however, Wilson took the oath in the Capitol, not the White House.

About an hour before noon, Sunday morning, the Wilsons left the White House and, accompanied by Secret Service men, drove to the Capitol, where Wilson plunged into work on some last-minute legislation sent to him in the president's room. Just before noon, he finished his work and got to chatting with Chief Justice Edward D. White, who was on hand for the ceremony. So absorbed did the two men become in their conversation that they paid no attention to the four sharp rings that sounded from the Senate chamber, across the corridor outside, and indicated that twelve o'clock had arrived and the Senate stood adjourned. Supreme Court clerk James D. Maher hovered uncertainly around them for a few minutes, reluctant to intervene, and then suddenly ventured, "Pardon me, Mr. Chief Justice, it is 12 o'clock." At that Wilson and White jumped up and moved at once into the little oath-taking ceremony.[7]

With about thirty people in the room, and several more watching from the corridor, the chief justice read the presidential oath and Wilson repeated it slowly after him and then kissed the Bible (which he had also used during his first inauguration in 1913). Afterward White exclaimed, "I am very, very happy," and Wilson returned, "Thank you, sir." During the brief ceremony, Mrs. Wilson watched her husband "with shining eyes," according to a White House staff member, "proud of him, her head held high, a little smile on her lips."[8] Then both Wilson and White signed their names to the oath, which had been copied on the fly-leaf of Wilson's Bible, and, entrusting the Bible to Mrs. Wilson, who tucked it under her arm, they prepared to leave for the White House. Wilson had his formal installation the following day on the inaugural platform outside the Capitol, but the *New York Times* regarded the March 4 ceremony as the "real inauguration."[9]

Forty years later, in 1957, inauguration day fell on a Sunday again, but this time the inaugural date was January 20, not March 4, and the public ceremony was postponed until the twenty-first. Like Monroe, Taylor, Hayes, and Wilson, Dwight D. Eisenhower, ready to launch his second term, took his oath twice in 1957: at a simple ceremony on Sunday and at the customary public ceremony on Monday. On Sunday morning, the Eisenhowers attended services at the National Presbyterian Church, where they were members, and listened to a sermon by the Reverend Edward Elson, which took as its text the passage from the Bible that Ike planned to use himself when taking his oath later that morning. Back at the White House around ten, he and his wife, Mamie, were ready to go ahead with the private oath-taking in the East Room. At Ike's request, newspaper reporters and television cameras were barred from the room, but the public later learned that President Eisenhower wore a short morning coat and striped trousers for the ceremony and that Mrs. Eisenhower wore a black taffeta dress.

In 1957, for the first time, the vice president—Richard M. Nixon—with his wife, Pat, took part in the private ceremony, with Nixon's swearing in coming first, as it did in the inauguration the following day. Witnessing the ceremonies were fifty members of the Eisenhower family, ten members of Nixon's family, a handful of old friends, and some White House officials, maids, ushers, and cooks. Watching the proceedings was the eight-year-old Julie Nixon, sporting a black eye from a sled accident a few days before. Ike's four grandchildren were also there, including the thirteen-month-old Mary Jean, and they watched the proceedings with varying degrees of attention. At 10:26, California's William F. Knowland, Senate Minority Leader, administered the vice presidential oath to Nixon, with the latter resting his hand while taking the oath on a Bible, published in 1829, that had been in his family for five generations.

Two minutes after Nixon completed his oath, Chief Justice Earl Warren (an Eisenhower appointee) swore Eisenhower into office for a second term. "With his 42-word oath," reported *Newsweek,* in almost breathless (if not deathless) prose, "Mr. Eisenhower shouldered perhaps the greatest burden ever thrust upon a peacetime President. By swearing to preserve, protect, and defend the Constitution, the President, in effect, swore to preserve, protect, and defend the entire free world. And arrayed against his leadership was a massive combination of Communist power that had just denounced him as a warmonger."[10] As in 1953, Eisenhower took his oath with his left hand on the Bible that his mother had given him when he graduated from West Point in 1915, and he had it opened to Psalm 33: "Blessed is the nation whose God is the Lord; and the people whom he hath chosen for his own inheritance."[11]

After Eisenhower finished taking his oath, he shook hands with his guests and then led them into the State Dining Room for coffee, sweet rolls, and coffee cake. After the brunch, "Legally assured of his right to his job," as *Time* quipped, he buckled down to a hard day's work, putting finishing touches on his second inaugural address. Monday, January 21, started off badly, with clouds and some rain, but by the time Ike arrived on the inaugural platform outside the Capitol to take his oath a second time, the sun had come out with what some reporters called "typical Eisenhower luck."[12]

Before the twentieth century came galloping to an end, there was one more January 20 falling on a Sunday: This one was in 1985, on the occasion of Ronald Reagan's second inauguration. As in 1957, the inaugural planners remembered to keep the Sabbath day holy by postponing the public inauguration ceremony until Monday, the twenty-first, while arranging to have President Reagan sworn in privately beforehand in the White House. First, however, the Reagans attended services in the National Cathedral with Vice President and Mrs. George Bush, listened approvingly to Reverend Billy Graham's sermon, and joined the congregation in singing the hymn, "We Shall Gather Together." In his sermon, the Reverend Mr. Graham recalled that Reagan once praised football players for kneeling in prayer in the locker room before the game, and then Graham told the congregation: "Prayer should be the habit of everyone on this team we call America."[13]

After the service, a little before noon on January 20, Reagan took his second oath as president in the White House. Dressed in a dark business suit and flanked by his wife, Nancy, who wore a vivid red dress, Reagan stood on the carpeted landing of the grand staircase, right hand high and left hand flat on a family Bible opened to Chronicles

7:11, and took the oath administered by Chief Justice Warren E. Burger, as ninety-five guests, including his family,
cabinet members, friends, aides, and congressional leaders
(plus the television audience) looked on. Vice President
Bush took his oath, too, at this time. Former Supreme Court
Justice Potter Stewart administered it, and Bush's wife, Barbara, and their family looked on proudly.

After the brief ceremonies, Reagan and Bush stepped
outside at the north portico to pose for photographers.
"Wow!" exclaimed Reagan, as he felt the icy wind; he and
Bush quickly darted back into the warmth of the White
House. There was a buffet luncheon for the guests afterward, and then Reagan did something else important: he
went to the White House Map Room to go on live television once more and toss the coin that would open the Super
Bowl game that Sabbath day between the Miami Dolphins
and the San Francisco 49ers.

GETTING TO WASHINGTON

UNTIL THE MIDDLE OF THE TWENTIETH century, when plane travel became common, the journey of the president-elect to the nation's capital for induction into office was an integral part of the inaugural celebration, consisting of a friendly send-off from his hometown, a warm reception by his well-wishers en route to Washington, and a rousing welcome when he arrived in the capital a few days before his inauguration. Not all the presidents-to-be, to be sure, engaged in these preinaugural warm-ups. Vice presidents, secretaries of state, and members of Congress moving up to the presidency, as well as presidents who had been elected for another term, were already residing in Washington, and the only trip they looked forward to making was the one up Pennsylvania Avenue to Capitol Hill on inauguration morning. But for those with a lengthy itinerary, particularly in the nineteenth century, the trip to Washington was a morale booster for thousands of people gathered along the route to celebrate, as well as for the president-elect himself. No preinaugural journey matched the impressiveness of Washington's in 1789, but some of the trips attracted a great deal of attention and added to the festive mood sweeping the country at inauguration time.

Andrew Jackson was the first president-elect after George Washington who wasn't residing in the Federal City when he was elected. The Democrats planned "a great commotion" upon Jackson's arrival in Washington for the inauguration, but the president-elect made it clear that he wanted no "public shows and receptions," either on his journey to Washington or upon his arrival there.[1] His mood was mournful, not triumphant, on the eve of his inauguration, despite his victory over John Quincy Adams in the heatedly fought election of 1828. He was still grieving over the loss of his beloved wife, Rachel, who died of a heart attack shortly after the election, in great part, Jackson was convinced, because of the slander his political enemies hurled at her during the vituperative 1828 campaign.

During the three-week journey from Nashville to Washington, Jackson wore a black suit, black tie, a black armband, and a black band, called a weeper, that circled his tall beaver hat and drooped down the back of his neck. Accompanied by relatives and friends, he boarded the steamboat *Pennsylvania* on January 19, 1829, and headed for Cincinnati and then Pittsburgh, where he shifted to a two-horse carriage for the rest of the trip. Wherever he stopped along the way, cannons roared, rifle companies saluted him, and people lining the shores shouted their huzzahs. At Cincinnati, two steamboats escorted the *Pennsylvania* into port, and when Jackson came ashore the people gathered there to greet him shouted their approval and pressed forward to shake his hand.

Frances Trollope, a sharp-eyed British visitor, watched the scene with mixed feelings. She was impressed by Jackson. "He wore his gray hair carelessly but not ungracefully arranged," she observed, "and in spite of his harsh, gaunt features he looked like a gentleman and a soldier." But she deplored the fact that "the decent dignity of a private conveyance" was not "deemed necessary for the President of the United States." She was shocked, too, when she later learned of the "brutal familiarity" with which Jackson was treated on the boat taking him to Pittsburgh. "There was not a hulking boy from a keel-boat who was not introduced to the president," she reported, "unless, indeed, as was the case with some, they introduced themselves." At one point, she noted, a "greasy fellow" accosted Jackson with the exclamation: "General Jackson, I guess?...Why, they told me you was dead." "No!" cried Jackson. "Providence has hitherto preserved my life." Persisted the fellow: "And is your wife alive too?" Jackson bristled at the mention of his wife, and the man quickly ended the exchange by remarking, "Ay, I thought it was the one or t'other of ye."[2]

When Jackson reached Rockville, Maryland, his friend John Eaton (soon to become secretary of war) had a carriage waiting to take him to Washington. Learning from Eaton that his admirers planned to meet him at the city limits to escort him to the National Hotel, owned by John

Gadsby, with bands playing and cannons booming, Jackson decided to leave Rockville at once so he could reach the city several hours before he was expected. The minute he reached town, however, his fans hastily organized a company of artillery to accompany him the short distance to Gadsby's.

A young army officer who happened to witness Old Hickory's quiet entry into Washington on February 11 was deeply impressed by the lack of fanfare, so unlike "'the entrance of European potentates into their capitols to take possession of their thrones.... There passed my window about half past 10 o'clock,' he wrote his sister, 'a plain carriage drawn by two horses followed by a single black servant, & preceded by perhaps 10 horsemen who had perhaps joined it by accident on the road.'" It was a "'highly remarkable' entry," he noted, "one possessing...a great deal of moral sublimity."[3] Davy Crockett was also impressed by what Jackson had done. He had "stolen a march upon his friends," chortled Crockett, "as he always had done upon his enemies." But Jackson's unpretentious behavior only increased his stature in the eyes of his admirers.[4]

WILLIAM Henry Harrison's arrival in Washington for his inauguration in February 1841 was far different from Jackson's in 1829. Francis P. Blair's resolutely Jacksonian *Washington Globe* scornfully contrasted Harrison's noisy journey from Ohio to the nation's capital with the dignified simplicity of Jackson's entry into Washington. Blair couldn't resist turning Harrison's whole trip into a joke. "An earthquake" marked "his setting out," he wrote, and "the explosion of the banks welcomed him at Baltimore. From Baltimore he brought with him a snowstorm, and no sooner had he set foot on Pennsylvania Avenue than the robbing commenced, and a multitude had their pockets picked in the course of five minutes. These indications presage that the President is not likely to make times better for all." There was more. Soon after Harrison entered Washington, according to the *Globe,* the scroll bearing the motto of the Union, *E Pluribus Unum,* fell from the talons of the eagle in the Senate chamber, and the hand of the Goddess of Liberty in front of the Capitol holding the Constitution of the United States, dropped off. So much, concluded Blair, for the "arrogance and ostentation" of a president-elect who during the campaign of 1840 had promised "log cabin plainness, simplicity, and modesty, that were to win the confidence of the yeomanry of the country."[5]

Harrison's journey to Washington was unquestionably more showy than Jackson's. Jackson was in mourning; Harrison was trying to demonstrate his stamina. Harrison's sixty-eighth birthday fell on February 9, the day he reached Washington, and he was anxious to show people that he was the rugged "Hero of Tippecanoe" his supporters had portrayed him to be during the recent campaign.

At Cincinnati, where Harrison boarded the steamer, *Benjamin Franklin,* on the cold morning of January 26, he made a little address to the crowds gathered on the wharf, and as the boat left, the people waved and shouted, the military fired volleys, and the band on board played some lively tunes. "Gentlemen and fellow-citizens," Harrison told the crowd, "perhaps this may be the last time I may have the pleasure of speaking to you on earth or seeing you. I will bid you farewell, if forever, fare thee well."[6]

Harrison's words proved sadly true. He lasted only a month after the inauguration, partly because of the way he exposed himself to the elements during and after his trip to Washington in an effort to prove what a sturdy fellow he was. Time and again he appeared outdoors without a hat or coat despite the snow, ice, and cold.

Harrison's was a rigorous itinerary and the weather was bad all the way. In Wheeling he was greeted by cannons, bells, and flags, shook hands with thousands, attended a reception and dinner in the evening, and left for Pittsburgh that night. In Pittsburgh, ten thousand people were waiting to welcome him, and three companies of militia marched him to his hotel, where he heard several speeches in his honor and responded appropriately to each of them. From Pittsburgh, the Hero of Tippecanoe and his party of associates (which did not include his ailing wife, Anna, who expected to join him after the inauguration) set out in four coaches ("No monarch was so wonderfully coached") for the next leg of his journey, riding in state, so to speak, to Frederick, Maryland, where he received another noisy greeting.[7] "The General is looking remarkably well," it was reported, "and has borne the fatigue of the traveling and 'shaking hands' (which he complains of more than all) with good humor."[8]

Harrison was the first president to arrive in Washington by train. He boarded the Baltimore and Ohio Railroad in Frederick, Maryland, stopped for a while at Baltimore (where a crowded reception left his hand tired and sore), and when he reached Washington, a snowstorm was raging and it was impossible to hold the welcoming ceremony and parade planned in his honor. But a committee of Whigs met him at the station, offered him an umbrella, which he declined, and walked him through the snow to city hall, where he exchanged speeches with the mayor, and then settled down in Gadsby's Hotel. Fond of quoting the classics, Harrison compared his progress from Ohio to Washington to the return of Cicero to Rome after his exile.

HARRISON was the oldest president up to that time; James K. Polk, at forty-nine, the youngest. Like Harrison, former House Speaker Polk had a triumphant journey from his hometown in Tennessee to the nation's capital for his inauguration in 1845, but, unlike Harrison, he took his wife, Sarah, with him. On February 1, the Polks boarded a brand-new steamer made of cedar (called "the cedar boat") at Nashville and proceeded up the Ohio River, receiving congratulatory welcomes and friendly demonstrations all along the way. At Jeffersonville, Indiana, a rough-hewn farmer boarded the vessel, pushed his way through the crowd in the saloon surrounding Polk, offered his hand, and exclaimed: "I am glad to see you. I am a strong democrat, and did all I could for you. I am the father of twenty-six children, who were all for *Polk, Dallas,* and Texas!" Polk smiled, took the man's hand, and told him he was "happy to make his acquaintance, feeling assured that he deserved well of his country, if for no other reason than because he was the father of so large a republican family."[9]

During the voyage, an angry storm suddenly exploded, blowing Polk's boat ashore amid some trees, but while the skipper was regaining control, the Polks remained calm, and Polk himself continued busily at work on some papers in his cabin. The boat passed Louisville in the middle of the night, but there were swarms of people on the wharf ready to cheer the cedar boat as it steamed by. On Sunday, a band boarded the ship to play some music in Polk's honor, but the straitlaced Mrs. Polk put her puritanical foot down. Music, she insisted, would desecrate the Sabbath. The crestfallen musicians quietly departed. "Sarah directs all domestic affairs," Polk explained with a smile, "and she thinks that is domestic."[10]

At Madison, Indiana, an old-time Irish schoolmaster came aboard, along with a large number of his fellow townsmen, marched up to Polk, bowed low, and declared: "Yure koontenance is indicative of a bro-a-d basis." He then stationed himself behind Polk for a moment or two, bowed again, and repeated the cheery accolade. At Cincinnati, people on shore shouted approval of the president-elect, and he responded with a few words of thanks.[11] And at Wheeling, the Polks spent some time ashore, receiving a stream of callers.

From Wheeling to Cumberland, the Polks traveled by carriage over the National Road (which Polk had opposed funding when he was in Congress), and at Cumberland they boarded a train for Washington. When they reached Baltimore, an official welcoming committee came aboard to greet Polk, and soon after, former Pennsylvania senator George M. Dallas, the vice president–elect, joined the presidential party.

The Polks reached Washington on February 18 and took up residence in the National Hotel. Shortly after they checked in, a congressional committee called to inform Polk that the electoral college had chosen him president. Polk formally accepted the office and asked the committee to tell Congress that "in executing the responsible duties that would devolve upon him, it would be his anxious desire to maintain the honor and promote the welfare of the country."[12]

FOUR years later, the sixty-four-year-old president-elect, Zachary Taylor ("Old Rough and Ready"), made arrangements for his wife, Margaret, to travel to Washington by a separate route from the one he intended to use, because he was determined to spare her the fanfare accompanying the presidential treks to the nation's capital. A frail little woman who smoked a corncob pipe, Mrs. Taylor was markedly unenthusiastic about the prospect of life in the White House. In 1848 she had prayed for Henry Clay to get the Whig nomination for president, and when it came to her husband instead, she called it "a plot to deprive [me] of his society; and to shorten his life by unnecessary care and responsibility."[13] His life was shortened all right. Less than two years after his 1849 inauguration, he died of "cholera morbus" on July 9, 1850.

Just before his inauguration, Taylor seemed to be dragging his heels about going to Washington. Some of the Whig leaders, afraid he might decide not to come at all, put pressure on him to leave Baton Rouge as soon as he could, and early in February, after resigning his army commission, he finally started off for Washington. He was well prepared, he thought, for inauguration day. Known for his casual, even at times slovenly, attire, Taylor ordered two new suits, and when they arrived, he found both of them stuffed with letters from office seekers who paid the tailor handsomely to gain access to the president-elect this way. To well-wishers who gathered to see him off, Taylor declared he "should have much preferred to retain the office I am now about to vacate, and have remained among you."[14]

Taylor's journey from Baton Rouge, Louisiana, to Washington, D.C., took three weeks, and it was punctuated, as his wife had feared, with uproarious welcomes all along the way: parades, banquets, receptions, musical tributes, fireworks, bonfires, gun salutes. Taylor remained as informal and easy-mannered as ever through it all. "Ain't he a hoss!" exclaimed a boatman who saw him in Nashville. "Kentucky to the backbone!" pronounced another man who knew that Old Zach had once resided in the Bluegrass State. An elderly farmer who journeyed forty miles to get a look at the former Mexican War general pushed through the stevedores, grasped Taylor's hand, and announced: "I've voted for nine Presidents, but never with as much good will as I put into my vote for you." Returned Taylor somewhat uncertainly, "I belong to the old school."[15]

On his way to Washington, Taylor learned to make informal little speeches, exchange pleasantries, shake hands with men until his palms blistered, accept the kisses of ladies without blushing, tease the children, and ingest the food proffered at celebratory dinners until he got indigestion. He also met several crises along the way with the kind of grit and grace that had made him a military hero during the Mexican War. At one point, the boat on which he was traveling hit a snag, and the captain sent the passengers ashore in a small skiff while the steamer was being repaired. But as the skiff was ready to leave, a drunken passenger leaped down and almost capsized it when he hit the deck. Taylor told the man to sit down, and when the fellow defiantly grabbed hold of the lines from the steamer and pulled the skiff around, Taylor thundered: "Sit down, you drunken rascal, or I'll throw you overboard!" The man meekly obeyed.[16]

Taylor seemed to enjoy his triumphal preinaugural journey, just as Harrison had four years before, but Old Rough and Ready had more than his share of mishaps on the way. At Madison, Indiana, a trunk slid down the gangway, slammed into him, and painfully injured his left arm and side; and at Cincinnati, Ohio, a crowd of eager welcomers inadvertently pushed him against the boat's guardrail with such force that his right hand was also severely bruised. By this time he had developed a bad cold and had to excuse himself from attending a banquet in his honor. He did, though, meet briefly with some wartime volunteers. Later on, he and his associates took to the sleighs when their boat got jammed in the ice fifteen miles south of Wheeling.

When Taylor finally reached Baltimore by train late in February, there were three thousand people, including committees from Washington, waiting to greet him at the station. He made a little speech to the crowd, insisting that "the battles attributed to his valor were won by the bravery of the soldiers," and then, striking a lighter note, called out to a ragamuffin he spied nearby, "Come here, my little fellow, you may be a general yourself one of these days!" He also kissed a little girl in the crowd, and then singled out an older man for attention. "It does my heart good to see you, sir," he exclaimed, "for you are, like myself, an old man.... It seems to me this immense throng...is chiefly composed of young men, all in the prime of life." To those crowding around him for some handshaking, he held up his right hand and declared: "If it were not for this lame hand, my friends, I could make my way among you as well as the best of you."[17]

On the night of February 23, Taylor entered Washington and received an even livelier welcome than the one in Baltimore. Bonfires had burned along the railroad tracks all the way to the capital, and as soon as his train pulled into the station, horns sounded, bells rang, whistles shrilled, cannons thundered, and fireworks soared high in the sky. A writer for the *National Intelligencer* reported that the crowd gathered at the station to greet Old Zach was the largest ever seen in the city.

It took Taylor some time to get through the crowd to the carriage that was to take him to the Willard Hotel, his preinaugural headquarters, and even longer to get to the hotel. "I thought the mob would have torn the horses and carriage into a thousand pieces," recalled one spectator; "some were on the wheels, some *under* them, some had hold of the traces, and all were aiming to have a peep at the old Hero." There was a mob awaiting Taylor at the Willard, too, but, using all of his strength, he managed to fight his way into the hotel, where he rested a bit before going out on the balcony to greet his admirers.[18]

"The General was so much fatigued," wrote one observer, that "he couldn't come out for some time, but when he did come, the shout that rent the air and continued for ten minutes would have drowned the roar of the cannon of 'Buena Vista.' At length he raised his hand, and you could have heard the fall of a pin; I did not think it possible that such an uproar could have been changed into such silence in so short a time. He then commenced but was so fatigued and excited, that he could hardly utter a word, and had to stop before he had finished. He is not so ugly as I had expected to see him, but yet cannot be called *handsome*; and, although rather low in stature, has as commanding appearance as I ever saw."[19]

A story circulated afterward that when Taylor first came out to thank the crowd, some people mistook him for a popular Irishman named John Boyle (a Navy Department clerk) who looked a lot like Taylor, and jeered: "Ah! Get out, Johnny Boyle, you can't fool us!"[20] But they soon realized they were seeing the real thing.

UNTIL Abraham Lincoln's first inauguration in 1861, the preinaugural journeys were festive and celebratory. For Lincoln, it was different. With the nation on the brink of civil war, the mood of the president-elect—and of the American public—was somber. On the eve of his inauguration, Lincoln was "filled with gloomy forebodings of the future," according to Billy Herndon, his former law partner.[21] If so, the president-elect successfully concealed them from the public. In the speeches he made en route to Washington from Springfield, Illinois, he seemed confident that a compromise might somehow be reached that would preserve the Union. In his public remarks, however, he carefully avoided discussing the policies he planned to follow once he became president.

Lincoln left Springfield on February 11, and in saying farewell to his friends and neighbors, who had gathered at the railroad station, he made it clear that he was fully aware of the awesome responsibilities awaiting him. "My friends," he told them, "no one, not in my situation, can appreciate my feeling of sadness at this parting. To this place, and the kindness of these people, I owe everything. Here I have lived a quarter of a century, and have passed from a young to an old man. Here my children have been born and one is buried. I now leave, not knowing when or whether ever I may return, with a task before me greater than that which rested upon Washington. Without the assistance of that Divine Being who ever attended him, I cannot succeed. With that assistance, I cannot fail."[22]

When Lincoln boarded the train in Springfield, with his oldest son Robert, he was well aware that Samuel M. Felton, the president of the Philadelphia, Wilmington, and Baltimore Railway, was providing protection as well as accommodations for the presidential party as it proceeded eastward. Felton had hired Allan Pinkerton, the founder of a private detective agency in Chicago, to investigate threats against the railroad by Southern sympathizers, and on the first day, Pinkerton's operatives discovered a carpet bag on the train containing explosives, and, a little later, an obstruction on the railroad tracks that may have been the work of saboteurs.

For the most part, however, Lincoln's trip east went smoothly. Lincoln received "magnificent receptions," as he put it, wherever he stopped—at whistle-stops as well as in towns and cities—and he delivered dozens of little speeches along the way, filled with hope for a peaceful resolution of the sectional crisis agitating the nation. "If the great American people will only keep their temper, on both sides of the line," he declared at Pittsburgh, "the troubles will come to an end . . . and this great nation shall continue to prosper as heretofore." His policy, he said, was to do what he thought was "right for the North, for the South, for the East, for the West, for the whole country."[23]

In Indianapolis, where his wife, Mary Todd, and other two sons joined him, Lincoln celebrated his fifty-second birthday on February 12. While he was there, he received, as a kind of birthday present, a dispatch from Washington (which he read with a smile), notifying him that Congress had just counted the electoral votes and that he had received 180 out of 303, making him officially the winner of the 1860 contest. But at Cincinnati he turned somber. After the welcoming ceremonies were over and he returned to his quarters, he quoted a few lines from Shakespeare's *Henry IV* to his friends:

> Come, let us sit upon the ground,
> And tell strange stories of the death of kings;
> . . . They were all murdered.

He said the words had been running through his mind all day.[24]

At Westfield, New York, Lincoln was in a cheerful mood again. When a crowd of people gathered to welcome him there, he tried to find Grace Bedell, the little Westfield girl who had written months before suggesting he grow whiskers to improve his appearance. "I have done so," he announced, "and now, if she is here, I would like to see her." According to the *Philadelphia Inquirer,* a little boy, "mounted on a post, with his mouth and eyes both wide open," cried out, "There she is, Mr. Lincoln," and pointed to "a beautiful girl, with black eyes, who was blushing all over her fair face." Lincoln left the train platform, made his way through the crowd, and when he reached the girl, gave her "several hearty kisses" amid "the yells of delight from the excited crowd," and then returned to the train to resume his journey.[25]

There was more fun for Lincoln at Leman Place, Pennsylvania, where people asked to see his wife after he made an amusing little speech for them. "Loud calls being made for Mrs. Lincoln," according to the *Lancaster Evening Express,* "Mr. L. brought her out, and said he had concluded to give them 'the long and the short of it!' This remark—with the disparity between the *length* of himself and wife—produced a loud burst of laughter, followed by enthusiastic cheers as the train moved off."[26]

Things turned serious in Philadelphia. There Lincoln faced the first crisis of his trip. "You must go directly to Washington today," detective Pinkerton told him, soon after the president-elect reached the city on February 21. Through his operatives, Pinkerton explained, he had learned that Lincoln's enemies planned to start a riot when he reached Baltimore, and, amid the uproar, try to take his life. Lincoln was impressed by the news, of course, but he absolutely refused to leave Philadelphia at that point. He had promised to give a speech at Independence Hall the following morning, he told Pinkerton, and he was also scheduled to address the Pennsylvania General Assembly in Harrisburg in the afternoon. Pinkerton had no choice but to accept Lincoln's decision to stay and fulfill his commitments, but the detective went ahead with his plans for getting the president-elect safely through Baltimore to Washington.[27]

On the morning of February 22, Lincoln made his speech, as planned, in Philadelphia's Independence Hall, at a ceremony celebrating George Washington's birthday. It was the most thoughtful speech Lincoln had delivered on his inaugural journey, and it revealed in a nutshell the basic ideas animating the policies he was to follow as president. In the speech, he took the occasion to explain to the American people that his political outlook rested on the "sentiments" contained in the Great Declaration adopted in Independence Hall some eighty-five years before. "I have never had a feeling politically," he declared, "that did not spring from the sentiments embodied in the Declaration of Independence." It was "not the mere matter of the separation of the colonies from the mother country," he hastened to add, "but something in that Declaration giving liberty, not alone to the people of this country, but hope to the world for all time. It was that which gave promise that in due time the weights should be lifted from the shoulders of all men, and that *all* shall have an equal chance." He went on to say that he hoped the country could be saved "upon that basis," and then (possibly with Pinkerton's warning in mind), he added: "But, if this country cannot be saved without giving up that principle, I was about to say I would rather be assassinated on this spot than to surrender it." He ended his speech with the insistence that "there is no need of blood-shed and war."[28]

That afternoon, Lincoln took the train to Harrisburg, appeared before the Pennsylvania General Assembly, and made a speech filled with friendly remarks that, according to the local paper, elicited "rapturous and prolonged cheering." Lincoln then attended a dinner in his honor at the Jones House Hotel.[29] While he was dining, Pinkerton sought him out again to outline the plan to get him safely to Washington. Lincoln was to leave Harrisburg at once, Pinkerton advised, preferably in disguise, return to Philadelphia, and there board the night train to Washington, which would arrive early the next morning, several hours ahead of schedule. The president-elect didn't much like Pinkerton's plan. "What would the nation think of its President," he is said to have cried, "sneaking into the capital like a thief in the night?"[30] By this time, however, he had received a warning directly from Washington that made him more receptive to Pinkerton's proposals. In Washington, army General-in-Chief Winfield Scott had learned independently of the dangers awaiting Lincoln in Baltimore and alerted New York senator William Henry Seward (Lincoln's choice for secretary of state); Seward sent his son Frederick posthaste to Philadelphia with a letter of warning for Lincoln. "I concur with General Scott," Seward wrote in the letter his son carried to Lincoln, "in thinking it best for you to reconsider your arrangement."[31]

Lincoln agreed to change his plans. His original schedule, which had been made public, called for him to pass through Baltimore on Saturday, February 23, and arrive in

Washington that evening. Instead, on the twenty-second, he boarded a special train Pinkerton had waiting for him in Harrisburg, transferred to a sleeper on a train in Philadelphia around 11 P.M., passed quietly and uneventfully through Baltimore in the early hours of the twenty-third, and reached the Washington railroad station around 6 A.M., with only Illinois congressman E. B. Washburne at the station to greet him. Lincoln did not wear a "Scotch plaid cap and...a long military cloak" en route, as one reporter fancifully wrote a couple of days later. The president-elect simply replaced his top hat with a felt cap and slipped on a black overcoat for the secret trip.[32]

Still, the Scotch-plaid-cap story was picked up by newspapers hostile to Lincoln, and made much of by his critics, especially cartoonists, in an effort to portray him (as he had feared) as craven and cowardly. "Abe Lincoln tore through Baltimore," went one Southern parody,

> *In a baggage-car with fastened door;*
> *Fight away, fight away, fight away for Dixie's land.*
> *And left his wife, alas! Alack!*
> *To perish on the railroad track,*
> *Fight away, fight away, fight away for Dixie's land.*[33]

But the danger in Baltimore was real enough. Baltimore (and Maryland itself) was unfriendly; there were no "magnificent receptions" planned and no requests for speeches; Baltimore authorities refused even to guarantee police protection for the president-elect.

When Congressman Washburne met Lincoln at the Washington depot early Saturday morning, he took him to the Willard Hotel, where Lincoln was to stay with his family until the inauguration. Shortly afterward, Senator Seward arrived, a bit upset because he hadn't been at the station with Washburne to meet the president-elect. After breakfast, Seward took Lincoln to the White House to meet President James Buchanan, and then off to talk with General Scott about measures to guard the city on inauguration day. "He is very cordial and kind to me—," said Scott after meeting Lincoln, "simple, natural, and agreeable."[34]

FOR various reasons, the next few presidents rode into Washington without much to-do, and it wasn't until 1897, when William McKinley became president, that the Washington-bound journey was again an important part of the inaugural happenings. McKinley's trip from his home in Canton, Ohio, was one of triumphant joy. He left Canton, "as bright and cheerful as a boy," reporters noted, amidst flaming bonfires, strains of joyful music, and cheers of old-time friends. In his farewell statement at the station, where thousands gathered to see him off, he spoke of the "arduous responsibility, as great as can devolve upon any man" that faced him, and asked them for their prayers and goodwill. In every hamlet, town, and city through which the presidential party passed en route to Washington, there were crowds cheering and waving flags, as well as bonfires, torches, and rockets blazing in the night.[35]

McKinley asked the managers of the inauguration not to arrange any special demonstrations for him when he reached Washington, but hundreds of people were waiting when he arrived the following morning. As he descended from the train, carrying a bunch of white carnations, and walked with his family and friends to the waiting room, he doffed his hat to acknowledge the applause, bowed to the train crew and dining-car porters on the platform, then handed the carnations to the train engineer, who "fairly blushed," according to the *New York Times,* "through the soot on his face."[36] There were crowds at Ebbitt House (McKinley's preinaugural headquarters), too, when he arrived in the carriage provided at the station, and he waved and smiled as the people cheered. McKinley, the *Washington Post* observed, "wore a high silk hat and a closely buttoned Prince Albert coat, with vest and trousers, his usual costume. Spring, summer, autumn, and winter come and go, but McKinley's attire never changes as to style."[37]

IT wasn't until 1913, when Woodrow Wilson succeeded William Howard Taft as president, that the president-elect's trip to the capital, this time a short one, rivaled McKinley's in 1897 for excitement. Two days before Wilson left Princeton for Washington, about three thousand of the townspeople, led by the head of the town's Woodrow Wilson Club, marched to the president-elect's home, presented him with a silver loving cup, and begged for a speech. "If there is one thing a man loves better than another," Wilson told the crowd, "it is being known by his fellow-citizens." He went on to say that it would be a "very poor President" who lost consciousness of his home ties and a "very poor public servant who did not regard himself as part of the public," and he concluded: "I have never been inside the White House, and I shall feel very strange when I get inside of it. I shall think of this little house behind me and remember how much more familiar it is to me than *that* is likely to be.... One cannot be neighbors to the whole United States. I shall miss my neighbors."[38]

Wilson's departure for Washington on the morning of March 3 was another occasion for demonstrations in Princeton. A crowd of people gathered in front of the Wilson house with a band, to see him off, and there were several automobiles there to take the president-elect and his family to the railroad station. "With motor cars standing in line," Eleanor Wilson recalled, "father and mother suddenly rebelled and, leaving us to follow, walked alone to the station where the special train was waiting."[39] The Wilsons smiled and waved as they trudged the half mile to the station, and when a Presbyterian minister offered congratulations, Wilson (a Presbyterian himself) exclaimed: "I appreciate your good wishes, but had you not better pray for me?"[40] At the station a crowd was gathered to see them off; and six hundred Princeton students (Wilson had once been president of Princeton) were waiting to board the special train of nine cars and accompany the Wilsons to Washington. When the Wilsons boarded the car reserved for the presidential party, the students sang "Marching through Princeton" and gave the college yell, amended for the occasion: "Siss, boom, ah, Wilson!" Recalled Eleanor Wilson: "We stood on the back platform when the train pulled out and, although father and mother were smiling and waving, I thought they both looked very wistful as the lovely classic towers of Princeton faded in the distance."[41]

When the train reached Washington's Union Station that afternoon, the Princeton students lined up to give a series of lusty college yells as the Wilsons descended from their car, but there were no big welcoming demonstrations, largely because most of the Democrats in town for the inauguration were lined up along Pennsylvania Avenue at the time watching several hundred suffragists march from Capitol Hill to the White House on behalf of "Votes for Women." There were only five hundred people in Union Station waiting to welcome Wilson—although the *New York Times* insisted they "made up in noise for what they lacked in numbers"—and the presidential party quickly boarded the automobiles President Taft had sent to the station and, to avoid the suffragists' parade, headed through empty backstreets to the Shoreham Hotel, where the Wilsons were to stay until inauguration day. The president-elect, remarked one of Wilson's associates, "got his first glimpse of Washington as a deserted village."[42]

WILSON'S was the last presidential journey to play a significant part in the inaugural festivities. More and more, as the twentieth century wore on, the preinaugural activities centered on parties, receptions, concerts, and show-biz galas held in Washington itself during the days leading up to inauguration. In 1981, Ronald and Nancy Reagan, to be sure, received what *Newsweek* called "an epic send-off," with a "Reagan Day" ceremony at the Los Angeles City Hall, but their flight to Washington afterward was unexceptional.[43] Not until 1993, when William Jefferson Clinton became president did a journey to Washington just before the inauguration—the twentieth century's last such trip—once again become part of the inaugural festivities.[44]

Clinton started with a pleasant send-off in Little Rock, Arkansas, on January 16. He took a final jog, greeting people along the way, signed autographs, and paid last visits to old haunts like the YMCA, McDonald's, and the Community Baker, where he got his bagels. He also carried his daughter Chelsea's pet frog in a shoe box to the Arkansas River and, watched earnestly by his friends, deposited it in the water. Later on, wearing blue jeans, a Wharton School of Business sweatshirt, and a Georgetown University baseball cap, he watched the movers load boxes—one of them labeled B.C. SUITS, ROOM 219, WH—onto an eighteen-wheeler, as he talked to reporters about leaving Arkansas for the first time since settling there after finishing law school many years before. "I've worked through it," he said. "I'm ready to go, I'm eager." He had been writing his inaugural address the past few days, he revealed, and didn't know yet how long it would be, though his advisers hoped he would keep it to twenty minutes. "Most of it is easy," he said of the writing. "There are two or three things I'm having trouble figuring out how I want to say them."[45] Scores of people turned up at the Little Rock Regional Airport that afternoon for a friendly send-off. The *Arkansas Democrat and Gazette,* never friendly during Clinton's five terms as governor, took the occasion of his departure for Washington to lecture him on his propensity for breaking campaign pledges.

The Clintons' immediate destination was Charlottesville, Virginia. There they were planning to join Vice President—elect Al Gore, former Tennessee senator, and his family at Monticello, Thomas Jefferson's estate. From Monticello, the two families would board a bus for the 121-mile trip to the Lincoln Memorial in Washington. Their bus would lead a cavalcade of fifteen buses carrying friends, aides, advisers, and reporters. Clinton decided to follow the route Jefferson himself used when he traveled from Charlottesville to Washington, he said, because the third president "was sort of associated with the populism of his time," and the bus Clinton and Gore used during the 1992 campaign had become a symbol of his own populist political philosophy. During a tour of Monticello before beginning the trip, Clinton was ecstatic about Jefferson's library ("I love it"), and Gore was curious about some white plastic busts he noticed ("Who are these people?" he asked, and the tour guide identified George Washington and Benjamin Franklin for him). On the portico at Monticello, Gore told some schoolchildren that he and the president had been doing their homework, too: "We read the Declaration of Independence on the way over."[46]

At Monticello, Clinton made a short speech to the people gathered there. "I want," he said, "to be faithful to Jefferson's idea that about once in a generation you have to shake things up and face your problems. We owe it to Thomas Jefferson and George Washington and all our forbears to face the difficult problems of our time and try to solve them." Asked if he would name Jefferson to his cabinet if he could, Clinton exclaimed: "If Thomas Jefferson were alive today, I would appoint him Secretary of State, and then suggest to Senator Gore that we both resign so he could become President." After the tour, the Clintons and the Gores boarded the Washington-bound bus, which carried a license plate bearing the name of Clinton's Arkansas birthplace: HOPE 1.[47]

Clinton wore a dark suit on the bus trip and made informal remarks to spectators in the little towns along the way. "We know that you put us in the White House and we won't forget you," he told a little crowd during a stop at a gas station in one town. "On this wonderful day, we ask you to pray for us, to pull for us, to make sure we stay in touch, and when you think we are wrong, to tell us that, too." As the Clinton-Gore bus passed, some people held up placards announcing, BUBBAS FOR BILL; GOD BLESS OUR NEW PRESIDENT; GOOD LUCK, MR. CLINTON AND MR. GORE; WE ARE COUNTING ON YOU; and MAY GRACE BE WITH YOU. Outside the Culpeper Baptist Church, however, anti-abortion demonstrators waved signs protesting Clinton's pro-choice position: MR. CLINTON, DO NOT MOCK GOD. But Clinton and his entourage attended the 11 A.M. service at the church anyway, and there was a mad scramble after the service when people tried to touch Clinton and Gore as they left. "It was a once-in-a-lifetime experience for me," said the minister afterward. "I get nervous every week when I preach, and I guess I was a little more nervous than ever."[48]

At a truck stop in Ruckersville there was a big sign: MR. PRESIDENT-ELECT: OUR COFFEE'S BETTER THAN MCDONALD'S, but the buscapade did not stop there, and the waitress was shattered: "I wanted him to stop so bad!" At Gainesville, Virginia, where the buses did stop, three thousand people were to see the president-elect. Suddenly a forty-three-year-old woman darted over to the open doors of Clinton's bus, got past the Secret Service agents and state troopers, and shook hands with Clinton. Afterward, she explained, she felt "bubbly." When the procession of buses turned down Interstate 66 for the last lap of the trip, the Virginia Department of Transportation came up with a friendly jingle (modeled after the old Burma Shave advertisements that used to grace America's highways):

> Thanks, Mr. President
>> For Taking the Bus
>>> Fewer Cars on the Road
>>>> Helps All of Us
>>>>> White House 23 Miles.[49]

To everyone's surprise, Clinton, a notorious late arriver, reached the Lincoln Memorial at 3 P.M., the scheduled time for the telecast, and at the same time, it was reported, the sun actually sparkled upon his appearance. By that time, the "American Reunion on the Mall," the centerpiece of the "People's Inauguration," honoring the nation's diverse ethnic heritage, was in full swing, with some 300,000 people gathered on the Mall, taking in the various kinds of food, music, and crafts displayed in the tall white tents erected in the area. "Mom!" cried a boy on the Washington Monument hill gazing at the scene, "Look at how many people there are! It's sooo neat!"

The drums rolled, the trumpets sounded, and military jets whooshed overhead as Clinton stepped out from the pillars and descended the marble steps of the Lincoln Memorial, but almost no one could see him because an enormous scaffolding for lights, cameras, and TV equipment in front of the memorial completely blocked the view. "I don't understand," sighed a man in his mid-twenties to his companion. "This show is supposed to be performed on the steps of the Lincoln Mcmorial, but there's this huge structure in front of it." "That's so they can televise it," explained his friend. "Well," said the young man, "let's go home then, and watch it on TV."[50]

The "American Reunion on the Mall" was only the first of a series of celebrations in 1993 that in the late twentieth century came to replace the president's trip to Washington as the focus for preinaugural activities. True to the spirit of the times, these celebrations were practically made for television.

Coping with the Weather

No one knows what the weather was like on April 30, 1789, the day that George Washington took his oath as first president of the United States. There were no complaints above the weather, to be sure, in the reports of people who wrote about the event at the time, and that may well mean that it was a fair day. Still, one can't be absolutely sure. Years later, Washington Irving, on hand for the inauguration, was reported to have told friends that at 8 A.M. on the morning of April 30, it was cloudy, but that the sun came out by the time the inaugural ceremony commenced. But another eyewitness, Mary Hunt Palmer, fourteen at the time of the inauguration, recalled drenching rain when she wrote her recollections in her old age. "It never rained faster," she averred, "than it did that day," and Washington was forced to use an umbrella when he was outdoors.[1]

If Washington kept an umbrella handy in 1789, he wasn't the only president to do so on the day of his inauguration. There was "a sea of umbrellas" at Benjamin Harrison's rainy inauguration in 1889.[2] And thermal underwear was the order of the day for Lyndon B. Johnson's cold and windy oath-taking in 1965. Sometimes the weather on inauguration day was so frightful that the president canceled the outdoor ceremonies and swore his allegiance to the Constitution indoors. But cancellation has been a rare last resort, for, as Franklin Roosevelt remarked on the nasty day of his second inauguration in 1937, if the people gathered outside the Capitol on inauguration morning were willing to brave the cold, he should be out there, too.[3]

The first few inaugurations after Washington's first seem to have had decent enough weather: fair, sunny, chilly but pleasant, and, if lucky, "the freshness and beauty of early spring morning," as on James Madison's second inauguration in 1813.[4] James Monroe's first inauguration, on March 4, 1817, was especially nice. *Niles' Register* called it "auspiciously delightful," and historian James Schouler fairly raved over the "day of spring sunshine unusual for early March" that warmed the Federal City for the inaugural ceremony. "The softness of the air!" he wrote, "the radiance of the noonday sun, the serenity of the rural surroundings, from woody heights to the placid Potomac, carried a sense of tranquil happiness to the hearts of thousands of spectators who had assembled for the outdoor ceremonies on Capitol Hill."[5] Monroe's was the first inaugural ceremony to be held outdoors, and the spring weather added to its success.

But if 1817's weather was glorious, 1821's was glacial. Monroe's advisers had planned another outdoor ceremony for his second inauguration that year, but the snow and ice blanketing Washington produced a last-minute change, and Monroe took his oath in the recently renovated Capitol Building rather than on the platform erected outside a few days earlier. It was so bitterly cold and windy, moreover, that only a handful of people gathered in front of the President's House to greet him before the ceremony. Even fewer people lined Pennsylvania Avenue to watch him as he journeyed to Capitol Hill in a plain carriage with four horses and one footman, followed by members of his cabinet, each of them in "a carriage and pair."[6]

1833—Andrew Jackson's second inauguration—was colder and windier, if anything, than Monroe's in 1821, and Jackson abandoned plans for an outdoor swearing in and took his oath in the hall of the House of Representatives (called "the cave of the winds" only partly because it was so drafty). Four years later, almost as if to make up for the chill that greeted Jackson, his successor, Martin Van Buren, had a beautiful day—"clear sky," Missouri senator Thomas Hart Benton recalled, "balmy vernal sun"—and the crowds gathering in front of the east portico of the Capitol to see him take the oath of office reminded some observers of the multitudes assembled in front of St. Peter's in Rome waiting to receive the papal blessing.[7]

The 1840s were not so good. March 4, 1841, was "excessively disagreeable" and the icy outdoor ceremony that day may have contributed to the death of sixty-eight-year-old William Henry Harrison. To show his stamina, Harrison insisted on dispensing with hat and coat, and died from pneumonia a month after he took office.[8] James K. Polk's inauguration day in 1845 was cold, rainy, and muddy, but he at least survived the outdoor ceremony, though he was not particularly robust. In 1849, inauguration day was gloomy, cloudy, windy, and a bit snowy, but Zachary Taylor was able to swear his loyalty to the Constitution on the east portico of the Capitol without mishap. For Abraham Lincoln in 1861 it was damp and cold in the morning, but the sun came out about the time of the ceremony. His second inauguration in 1865 was accompanied by rain and hail, but the sun appeared while he was delivering his celebrated Second Inaugural Address.

SOME people seem to have thought that presidents got the kind of weather they deserved, particularly if the weather was good and they liked the president. The mild and sunny day of Grover Cleveland's first inauguration in 1885 was called a "Cleveland day," which his supporters thought he merited for his rugged honesty. The fair weather for the popular Calvin Coolidge's oath-taking in 1925 was considered well-deserved "Coolidge luck." For the likable Dwight D. Eisenhower's second inauguration in 1957, the day started with clouds and rain, but the sun came out, with "typical Eisenhower luck," for his oath-taking later in the day.[9]

The sunny weather for William McKinley's oath-taking in 1897 seemed particularly noteworthy, for he had heroically trounced William Jennings Bryan, that dangerous threat to the gold standard, in the stormy battle of 1896, and ably earned his good weather. The *New York Times* looked on the mild, sunshiny day of McKinley's first inauguration as a harbinger of good things to come. "If good weather for so important an event may be accepted as a favorable augury," wrote the *Times* reporter covering the event, "President McKinley has begun an administrative career that should be full of sunshine, good order, good humor, and general satisfaction. Not a cloud cast its shadow over any part of the inaugural proceedings." The *Times* writer toyed with the idea that the weather shared McKinley's affection for the gold standard. "The sun looked all day like a great disk of burnished gold," he observed. "It was weather truly emblematical of the victory which resulted in the ceremonies of today. In more senses than one it was a golden inaugural."[10] A silvery day—after free-silver crusader Bryan's smashing defeat in the 1896 election—was simply unthinkable.

There were no golden inaugurals for Ulysses S. Grant; both his inaugurations were conspicuously lacking in "Grant luck." His first inauguration in 1869 was cold and rainy, and the skies didn't begin to clear until it was almost too late to brighten things up. And his second induction into office, in 1873, was a disaster; it was one of the coldest days in inaugural history. The Republicans wanted Grant's second inauguration to be more impressive than his first, recalled Maine senator James G. Blaine, "but the skies were unpropitious, and the day will long be remembered, by those who witnessed the festivities, for the severity of the cold—altogether exceptional in the climate of Washington. It destroyed the pleasure of an occasion which would otherwise have given to unrestrained rejoicing over an event that was looked upon by the great majority of people as peculiarly auspicious."[11] People had flocked to Washington to be on hand for Grant's second inauguration, and all the hotels and boardinghouses were filled to the brim. But weather ruined the festivities they had anticipated with such eagerness.

At dawn on March 4, 1873, when the cannons sounded, it was four above zero, and a bitter wind from the icy Potomac River tore down flags and decorations along Pennsylvania Avenue and froze tree boughs. The temperature rose a bit during the day, but the wind continued to wreak havoc with the inaugural trimmings, and the snow left the streets icy and treacherous. "The imps come down and seize an old man's hat, and fly off with a woman's veil and blow a little boy into a cellar," wrote novelist and reporter Mary Clemmer Ames, with mordant playfulness. "The bigger air-warriors, intent on bigger spoil, sweep down banners, swoop off with awnings, concentrate their forces into swirling cyclones in the middle of the streets, and bang away at plate-glass windows until they prance in their sockets." The intense cold literally stopped the music in the inaugural parade. The condensation from the breath of the musicians froze the valves of their instruments and made playing impossible. Some of the paraders, half-frozen, dropped out of the ranks.[12]

But the inaugural show—the morning procession from the White House to the Capitol, the oath-taking ceremony on a platform outside the Capitol, the afternoon parade, and the inaugural balls in the evening—went bravely on. President Grant wore a dark blue beaver overcoat, with a velvet collar, in the procession to the Capitol, but the West Point cadets and the Annapolis midshipmen who marched down Pennsylvania Avenue after the presidential carriage were not garbed in overcoats and for them the procession was an ordeal. "What faces, what muscle, what manhood!" wrote Mrs. Ames of the young servicemen. "Their movement is the perfect poetry of motion, a hundred men stepping as one. What marching, and at what odds! They are so pitilessly dressed! Thousands of men come behind warmly muffled; but the West Point cadets have on their new uniforms, single jackets. . . . What wonder, that two while standing in the line sank insensible with the cold not an hour ago. . . . What cold and hunger, and delay on the way, and now, what nerve and will it takes to march in the wind like this!" Some of the civilians in the procession found comfort in the bottle as they marched.[13]

Despite the cruel weather, thousands of spectators gathered in East Capitol Park to witness Grant's second inauguration. An outdoor platform had been erected for the occasion on the east portico of the Capitol. The wind blew hard while Grant was reading his inaugural address, almost tearing it out of his hands, and few people were able to hear anything he said. But most of the audience, warmly bundled up, remained to the bitter end. The parade back to the White House after the inauguration was as grueling as the morning procession to Capitol Hill, even though the temperature had risen a bit. But Grant's review of the troops from a special pavilion erected in front of the White House produced more casualties: some cadets passed out from the cold, and the tears of the drummer boys marching past froze on their cheeks. Grant and his guests, warmly attired, sipped coffee as they watched, while the wind continued to rage and the temperature began dropping again.

The inaugural ball that ice-cold night was a fiasco. The men planning the party neglected to install heating equipment in the wooden building erected in Judiciary Square for the occasion, so the guests danced in their overcoats, neglected the champagne and punch for hot coffee and chocolate (though some of it was frappéed), and fled soon to the warmth of their homes and hotels. Some six thousand guests were expected, but only three thousand showed up and most of them left early. One woman with bronchial trouble collapsed on the dance floor and then expired. Canaries, brought to the ballroom to sing cheerfully while the guests danced, simply tucked their bills under their wings and froze to death in their cages. The Grants stood for a while, shivering in their overcoats on a carpeted platform at one end of the chilly ballroom, and then departed.

Next to the ballroom was a big dining room boasting one of the most lavish feasts ever prepared for an inaugural ball: fried scallops and pickled oysters; boned and roasted turkey; capons stuffed with truffles; mutton, beef, quail, chicken, ham, and partridges; baked salmon; stuffed boars' heads; cheese, ham, and beef sandwiches; chicken, lobster, and egg salad; charlotte russe, blanc mange, ice cream, cake, candies, and fruit. But most of this feast was cold, frozen, and tasteless by the time the guests began to dine. Some hardy souls hacked away at the frozen food, but most concentrated on the hot coffee. The number of guests braving the cold (at ten dollars a ticket) diminished rapidly after the Grants left. By midnight the place was still and empty—and freezing cold.

THE weather for Benjamin Harrison's inauguration in 1889 was rotten, too, though not as bad as for Grant's in 1873. "There was cold wind and rain, sometimes turning into snow," recalled Nicholas Murray Butler, "and a dark, heavy sky that was depressing in the extreme." After listening to the first few sentences of Harrison's inaugural address outside the Capitol, Butler fled to the Cosmos Club to enjoy "the glow of a bright fire and the delights of intimate conversation on men and things."[14] Reporters covering the inauguration couldn't help recalling the bad weather forty-eight years earlier, when William Henry Harrison, Benjamin's grandfather, took his oath, caught cold, and died a month later. A few superstitious people suggested that a "Harrison hoodoo" dogged the family, but if so, Benjamin Harrison defied it, for he insisted on going through with the outdoor ceremonies; and in spite of the wind, rain, and cold (and an inaugural address almost as long as his grandfather's), he was none the worse for wear when it was all over. His wife, Carrie, saw to it that he was warmly clad. "No inauguration pneumonia for him!" she exclaimed. To please the protectionists, Harrison let it be known that he wore American-made clothes that day, but he cheated a bit by wearing a shirt of European chamois leather underneath to keep his chest dry during the drizzle. The sergeant-at-arms of the Senate held an umbrella for him while he took his oath and read his address. Later on, the weather improved, and though the fireworks display, planned for inauguration night, was canceled, the inaugural ball went off nicely.[15]

IN 1893, Grover Cleveland replaced Harrison in the White House, but the "benign Cleveland weather" the Democrats had bragged about at his first inauguration in 1885 was notably absent during his second. On March 4, 1893, the weather was "as bad as mortal man ever endured," Congressman Champ Clark of Missouri recalled, "windy, stormy, sleety, icy."[16] In the end, though, the planners of the inaugural pageant stuck to schedule, and Cleveland's second inauguration took place in what the *New York Times* called "a delicate arctic setting" along Pennsylvania Avenue and around the Capitol.[17] When Cleveland appeared on the inaugural platform, took off his silk hat, and stepped to the front to deliver his address (before taking the oath), there were shouts from the crowd below: "Put on that hat!" But Cleveland ignored them, and with hat in his left hand and his right hand partly thrust into his overcoat pocket, he launched into his speech as flecks of snow played around his face. He and his supporters braved the rest of the day, too, going ahead with the afternoon parade and the evening ball. "The cold wind and the fatigues of the day did not appear to have had a prolonged effect," observed the *New York Times* the following day, "for the attendance at the ball was early, large, and brilliant." The ballroom was heated this time.[18]

One Democrat held the weather against Cleveland. Two days after the inauguration, when Cleveland appointed Walter Q. Gresham, a Republican, as secretary of state, South Carolina senator Benjamin "Pitchfork Ben" Tillman rose in the Senate to deliver a vitriolic attack on the president. "I stood out here in front of the Capitol two hours in the midst of a biting wind," he thundered, "where every inch of the ground was covered with snow and sleet and ice, where we were all nearly frozen to death by wintry blasts that swept down from the north, and gloried over the inauguration of a man whom we voted for and fought for as a

Democrat, but who turned out to be a traitor to the Democratic Party, and to everything to which it was pledged. God forgive me for being such an infernal fool."[19]

THE elements continued to be implacably nonpartisan as the United States entered the twentieth century, and horrendously unpredictable, too, at times. In 1909, Weather Chief Willis Moore forecast "plenty of sunshine" for William Howard Taft's inauguration, but instead, a raging blizzard hit Washington on the night of March 3, disrupting telephone and telegraph communications with other cities, tying up rail connections between Washington and New York, putting the Washington trolley out of commission, and destroying the inaugural decorations along Pennsylvania Avenue. By inauguration morning, when Theodore Roosevelt, the outgoing president, entertained the Tafts at breakfast in the White House, hundreds of workers from the street cleaning department were busy shoveling and sanding Pennsylvania Avenue, hoping to make it passable, even though the snow continued to fall.[20]

Roosevelt was convinced that the weather was too wretched to go through with the customary outdoor inaugural ceremony, and he suggested that Taft take his oath and deliver his inaugural address in the Senate chamber. Taft demurred; he wanted to wait as long as possible to see if the weather improved enough to hold the ceremony on the east portico of the Capitol Building. When Senator Henry Cabot Lodge, chairman of the arrangements committee, arrived, however, he seconded TR's proposal, and when Taft still hesitated, he reminded him that Chief Justice

Melville Fuller was neither young nor in good health, and that it would be unconscionable to subject him to the wind and cold in an outdoor ceremony. At this, Taft relented, and Lodge went to work revising the plans for the day, which included rushing a special resolution through Congress providing for Taft's inauguration in the Senate chamber. Taft's was the first indoor ceremony since 1833, when a blizzard forced Andrew Jackson to take his oath for a second term in the Senate chamber. TR joked that "as soon as I am out where I can do no further harm to the Constitution," the storm would cease. "You're wrong," retorted Taft. "It is my storm. I always knew it would be a cold day when I became President."[21]

IT was a cold day, too, when Herbert Hoover became president in 1929, and there was rain as well. "Well, Grace," wheezed Calvin Coolidge, Hoover's predecessor, glancing at his wife, after looking out at the South Lawn of the White House, "it always rains on moving day."[22] There was some talk of shifting Hoover's inauguration to the Senate chamber, but no one really wanted to, and in the end Hoover took his oath outdoors.

1937—Franklin Roosevelt's second inauguration—also came up with a cold and rainy day, January 20 (the worst inaugural day, some people thought, since 1909), but when Roosevelt peered out of the window and asked whether crowds were gathering in the rain and was told they were, he announced, "If they can take it, so can I." Writing about the inauguration afterward, *Life* called the Roosevelts "the wettest First Family ever to enter the White House," *Time* called it "a sentimental historical ducking in five acts," and *Newsweek* reported that it was "literally a washout—a mass of squishy shoes, ruined top hats, sodden music, and runny noses." Eleanor Roosevelt recalled "umbrellas and more umbrellas."[23] But far worse than 1937's storm was the blizzard that immobilized Washington the night before John F. Kennedy's inauguration in 1961. Fortunately, the storm had abated by inauguration morning, and Kennedy was able to take his oath and deliver his address in cold and windy, but sunny, weather, outside the Capitol.

Ronald Reagan had no such luck in 1985, when he faced his second inauguration as president. He took his oath privately on January 20, a Sunday, and looked forward to taking the oath again outdoors the following day. But it was not to be. That night the temperature in Washington declined steadily, and the inaugural planners' hearts sank with it. When hypothermia experts at the National Institutes of Health strongly advised against holding an outdoor parade the following day, Inaugural Committee chairman Ronald Walker went over to the White House to inform Reagan of the bad news. Reagan at once agreed to cancel the Monday parade and also to take his oath indoors instead of at the west front of the Capitol. At ten o'clock Sunday night, Maryland senator Charles Mathias convened the congressional committee on inaugural arrangements to make plans for the president's oath-taking in the Capitol Rotunda. Walker himself had the unhappy task of informing two hundred high school band leaders and equestrian commanders from all fifty states that they wouldn't be marching in an inaugural parade the following day. "I had tears in my eyes as I tried to explain," he said later, "and so had they."

He promised the high schoolers that the president would meet them at the Capital Center in suburban Landover, Maryland, after the Rotunda ceremony.[24]

Reagan issued a statement Sunday evening explaining that he had decided to cancel the parade and the outdoor ceremony after medical experts said the temperature and wind would "cause significant risks to the well-being of many of the thousands who would attend and work at these events," and that he hoped it would be possible to organize an event following the inaugural ceremony in the Capitol Rotunda "to allow those who have traveled so far and have given so unselfishly an opportunity to be part of this historic occasion." He ended on a cheery note: "It may be cold outside, but our hearts will always be warmed by the many wonderful memories of thousands of our fellow citizens coming to Washington this weekend to join in as we continue to work to make America great again." *Newsweek* quipped that Reagan's second inaugural might be long remembered as "a moment literally frozen in time."[25]

By early Monday morning, the temperature was four degrees below zero and blasts of frigid arctic air were knifing their way through Washington. But the Reagans braved the weather to attend the customary inauguration day worship service at St. John's Church across from Lafayette Park, and then made the trip to the Capitol by limousine, past the now useless $12-million reviewing stand and the empty bleachers along Pennsylvania Avenue. *Time* called the Capitol Rotunda where Reagan took his oath that day an "*ad hoc* theater-in-the-round," and thought the ceremony was "all the lovelier for its make-do, understated quality." The newsweekly also thought it was high time the Californian took his oath inside. "It seemed fitting that this President should rechristen his Administration indoors, and inside the Capitol at that: Reagan still enjoys posing as an outsider, a people's crusader battling Washington, but after four years in the White House, and with four more ahead, the role no longer really fits. To govern is to be an insider."[26]

After lunch in the Capitol's Statuary Hall following his inaugural address, Reagan proceeded to fulfill the promise he had made the day before when the weather forced him to cancel the afternoon parade: he went over to the Capital Center in Landover, with his wife, Nancy, to meet the thousands of youngsters who had come from all over the country with their bands and floats to march proudly down Pennsylvania Avenue that inaugural afternoon. Mrs. Reagan spoke first. "I know how hard and how long you worked," she told the youngsters. "But you wouldn't have liked frostbite." After a few more remarks, she sat down, then suddenly jumped up, as if mortified, one hand covering her face, and exclaimed: "I was supposed to introduce my roommate, who happens to be my husband, who happens to be the President of the United States." Reagan made a few remarks, too, explaining his reluctance to call off the parade. "I had a pair of long johns," he told the boys and girls. "We were rarin' to go!" Inaugural night was bitterly cold, but the nine inaugural balls went off nicely, and the Reagans went to them all, making the rounds in about three and a half hours.[27]

The twentieth century ended decently enough as far as inaugural weather was concerned, and there were no further crises. It was clear and cold for George Bush's inauguration in 1989, magnificently sunny for Clinton's in 1993, and for Clinton's second inauguration in 1997, the day began rather cold, but the sun came out as the inaugural ceremony began, and the day's temperature rose steadily. So did that of Clinton's right-wing enemies.

On the Eve of Their Inaugurations

Most presidents looked forward to their induction into office with eagerness and anticipation. They expressed profuse thanks in their inaugural addresses for the honor conferred upon them, modestly deprecated their ability to live up to the tremendous responsibilities facing them, and promised to do the very best they could, with the help, to be sure, of the wonderful American people. Some presidents probably believed what they said. But for most of them it was simply the proper thing for the president of a democratic republic to say, even though, deep down, they were convinced that they would do a good job in the White House and almost certainly a better job than the man they had just defeated for the presidency.

George Washington, it is true, said he felt like a "culprit" on his way to prison when he learned he had been picked as the first president of the United States, but his triumphal journey from Mount Vernon to New York buoyed his spirits, and though he was a bit nervous when delivering his inaugural address, he seemed to enjoy inauguration day thoroughly and to look forward to meeting the next big challenge in his noteworthy career with courage and resolve. Like Washington, Abraham Lincoln was sober-minded as he traveled from Springfield to Washington, D.C., to take his oath on the eve of the Civil War, but though he had presentiments of death at times, he was mostly upbeat on the journey and enjoyed his exchanges with the crowds that greeted him along the way; he was steeled to do all he could to hold the nation together. As for Franklin D. Roosevelt, he was brimming with confidence as he faced his inauguration as president in the midst of the gravest economic crisis that ever faced the nation. "I am not the least worried about Franklin," said his mother airily, on the train from Hyde Park to Washington. "His disposition is such that he can accept responsibilities and not let them wear him down."[1]

But some presidents-to-be did not feel so good on the eve of their inaugurations. John Adams fussed and fretted about whether he could afford to furnish the Executive Mansion after the Washingtons moved out, and, as he wrote his wife soon after the inaugural ceremony: "I was very unwell, had no sleep the night before, and really did not know but I should have fainted in the Presence of the world. I was in great doubt whether to say anything or not besides repeating the oath."[2] His son, John Quincy Adams, was in even worse shape just before his inauguration, but he had more reason than his father to be glum, for in 1824 the younger Adams had won the presidency only by the skin of his teeth. His major opponent, Andrew Jackson, actually won more popular and electoral votes in the election, but not enough electoral votes to win, and when the House of Representatives, voting by state, picked Adams as the winner, the Jacksonians exploded in wrath, and JQA himself was painfully conscious of the inauspicious way he won the contest. When a congressional committee called to give him official notice of his election, he was bathed in sweat, confessed he had misgivings about the way he was chosen to lead the country, and told the committeemen that if there had been some way, under the Constitution, for voters to express with a "nearer approach to unanimity the object of their preference," he would certainly have acquiesced in their decision. He even mentioned the predicament he was in toward the end of his inaugural address. "Fellow citizens," he said, "you are acquainted with the peculiar circumstances of the recent election. . . . Less possessed of your confidence in advance than any of my predecessors, I am deeply conscious of the prospect that I shall stand more and oftener in need of your indulgence." No wonder he had "two successive sleepless nights" (as he wrote in his diary) just before the inauguration.[3]

Four years later, Andrew Jackson easily defeated JQA's bid for reelection, but Old Hickory was not in a celebratory mood, for he was still mourning for his wife, Rachel, who died shortly after the 1828 election. Still, he had no doubts about his capacity for leadership and he was still convinced that he should have become president in 1825. In 1841, William Henry Harrison was similarly confident about his ability to become a good president, despite his age (at sixty-eight, the oldest president before Ronald Reagan). As if to prove his physical fitness, he was continually on the go in the days before his inauguration. He called on President Van Buren, made a surprise visit to the Senate chamber, attended a preinaugural ball, and visited his ancestral home in Virginia. "The President is the most extraordinary man I ever saw," exclaimed Van Buren. "He does not seem to realize the vast importance of his elevation. He talks and thinks with...much ease and vivacity." Vice President John C. Calhoun was irritated by Harrison's refusal to face the fact that at his age he "lacked the physical strength" to handle presidential responsibilities. The president-elect, moaned Calhoun, was "as unconscious as a child of his difficulties and those of his country," and "he seemed to enjoy his elevation as a mere affair for personal vanity." Calhoun wasn't surprised when Harrison took sick and died soon after becoming president.[4]

Franklin Pierce was, like Jackson, in mourning just before he became president in 1853, but unlike Jackson his mental state bordered on deep depression. A few weeks earlier, he and his wife were in a train accident in New Hampshire and their little boy, Benjamin, only eleven, was crushed to death before their very eyes. Pierce, like his wife, Jane, was devastated; but, with his Calvinistic outlook, he was unable to look on the tragedy as a mere accident. Instead, he decided, he was being punished for his inability to experience a genuine state of grace, despite faithful church attendance, daily prayers, regular Bible reading, and intense heart-searching. His overwhelming guilt may explain why he chose to affirm his loyalty to the Constitution at the inauguration ceremony rather than swear on a Bible, as all the other presidents had. There were other family tensions that haunted Pierce on the eve of his inauguration. Jane Pierce, who loathed politics, had persuaded her husband to take up law after he had served a term in the U.S. Senate, but after a while he quietly returned to politics. She collapsed in shock when he won the Democratic nomination for president in 1852, and when she learned just before the inauguration that he had actively sought the presidential nomination, she was unable to contain her bitterness and resentment. She stayed away from the inauguration, "confounded" by her husband's duplicity, and withheld a locket containing some of Bennie's hair that she had previously wanted him to wear next to his heart on the inaugural platform. Pierce slept poorly the night before his inauguration, grumbled his way through breakfast the next morning, and seemed interested only in getting the inaugural ceremony over and done with as quickly as possible.[5]

Ulysses S. Grant was another president who approached his inauguration without any particular pleasure. He certainly had no gnawing doubts about his qualifications to be president, but in the days before his induction into office in 1869, he was more uncommunicative and closemouthed than usual. "He was very reserved and even restrained," reported his secretary, Adam Badeau, "colder in manner than ever before." He kept his cabinet choices to himself, and when Republican leaders told him they wanted to know his choices, he murmured, "So does Mrs. Grant." Cartoonist Thomas Nast sent him a sketch he had made of the president-elect letting seven cats out of a bag, but without heads, and Grant laughed, but stayed mum. He seemed to be lukewarm about the forthcoming inaugural festivities, even suggesting at one point, to the horror of Washington socialites, that the customary inaugural ball be omitted. On inauguration day, Badeau observed, Grant "bore himself with a distant and almost frigid demeanor that marked how much he felt removed from those who had hitherto been in some sort his associates. That day there was no geniality, no familiar jest, hardly a smile." Badeau could only explain his chief's utter lack of emotion by his awe at joining "the ranks of the earth's mightiest potentates."[6]

The only other president who approached his inauguration with as much seeming indifference as Grant was Calvin Coolidge. The White House's chief usher, Irwin "Ike" Hoover, was astonished at Silent Cal's apparent unconcern about his oath-taking in 1925. It "seemed unnatural," he wrote later, "that such an important event should arouse so little outward feelings. It seemed as if, could it have been so arranged, the president would have liked to keep on with the regular routine, just merging one day into the next, one administration into the other. He would have preferred to take his little walk of ten or fifteen minutes in the morning, spending the day at the office, take another short walk in the late afternoon, retire early, and let it go at that!"[7] But Coolidge had good reason for his restraint. He was still grieving over his sixteen-year-old son, who had died from blood poisoning the summer before.

Two presidents—James A. Garfield and Grover Cleveland—were so depressed by the unremitting pressure of aggressive office seekers after their elections that they couldn't help wondering why they got into the presidential mess in the first place. "From an early hour on the morning after his election...," reported one of Garfield's admirers, "his time was taken, his footsteps dogged, or his sickbed disturbed with the ceaselessly importuning office seekers.... They invaded his private house in swarms. They stopped his carriage in the street; they called him out of bed; they bored him in the railroad carriages and stations; they wrote to his wife and his sons; they courted, fawningly, all his old neighbors and relatives. They covered him with flattery more contemptible than slander; they filled his office with piles of letters it was impossible to read or answer; they sent him tempting presents ... and teasing, coaxing, threatening, they made anxious and unhappy nearly every hour of his life after his election." Though Garfield was an experienced member of Congress, he seemed surprised, even bewildered, by the assaults on his time by people seeking appointments, high and low, in the federal government. "I have been dealing all these years with ideas," he told Maine senator James G. Blaine, his choice for secretary of state. "I have been heretofore treating of the fundamental principles of government and here I am considering all day whether A or B should be appointed to this or that office.... My God! What is there in this place that a man should ever want to get into it?"[8]

In a speech to some Williams College classmates just before the inauguration in 1881, Garfield took a gloomy view of what he was getting into. "Tonight I am a private citizen," he said. "Tomorrow, I shall be called to assume new responsibilities, and, on the day after, the broadside of the world's wrath will strike. It will strike hard; I know it and you know it." He went on to insist that he had never actively sought the presidency. "The honor comes to me unsought," he declared. "I have never had the presidential fever, not even for a day, nor have I it tonight. I have no feeling of elation in view of the position I am called upon to fill and I would thank God were I today a free lance in the House or the Senate."⁹

Garfield's preinaugural unhappiness even produced a strange dream one night. In the dream, he wrote in his diary, he was traveling on a canal boat (as a youngster he was a canal boy) with Vice President–elect Chester A. Arthur and his friend, Major David G. Swaim, when suddenly a rainstorm struck, and as he and Swaim leaped ashore, they saw Chester Arthur lying on a couch in the boat, "very pale, and apparently very ill." Garfield wanted to return to save Arthur, "but Swaim held me, and said he cannot be saved, and you will perish if you attempt it." The next thing Garfield knew, he and Swaim were "naked and alone in the wild storm" and in hostile country. "In this dream," he wrote, "for the first time, for the first time in a dream, I knew I was President-elect. After a long journey, we somehow found a few yards of calico each for partial coverings. After a long and tangled journey we entered a house, and an old negro woman took me into her arms and nursed me as though I were a sick child. At this point I awoke."¹⁰ Despite the anxiety dream, Garfield performed creditably on inauguration day and plunged earnestly into his work as president. A few months later he was assassinated by a disappointed office seeker.

Grover Cleveland had no disturbing dreams about the presidency in 1885, when he took his oath as president for the first time, but he shared Garfield's disgust with the importunities of the pushy office seekers and his lack of enthusiasm at the prospect of becoming president. "I look upon the next four years to come as a cheerful self-inflicted penance for the good of my country," he told Wilson S. Bissell, his former law partner in Buffalo. "I can see no pleasure in it and no satisfaction, only a hope that I can be of service to my people." Not only did the office seekers bother him, he was also upset by the unsolicited but insistent advice on policies from his political associates. "I am sick at heart and perplexed in brain during most of my working hours," he told Bissell. "I almost think that the professions of most of my pretended friends are but the means they employ to accomplish personal and selfish ends. It's so hard to discover their springs of action and it seems so distressing to feel that in the question as to who shall be trusted, I should be so much at sea." At one point he was ready to drop everything, he said, and head for the "North Woods" to think things over.

Still, like Garfield, Cleveland performed ably at his inauguration, and worked hard as president. He also ran for reelection in 1889, losing to Benjamin Harrison, and then, in another try, he beat Harrison in 1892. But the pressure for federal appointments and pensions lowered his spirits again, just before his second induction into office. "Every feeling of jubilation," he confessed to a friend, "and even my sense of gratitude is so tempered as to be almost entirely obscured by the realization, nearly painful, of the responsibility I have assumed in the sight of the American people."[11] Cleveland simply wasn't the cheerful type.

IN the twentieth century most of the presidents—except for Coolidge—approached their inaugurations with great expectations. Theodore Roosevelt (who became president in 1901 upon the assassination of William McKinley and won the presidency on his own in 1904) was exultant on March 3, 1905. "Tomorrow I shall come into office in my own right," he cried just before his inauguration. "Then watch out for me!" Woodrow Wilson eagerly looked forward to outlining his political philosophy in his inaugural address and then presenting his ambitious program for progressive reform to Congress right afterward. Even Warren G. Harding hoped somehow to become America's "best-loved President" in 1921. Dwight D. Eisenhower helped plan the inaugural celebrations in 1953 (he decreed homburgs instead of silk hats and asked for a shorter parade); John F. Kennedy displayed as much youthful exuberance about his inauguration in 1961 as TR had in 1905; Lyndon B. Johnson involved himself in the nitty-gritties of the inauguration in 1965, scrutinizing every detail of the preparations; and Richard M. Nixon's inauguration in 1969 (which he centered on the theme Forward Together) was, *Newsweek* reported, "a triumph of Nixon technique—as precise—and as spontaneous—as clockwork."[12]

For some reason, however, Nixon turned reclusive, closemouthed, and uncommunicative on the eve of his second inauguration in 1973, despite his overwhelming victory in his bid for reelection. Washington, reported *Newsweek,* "has been mystified—and troubled by Richard Nixon's behavior since his re-election. The President's imperious behavior toward Congress, his remoteness from the press and his aloofness from the capital city in which he is supposed to be the leading resident all seemed more appropriate to the royal court of Versailles than to the White House—altogether an air of 'L'état, c'est moi.'"[13] Even Nixon's friends were bothered by the president's increasing isolation from Congress and the press and his bitterness toward his enemies, particularly the anti–Vietnam War protesters. He spent so much more time in the presidential retreat at Camp David than in the White House that some people joked that the inaugural parade would be routed past Camp David after Nixon took his oath as president, and he would send out some of his aides to review it. Fortunately for the Republicans, Nixon's mood lightened as inauguration day approached.

PERHAPS the most laid-back president of them all was Ronald Reagan. "We do have a rendezvous with destiny," he announced at a luncheon in his honor in Los Angeles just before flying to Washington for his first inauguration in 1981. "There is a divine plan that created this union and put us here for the service of mankind." When he got to Washington he was excited and deeply moved by the "Inauguration Spectacular" organized on his behalf, and he attended many of the preinaugural events with pleasure and appreciation. But when the morning of the inauguration arrived, Reagan surprised himself by not having any special feelings about the prospect of becoming, at long last, the president of the United States. He mentioned this to his wife, Nancy, and she confessed similar feelings. "Both of us," he said years later, "kept thinking there was going to come a moment when all of a sudden it hits us, but things kept happening and there you were making a speech, and the crowd, and you still did not have that thing you thought would happen, that moment of awareness."[14]

Unlike John Adams and John Quincy Adams, Reagan slept comfortably the night before he became president. A little before nine on inauguration morning, Michael Deaver, one of his aides, arrived at Blair House to help the president-elect get ready for the inaugural ceremony and found Mrs. Reagan getting her hair done. "Where's the Governor?" he asked. Without moving her head, Mrs. Reagan answered: "I guess he's still in bed." "In bed?" exclaimed Deaver. "If it was me, if I was about to become President of the United States, I don't think I could still be asleep at nine o'clock on the morning of my swearing in." He then opened the door to the bedroom, found it pitch-dark, curtains still drawn, with an indistinct heap of blankets on the bed. "Governor?" he called. "Yeah?" came the sleepy response. "It's nine o'clock!" said Deaver. "Yeah?" repeated Reagan. "Well, you're going to be inaugurated in two hours," said Deaver firmly. Sighed Reagan: "Does that mean I have to get up?"[15] Once he was up, though, he quickly got into the swing of things. He was on location again.

THE MORNING PROCESSION

GEORGE WASHINGTON RODE TO NEW York's Federal Hall in an elegant coach, drawn by four handsome horses, to take his oath as president. John Adams acquired a new carriage, "simple, but elegant enough," to get to Philadelphia's Congress Hall for his induction into office.[1] With Washington, D.C., at last the new nation's capital, Thomas Jefferson walked to Capitol Hill for his first inauguration and rode in a carriage for his second, accompanied by his secretary and a groom. James Madison, Jefferson's successor, was the first president to have an official escort—some militiamen from the area—when he traveled to the Capitol for his inaugurations in 1809 and 1813, and after Madison it became the custom for the president-to-be to head a little procession to the Capitol just before noon on inauguration morning. Madison asked his friend Jefferson to ride with him at his first swearing in, but Jefferson politely declined. "Today I return to the people," he told Madison, "and I wish to join them in doing you honor."[2] The custom of the outgoing and incoming presidents riding together at the head of the procession to the Capitol had not yet become a regular part of the inaugural proceedings.

Madison's processions were small ones, though lustily cheered by people lining Pennsylvania Avenue to see the show, but with subsequent inaugurations the processions increased steadily in size, complexion, and importance. Madison's consisted only of militiamen from Washington and Georgetown. James Monroe's in 1817 included hundreds of people on horseback, as well as militiamen; and Martin Van Buren's in 1837 included mounted representatives of various political organizations that had supported him in the recent election, as well as a voluntary brigade of infantry and cavalry. With William Henry Harrison's inauguration in 1841, however, the morning procession took its place as an event of major significance in the inaugural festivities.

The Whig campaign for the election of Harrison in 1840 had been energetic and boisterous—centering on "log cabins and hard cider" to demonstrate General Harrison's democratic virtues—and the Whigs were determined to make his inauguration equally rambunctious, as thousands of his supporters flocked to Washington to march, cheer, sing, and shout on the "Glorious Fourth of March." Party workers organized a long procession for inauguration morning, made up of militia companies, members of Tippecanoe Clubs from near and far, college students, schoolboys, and veterans who had fought under Old Tippecanoe during the War of 1812. But the organizers also introduced something new and striking for the celebration: inaugural floats. One of the most spectacular was a large platform on wheels, drawn by six white horses, on which rested a power loom from the Laurel Factory, with several operators busily at work producing pieces of cloth and tossing them out to the people lining Pennsylvania Avenue. Most of the other floats were log cabins on wheels, surrounded by cider barrels, coonskins, and other frontier goods celebrating the aristocratic Harrison as a genuine man of the people. Whig marchers also rolled a huge paper ball (as they had done during campaign rallies), covered with Tippecanoe-and-Tyler-too slogans, while singing one of 1840's popular campaign songs: "Keep the ball a-rolling on, For Tippecanoe and Tyler, too!" The crowds gathered along Pennsylvania Avenue liked the parade so much that the inaugural managers asked the participants to troop back and forth for a couple of hours on that joyful morning.[3]

After 1841, organizers of the morning processions added new components—firemen, clergymen, native Americans—and included as many features as they could dramatizing the persona of the president-elect being honored. The marshals for the procession of James K. Polk (Young Hickory) to the Capitol in 1845 carried batons made of young hickory, decked with ribbons, and many of the people lining the street waved branches of hickory as Polk's carriage passed by. For the procession in honor of Zachary Taylor (Old Rough and Ready) in 1849, there were members of Rough and Ready Clubs in the ranks, as well as governors, militiamen, members of state legislatures, Washington and Georgetown officials, army and navy officers, clergymen, and students from Georgetown College.

But floats continued to be the most popular features of the morning marches. During the procession of the feckless James Buchanan in 1857, two special floats attracted a great deal of attention from both the press and the public: one, a flatcar, drawn by six white horses, on which stood a woman dressed like the Goddess of Liberty; the other a sizable replica of the frigate *Constitution* (Old Ironsides), symbolizing the Union, with sailors busily running the sails up and down. The pair of floats suggested that the Union, like Liberty, was in good shape, though neither actually was. For Abraham Lincoln's first inauguration, in 1861, a long float, decorated in red, white, and blue, drawn by four white horses, featured thirty-four pretty girls–representing the states and territories–wearing white frocks and waving little flags. Several newspapers reported that Lincoln bestowed a hearty kiss on each of the little girls, but, as Lincoln biographer Carl Sandburg put it, the story "made interesting reading," but was "neither true nor important."[4]

Blacks appeared for the first time in the procession for Lincoln's second inauguration in 1865, some of them soldiers wearing the Union Army blue and others, members of an Odd Fellows Lodge, in full regalia.

As morning processions developed into major attractions of presidential inaugurations, the protocol for encounters between the outgoing and the incoming president was also taking form. The standard procedure became for the president-elect to make a courtesy call on the president when he first arrived in Washington, and for the president to return the call. It also became customary for the president, sitting on the right, to ride with his successor in the procession to Capitol Hill to witness the latter's oath-taking. Jackson was the first president to do so, in 1837, and his ride with the president-to-be, Martin Van Buren, was a pleasant one, for the two liked and respected each other.

But some of the journeys of the presidents and their successors to the Capitol were not so pleasant. When Zachary Taylor joined President Polk for the procession in 1847, he set the expansionist Polk's teeth on edge (perhaps purposely, since the two had clashed during the Mexican War) by remarking that California and Oregon were too distant to become members of the Union and ought to become independent. Fumed Polk about Taylor in his diary that night: "Uneducated, exceedingly ignorant of public affairs, and, I should judge, of very ordinary capacity."[5]

Buchanan and Lincoln's ride on inauguration morning in 1861 was much more pleasant than the Polk-Taylor trip. But it was a tense day, for the sectional strife was reaching the breaking point, and Lincoln looked as "grave and impassive as an Indian martyr," observers noted, while Buchanan was "pale, sad and nervous." En route to the Capitol, the story goes, Buchanan turned to Lincoln and exclaimed: "My dear sir, if you are as happy in entering the White House as I shall feel on returning to Wheatland, you are a happy man indeed." "Mr. President," Lincoln is reported to have replied, "I cannot say that I shall enter it with much pleasure, but I assure you that I shall do what I can to maintain the high standards set by my illustrious predecessors who have occupied it." This sounds too stilted for Lincoln; indeed, there is no solid evidence that the exchange ever took place. Lincoln himself left no record of the conversation, and all Buchanan mentioned afterward was that "both on the way to the Capitol and the return from it," the president-elect "was far from evincing the slightest apprehension of danger."[6]

But there were threats against Lincoln that day, and General-in-Chief Winfield Scott took no chances. He arranged for the presidential carriage to move along Pennsylvania Avenue between double files of District of Columbia cavalry, with a company of sappers and miners marching in front of the carriage and some infantry and riflemen of the District following behind. Scott also saw to it that cavalrymen patrolled the side streets crossing the parade route, and that riflemen were stationed on the roofs and at the windows of buildings along the avenue, with orders "to watch the windows on the opposite side and fire upon them in case any attempt should be made to fire from those windows on the presidential carriage." After everything went off peacefully that day, General Scott, stationed on a hill nearby, raised his hands and exclaimed: "God be praised! God in his goodness be praised!"[7]

The *New York Times* once observed that on inauguration day, American history centered on "an outgoing President riding up Pennsylvania Avenue with his successor, each trying to make pleasant conversation while each hears the loud ticking of the clock that brings noon nearer."[8] One of the most pleasant clock-ticking exchanges took place between Grover Cleveland and William McKinley at the latter's inauguration in 1897. "Mr. President," ventured McKinley, as they joined the procession to the Capitol, "you are a happier man than I am." Returned Cleveland, almost as if on cue, "I am sure of that, Major."[9] But not all the morning encounters were as cordial as that; some were distinctly chilly, others merely silly.

One of the most amusing presidential chats took place in 1921, when Woodrow Wilson rode down Pennsylvania Avenue in an automobile (the first ever used in the morning procession) with President-elect Warren G. Harding. Harding felt ill at ease when he joined Wilson for the ride, he told friends later, but when the latter began the conversation at once by saying he had discarded horses for an automobile, they got to talking about animals and that put the president-elect at ease right away. "I suppose," Wilson said with a smile, "that your favorite animal is the elephant." Harding admitted that it was, but not because it was a Republican symbol. "And I told him a story about a sister of mine who lived in Siam for many years as a missionary," he recalled, "and had become very fond of a pet elephant. This beast had worked for her and protected her for years, in fact, most of my sister's life. And upon my sister's death in Siam, the elephant would not eat, and obviously was most unhappy. This continued for days. Finally the elephant crouched on its knees over my sister's grave, raised its trunk in the air, and died." That, Harding said, was why he was fond of elephants. "I told this story in some detail," Harding added, "and by the time I had finished, I was much relieved to see that we had almost reached the Capitol." Wilson listened, somewhat bemused, to Harding's tale, and when Harding told him he had always wanted to own an elephant, he murmured: "I hope it won't turn out to be a white elephant."[10]

The Wilson-Harding encounter was a love feast compared to the encounter between Herbert Hoover and his successor, Franklin D. Roosevelt, in 1933. Hoover was horrified by FDR's New Deal proposals for coping with the Great Depression and could scarcely conceal his disdain. Roosevelt made the customary courtesy call on Hoover just before inauguration day, taking his son James (to help him walk), as well as his wife, Eleanor, with him. Hoover served tea, but it "was a rather cool affair all around," one White House staffer recalled. "No one seemed comfortable and everyone was glad when it was over." When FDR was getting ready to leave and adjusting his leg braces, he told Hoover politely, "Mr. President, I know it is customary to do so, but you don't have to return our call if you don't want to." Hoover stiffened. "Mr. Roosevelt," he said coldly, "when you have been in Washington as long as I have, you will learn the President of the United States calls on nobody." Before Roosevelt could respond, Mrs. Roosevelt jumped up and exclaimed: "It's been very pleasant, but we must go now." FDR's son had never seen his father as angry as he was on that occasion.[11]

But Roosevelt tried to be friendly two days later when he rode to Capitol Hill with the anti–New Deal president to take his oath as Hoover's successor. Thousands of people lined Pennsylvania Avenue, waving, shouting, cheering, and singing "Happy Days Are Here Again!" but while FDR grinned, waved, and raised his silk hat in obvious pleasure, Hoover stared bleakly ahead and resisted all of Roosevelt's efforts to make conversation. FDR prided himself on his ability to make small talk, but on this occasion it failed him completely. In desperation at one point, he spied a building under construction along the way and exclaimed: "My dear Mr. President, aren't those the nicest steel girders you ever saw!" There was no response, so he gave up and concentrated on the crowds outside. As he told his secretary, Grace Tulley, later: "I said to myself, 'Spinach!' Protocol or no protocol, somebody had to do something. The two of us simply couldn't sit there on our hands, ignoring each other and everybody else. So I began to wave my own response with my top hat and kept waving it until I got to the inauguration stand and was sworn in." One of Roosevelt's Harvard classmates, watching the procession from a grandstand along the way, couldn't help being struck by the contrast between the faces of the two men in the car: Roosevelt's, full of cheer and confidence; Hoover's, like a lump of dough before it goes into the oven, puffy and expressionless.[12]

Even more strained than the relations between Hoover and Roosevelt in 1933 were those between Harry Truman and Dwight D. Eisenhower in 1953. Once on good terms, the two became alienated during the campaign of 1952 when Ike talked about the "mess in Washington" and Truman dismissed Ike's pledge to visit Korea in person if he became president as "a piece of demagoguery."

On the morning of Ike's inauguration, Truman was in a sour mood. He was hurt because the Eisenhowers had declined his invitation to lunch in the White House right after the inaugural ceremony and irked by the order sent him by inaugural planners to wear a homburg instead of a silk top hat, and though he agreed to do so, he absolutely refused another instruction: to go to the Statler Hotel to pick up Eisenhower for the trip to the Capitol, thus breaking the time-honored tradition that the president-elect call on the president at the White House for the inaugural trip. When Ike learned that Truman wasn't coming to the Statler, he revised his plans and drove to the White House after all, but once he was there, he stayed in the limousine instead of going into the White House, as was the custom, to greet the president. Truman waited impatiently inside for a few minutes, and then decided that with Ike waiting outside, he had made his point, so he went out, shook hands with Ike, and took his place beside him in the car.[13]

Truman and Eisenhower's trip to the Capitol that morning seems to have been extremely painful for both men. Afterward, when Truman was queried by reporters about the ride, he said lightly: "Oh, we talked about the weather, the crowd, the turnout, and how I hoped he would have a very successful regime." Years later, however, he wrote an article for *Look* magazine in which he gave a quite different report of what went on when he and his successor traveled to the Capitol with their congressional escorts, Senator Styles Bridges of Maine and Massachusetts congressman Joseph Martin. There was almost no conversation at first, he recalled, and then suddenly Eisenhower remarked, as he looked out at the crowds along Pennsylvania Avenue, "I did not attend your inauguration in 1949 out of consideration for you, because if I had been present I would have drawn attention away from you." Since Ike was Army Chief of Staff at the time, Truman remembered retorting: "You were not here in 1949 because I did not send for you. But if I had sent for you, you would have come."[14]

But the two men misremembered. Ike had, in fact, attended Truman's inauguration four years earlier; at the request of Kenneth Royall, Truman's secretary of the army, he had appeared in the afternoon parade in 1949, along with General Omar Bradley. Still, Truman's report of the exchange in the car seems to have been accurate. On the night of Eisenhower's inauguration, Truman made an entry in his diary about the ride to the Capitol that morning that confirms what he wrote in *Look* in 1960. "Conversation is general—on the crowd, the pleasant day, the orderly turnover, etc.," he wrote. "Ike finally said that Kenneth Royall tried to order him home in 1948 [1949] for the inaugural ceremony but he wouldn't come because half the people cheering me at that time told him they were for him. I said, 'Ike I didn't ask you to come—or you'd have been here.' Bridges gasped and Joe Martin changed the subject." Ike, like Truman, was unquestionably in an unfriendly mood that morning. Just before joining Truman at the White House, he told some of his associates that he wondered "if I can *stand* sitting next to the guy."[15]

By the time Truman and Eisenhower reached the Capitol, they got into another clash. According to Truman's article in *Look,* Ike suddenly asked him who had ordered his son, John, a major stationed in Korea, to fly to Washington to attend the 1953 inauguration. Truman had issued the order himself, as an act of courtesy, but he got the impression that Ike was suggesting that by giving his son special privileges as an officer, "it was just a way to embarrass him," so he shot back: "If it is, I embarrassed you because I ordered your son to come and he ought to be here."

Eisenhower remembered the exchange with Truman differently. He was delighted to have his son in town, he recalled, but, curious as to who had arranged his son's leave; he had already asked several people, including General

Bradley, Army Chief of Staff, the same question without getting a satisfactory answer. In his memoirs he simply reported that he asked Truman who arranged for his son to go to Washington on leave, and when the latter said, "I did," he "thanked him for his thoughtfulness."

In any case, if Ike had a chip on his shoulder, as Truman thought he did, he soon cooled off. Three days later he sent Truman a letter "to express my appreciation for the very many courtesies you extended to me and mine during the final stages of your Administration....I especially want to thank you for your thoughtfulness in ordering my son home from Korea...and even more especially for not allowing either him or me to know that you had done so." Ike's son also wrote to thank Truman.[16]

Truman politely congratulated Eisenhower after the latter took his oath and delivered his inaugural address, and then joined his wife, Bess, for a farewell party in his honor before leaving Washington for retirement in Independence, Missouri.

In the nineteenth century, inaugural protocol dictated that the ex-president accompany the new president back to the White House before retiring from the scene, but by the twentieth century the custom had been largely abandoned, partly because the afternoon parade had replaced the morning procession as the major celebratory event of the day and partly because there didn't seem to be much point in having the former president hanging around after his administration was over and done with.

Theodore Roosevelt was the first president to abandon the old custom. In 1909, right after his successor, William Howard Taft, finished his inaugural address, TR rushed over, shook his hand, and congratulated him. "God bless you, old man," he cried. "It is a great state document." He then bounded out of the Senate chamber (it was too cold in 1909 to hold the inaugural ceremony outdoors), headed for Union Station to meet his wife, and, before leaving for Oyster Bay, assured reporters that he had had "a bully time" in the White House. TR skipped the ride back to the White House with Taft because he thought it was a "peculiarly senseless performance."[17]

TR's action opened the way for Taft's wife, Helen, to break precedent, too, by becoming the first president's wife to join her husband on the return trip to the White House. Her decision to replace TR provoked objections from members of the congressional inauguration committee (some of whom wanted to ride with Taft themselves), but she stood firm. "I had my way," she wrote triumphantly in her memoirs, "and in spite of protests took my place at my husband's side. For me that drive was the proudest and happiest event of Inauguration Day. Perhaps I had a little secret elation in thinking I was doing something no woman had ever done before. I forgot the anxieties of the preceding night; the consternation caused by the fearful weather; and every trouble seemed swept aside." She was thrilled, too, when she and her husband descended from their carriage and walked together into the White House. "I stood for a moment," she wrote, "over the great brass seal, bearing the national coat of arms, which is sunk in the floor in the middle of the entrance hall. 'The seal of the President of the United States,' I read around the border, and now that meant my husband!"[18]

If Mrs. Taft was the first president's wife to join her husband in the procession back to the White House after the inaugural ceremony, Woodrow Wilson's wife, Edith, was the first to ride with her husband from the White House to the Capitol on inauguration morning for the swearing in. The occasion was Wilson's second inauguration in 1917, and the situation was tense, for the United States was on the verge of war with Germany, and federal and local authorities had taken the most elaborate measures to protect a president since Lincoln's first inauguration in 1861. "The President," reported the *New York Times,* "literally rode to the Capitol and back again through a lane of armed men." Secret Service men, troops of the Second U.S. Cavalry, detectives, and policemen formed a kind of hollow square around the president's carriage as it moved toward the Capitol. National Guardsmen lined Pennsylvania Avenue, and dozens of armed men were stationed on the roofs of buildings overlooking the Avenue. Mingling with the people on the sidewalks, moreover, were plainsclothesmen—"silent, sharp-eyed men"—on the lookout for suspicious activities.

"The heavy escort of Regular troops and Secret Service men which attended us during the procession to the Capitol," wrote Mrs. Wilson years later, "had a look of grim preparation—as indeed was the fact, for letters had been received threatening the President's life." One letter, she recalled, contained details of a supposed plot to throw a bomb at the president's carriage from the roof of a house overlooking the route to the Capitol, and just beyond the Peace Monument "there was an unaccountable halt in the procession and suddenly *plump!* something fell in my lap. *The bomb!* I thought. Happily, only a clump of flowers had been thrown from a window." In the end, the 1917 inauguration, like the 1861 ceremony, went off without incident.[19]

In accompanying her husband to the Capitol in 1917, Edith Wilson set no precedent. Only two presidential wives followed her example in later years: Mamie Eisenhower in 1957 and Nancy Reagan in 1985. To the end of the twentieth century, the majority of the presidents' wives rode in separate conveyances in the presidential procession to Capitol Hill on inauguration morning, and joined their husbands on the inaugural platform outside the Capitol for the swearing in. In 1921, however, Florence Harding, like Helen Taft in 1909, rode back to the White House with her husband after the inaugural ceremony, and that eventually became the accepted practice.

In 1977, Jimmy and Rosalynn Carter did something different. After the inaugural ceremony they boarded the presidential limousine with their daughter, Amy; rode to nearby Constitution Avenue; and then, to the surprise and delight of the people lining Pennsylvania Avenue, they stepped out of the bullet-proof car and started up the avenue toward the White House. Their sons, Jack, Chip, and Jeff, and their daughters-in-law Juliette, Caron, and Annette, fell in behind them and soon their nine-year-old daughter, Amy, caught up with them and skipped alongside as they trekked to the reviewing stand in front of the White House. Vice President Walter Mondale and his wife, Joan, waving to the crowds from the sunroof of their limousine, brought up the rear. "I didn't want to upstage him," explained Mondale later. "I was proud of him—and warmer too."[20]

The *New York Times* was impressed by Carter's action. "In a city where insecurity had bred extraordinary security precautions," the *Times* observed, "and where the commonplace had become uncommon for First Families, the amble down Pennsylvania Avenue by Mr. Carter and his wife, Rosalynn—their 9-year-old daughter, Amy, skipping between them part of the way—was both a rarity and a statement. It dramatized in deed the tone of the new President's Inaugural Address, in which he proposed to help Americans to unite in regenerating a spirit of national comity and openness."

The crowds lining the avenue, startled to see a president fifty feet away in the center of his family, responded enthusiastically. "Hundreds of youngsters raced along the icy perimeters of the avenue beside Mr. Carter," the *Times* reported. "People cheered and waved. 'Jimmy! Jimmy!' yelled one young man. He wore a beard, which was once symbolic of an antiestablishment mood in his generation. Mr. Carter glanced at him, grinning, and waved back. 'All right!' the young man shouted."

A woman in the crowd, holding an empty champagne glass, cried, "Isn't Rosalynn brave? She hasn't even got a hat on." A black Washingtonian exclaimed his approval: "Man, he got out and walked among the people like a man. Not like Nixon. He has got no reason to be scared." The walk took forty minutes, and though some presidents (including Bush in 1989 and Clinton in 1993) walked portions of the route, Carter was the only president to walk the whole distance on inauguration day.[21]

INSTALLING THE VICE PRESIDENT

JOHN ADAMS WAS THE NATION'S FIRST vice president; Adams served two terms with George Washington, but, like most of his successors, he didn't think much of the position. When he first became vice president in 1789, he tried to extract some kind of meaning out of the fact that the U.S. Constitution provided for the vice president to be the president of the Senate. If so, he reasoned, it followed that whenever the president of the United States entered the Senate chamber while the vice president was presiding, there were, in effect, two presidents there.

"Gentlemen," he told the senators, "I feel great difficulty how to act. I am possessed of two separate powers; the one *in esse* and the other *in posse*. I am Vice President. In this I am nothing, but I may be everything. But I am President also of the Senate. When the President comes into the Senate, what shall I be?...I wish Gentlemen to think what I shall be."

Most of the gentlemen in the Senate thought he was a little dotty; they doubted that the heavens would fall if Washington and Adams were in the Senate chamber at the same time, and when Washington walked into the Senate where Adams was presiding on inauguration day, 1789, they turned out to be right.[1]

In 1789, Adams's official swearing in came a couple of months after Washington took his oath as the first president. It wasn't until June that Congress passed a law providing an oath for vice presidents (and for members of Congress and executive officers of the government), and that oath was longer than the presidential oath contained in the Constitution. But length didn't mean importance. During Adams's stint as vice president, he rarely saw the president, was never called on for advice, and found that his activities were confined to presiding over the Senate and attending a few cabinet meetings. He continually complained about his lack of clout. "My country in its wisdom," he told his wife, Abigail, "has contrived for me the most insignificant office that ever the invention of man contrived or his imagination conceived." As far as Adams was concerned, the person who suggested that the vice president be addressed as "His Superfluous Excellency" was right on track.[2]

The president pro tempore of the Senate, New Hampshire's John Langdon, elected by the Senate, swore Adams into office in June 1789 and also administered the oath to Thomas Jefferson, who became vice president when Adams succeeded Washington as president in 1797. Jefferson took a more indulgent view of the office than Adams did. "The second office of the government is honorable and easy," he said, "the first is but splendid misery." But not many vice presidents found the position particularly honorable. Thomas R. Marshall (Woodrow Wilson's teammate) said he felt "like a man in a cataleptic state" when presiding over the Senate; Calvin Coolidge (Harding's) said he didn't feel half as important when he took the vice presidential oath as he did "on the day I graduated from Black River Academy"; and John Nance Garner (Franklin Roosevelt's first vice president) said the vice presidency wasn't worth "a pitcher of warm spit." Garner even joked about the position's inconsequentiality when he took his oath in 1933. "Senators," he said, in some remarks he made on the occasion, "this is my first and possibly it may be my last opportunity to address the Senate." Hubert H. Humphrey also made light of the position when he became vice president (under Johnson) in 1965. He had done some research on former vice presidents, he announced, and learned that they were an illustrious group. "Who can forget those storied Vice Presidents of the past!" he exclaimed. "William A. Wheeler! Daniel D. Tompkins! Garret A. Hobart! And Henry Wilson!"[3] It was a cold, hard fact, he knew, that only if vice presidents went on to become presidents did they make much of a mark on history.

PRESIDENTS pro tempore of the Senate, like John Langdon, did a lot of the swearing in of vice presidents through the years, but they weren't the only ones. Sometimes outgoing vice presidents did the honors; so, on occasion, did senators and representatives (usually friends of the vice president–elect) and associate justices of the Supreme Court. The chief justice was reserved for the president's swearing in, but on two occasions, the venerable Chief Justice John Marshall swore in both the vice presidents (George Clinton and Martin Van Buren) and the presidents (Thomas Jefferson and Andrew Jackson). The procedure was simple: the vice president took his oath in the Senate chamber, made a few remarks if he so desired, swore the newly elected Senators into office, and then joined the procession of dignitaries and their guests to the platform erected outside on the east portico of the Capitol to witness the president's oath-taking and listen to his inaugural address.

Two vice presidents were out of town on inauguration day and took their oaths elsewhere. In 1813, former Massachusetts governor Elbridge Gerry (the "Gentleman Democrat") didn't make it to Washington for the ceremony and was sworn in by a federal judge in Gerry's home in Cambridge. And in 1853, Vice President–elect William King of Alabama took his oath in Cuba. He had gone to Cuba for his health a few weeks before the inauguration, and Congress arranged for his oath to be administered by the U.S. consul in Havana, at a plantation near Matanzas. After he took the oath, some of the Cubans who happened to be there shouted: "*Vaya vol con Dios!* [God be with you!]."[4] But King never got to preside over the Senate, for he died soon after returning to his plantation in Alabama.

In 1937, for the first time, the vice president–elect took his oath on the inaugural platform with the president-elect rather than in a special ceremony beforehand in the Senate chamber. On inauguration day that year, Arkansas senator

Joseph T. Robinson, the Senate majority leader, administered the oath to Texas's John Nance Garner, who responded with a vigorous, "I do!" and then stepped back, without making any inaugural remarks, so that FDR could promptly take the oath. The end of vice-presidential ceremonies in the Senate chamber meant the end of the little addresses that vice presidents customarily gave after they were sworn into office; no doubt this was a good thing. Most of the new vice presidents' remarks in the Senate chamber after taking their oaths were brief, perfunctory, and forgettable. They simply expressed gratitude for the position they were taking over and promised to preside over the Senate with fairness, justice, impartiality, generosity, restraint, thoughtfulness, forbearance, efficiency, and in numerous other kindly ways.

To the senators' dismay, however, in the old days, a few vice presidents insisted on speaking at length after taking their oaths; they gave, in effect, little inaugural addresses of their own, sometimes offering unsolicited and unwelcome advice to the assembled solons. One of the worst offenders was Andrew Johnson, who became vice president in 1865 when Abraham Lincoln took his oath as president for the second time. Johnson wasn't feeling good on inauguration morning; he was recovering from typhoid fever and fortified himself with brandy just before going into the Senate chamber for his swearing in. When Vice President Hannibal Hamlin rose, thanked the Senate for the kindness shown him during the past four years, and then asked whether the vice president–elect was ready "to take and subscribe the oath of office," Johnson jumped to his feet, cried, "I am," launched into a lengthy disquisition on the way the American people were the source of power for all federal officials, including senators, in the American system, and then called proud attention to the fact that he, Andrew Johnson, was a man "who claims no high descent," but "comes from the ranks of the people." Ignoring the susurration welling up from the ranks of his auditors as he rambled on, he drove his point home time and again. Members of Congress derived their powers from the people, he reiterated, and so did Supreme Court justices and cabinet members. Then he started naming names. "You, Mr. Secretary Seward," he cried, looking over at Lincoln's secretary of state, and "Mr. Secretary Stanton," glancing at Edwin Stanton, the war secretary, and then, running out of names, he adverted to his humble origins again and announced: "I, though a plebeian boy, am . . . a man, and grave dignitaries are but men."[5]

As Johnson showed signs of going on indefinitely, Hamlin began pulling at his coattails, and John W. Forney, the clerk of the Senate, made shushing noises, hoping to stem the tide of words. But Johnson was not done; he had some proud words to say about his native state before presenting himself to Hamlin for the oath. When he finished bragging about Tennessee, he repeated his oath inaudibly, his hand on a Bible, and then turned, picked up the Bible, and, facing the audience, announced dramatically: "I kiss this Book in the face of my nation of the United States."[6]

For many people, Johnson placed himself beyond the pale, once and for all, by his behavior that day, but Lincoln was more forgiving. "I have known Andy for many years," he said a day or two later. "He made a bad slip the other day, but you need not be scared. Andy ain't a drunkard." Still, right after Johnson took his oath, a Senate marshal reported that it had stopped raining and Lincoln approved the outdoor ceremony for his own oath-taking, telling the marshal: "And don't let Johnson speak outside."[7]

For the rest of the nineteenth century, most of Johnson's successors confined themselves to brief and platitudinous tidbits after taking their oaths, and then, in 1901, at William McKinley's second inauguration, Vice President–elect Theodore Roosevelt decided to take the occasion of his induction into office as an opportunity to give the senators a lecture on a subject dear to his heart. This time the senators were more indulgent; TR, after all, was enormously popular, tried hard not to overshadow McKinley on inauguration day, and refrained from talking about himself in his little inaugural speech. Still, the *New York Times* reported, "no Vice President ever took the oath in quite the way in which Colonel Roosevelt took it today." When TR's oath-taking moment arrived, he mounted the steps leading to the vice president's desk so precipitously that the senator escorting him had to hold him back to keep pace with him. And as soon as Maine senator William Frye, the president pro tem of the Senate, indicated he was ready to administer the oath, TR snapped to attention, with his hand in a military salute, listened intently as Frye recited the oath, and then exclaimed, "I do," and brought his arm down sharply. He then bounded over to the desk and signed the official document recording his installation in office with a flourish. After that, he took his place as vice president, struck the desk forcefully with the gavel, bowed his head for the chaplain's prayer, and then barely waited for the audience to be seated before smiting the desk again with the gavel and launching into his speech.[8]

TR's speech centered on foreign policy. His main point was that the American people had incurred great responsibilities in the world as a consequence of their victory in the recent Spanish-American War, and that the United States simply had to abandon its traditional "isolationism" and take its (big) place in the sun, frankly and fearlessly, as one of the world's great powers. The U.S. Senate, moreover, said TR, had a vital role to play in seeing that the United States took "a leading part in the shaping of the destinies of mankind." After developing this thought at some length TR concluded: "A great work lies ready to the hand of this generation." At the very end of his talk, almost as an afterthought, he expressed appreciation for the high honor of presiding over the Senate for the next four years.

Francis E. Leupp, a writer covering the inauguration for *Harper's Weekly,* thought that the explosive way in which TR spit out one sentence after another in his speech gave the presentation dramatic force. "His is the manner of a man," wrote Leupp, "to whom the Vice-Presidency has come not as the crowning honor of a long career in the public service, but as a single state in a life overflowing with activity, an opportunity to make a neglected office notable." He also noted that when TR finished his talk, someone in the Senate chamber was "moved by enthusiasm to applaud. Others follow, and a wave of hand-clapping starts on a circuit of the chamber, but is interrupted by a blow of the gavel. . . . For a few glorious moments, Theodore Roosevelt knows how it feels to be the first citizen of the republic."[9]

TR got away with lecturing the Senate mainly because he avoided meddling in the senators' precious prerogatives. The next vice president to make a substantial inaugural speech—Charles G. Dawes, in 1925, when Calvin Coolidge became president—was not so wise. Dawes, in fact, did the unthinkable: he lectured the senators on their procedures in conducting debate and inevitably aroused their anger. His induction into office just before Coolidge's oath-taking turned out to be the sensation of the day, making front-page news in Washington and elsewhere.

It all started innocently enough. Iowa senator A. B. Cummins, president pro tem of the Senate, administered Dawes's oath and then handed him a special gold-mounted gavel made of wood from a piano stool Dawes had used as a boy. At this point, to the astonishment of the senators, Dawes began haranguing them in a loud voice, with much finger waving and desk pounding, on the duties and responsibilities of the upper house and the role the vice president played as the Senate's presiding officer. "Unlike the vast majority of deliberative and legislative bodies, the Senate does not elect its Presiding Officer," said Dawes pointedly. "He is designated for his duty by the Constitution of the United States." Having made it clear that he did not regard the vice president as a mere creature of the Senate, he went on to say that the vice president was concerned with procedural, not substantive, matters, and since he was accountable to the American people who elected him, rather than to the Senate, it was his duty to "express himself on the relations of its methods of transacting public business to the welfare of the nation." Then he lowered the boom: Senate Rule Number 22, which permitted filibustering, worked against the national interest by placing in the hands of one senator or a minority of senators a greater power than the veto power of the president of the United States, which could be overridden by a two-thirds vote in the Senate.

Dawes's blast against Rule 22 outraged the senators; even those who shared his opposition to filibustering resented being lectured to by a man who had never presided over a legislative body before and who was too impatient to get to know the Senate better before sounding off on senatorial procedures. There was some applause in the galleries when he finished his twenty-minute speech, and a great deal of amusement among members of the lower house, but the majority of the senators, Democrats as well as Republicans, sat in cold silence, and Coolidge (who had served as vice president under Harding) looked disgusted, too, though he had never liked Dawes much in any case.[10]

But there was more. Having offended the Senate by his inaugural address, Dawes managed to offend the senators even further by the way he rushed things through that inauguration morning when he came to swear in the newly elected senators. Ordinarily, the senators-elect would walk up to the rostrum in groups of four to take their oaths, and Dawes did allow two such groups to follow the accustomed procedure. But apparently he became impatient about the time it was taking and suddenly called out to the remaining twenty-four senators and their sponsors: "Bring 'em up faster, bring 'em all up!" Like "unruly soldiers being summoned to the guard house," noted one observer, "the bewildered solons were hustled before him, and the oath was administered *en masse*. Then, without awaiting a motion from the floor to adjourn, or the signature of the newly-sworn-in Senators—required by law before a new session could begin–the Vice-President announced that [they] would proceed forthwith to the front of the Capitol for the Inauguration of the President." Cried Missouri Senator Jim Reed afterward: "We'll have to tame him." Dawes never apologized for his behavior at Coolidge's inauguration, but four years later, when he gave a little farewell speech as he left office, he evoked laughter, not anger, among the senators, when, according to *Time,* "he swung his arms, shot his cuffs, and shouted that he took back nothing he had said about the Senate rules" in 1925.[11]

DAWES was the last vice president (up to the present time) to win headlines by talking longer than he should have at a presidential inauguration. Four vice presidents–John Adams, Thomas Jefferson, Martin Van Buren, and George Bush– went on to win elections as president after finishing their vice-presidential terms, and while Adams and Jefferson were famous before becoming President, Van Buren and Bush didn't become well known to the public until they entered the White House. Nine more vice presidents also became nationally known by becoming president when their predecessors died in office (John Tyler, Millard Fillmore, Calvin Coolidge, Harry Truman), were assassinated (Andrew Johnson, Chester A. Arthur, Theodore Roosevelt, Lyndon B. Johnson), or resigned (Gerald R. Ford).

John Tyler was the first of the "accidental presidents," as they were called, and the way he handled his accession to the presidency upon the death of William Henry Harrison in 1841 set precedents for such occasions in the future. Tyler, unlike Harrison, was a states-righter, but he insisted on all his rights and privileges as the nation's chief executive when Harrison died a month after his inauguration. Harrison's cabinet proposed calling Tyler "Vice-President of the United States, Acting President," but the ambitious Virginian would have nothing to do with such strict constructionism. He insisted that the oath he had taken as vice president was adequate for the purpose, but, just to be sure, since Chief Justice Roger Taney was unavailable at the time, he arranged for Judge William Cranch of the United States Circuit Court to swear him in as president.

Three days later Tyler issued a statement to the American people making it clear that he disagreed on fundamentals with the views of such Whig leaders as Henry Clay and Daniel Webster. Before long the Whigs disavowed him, and he became "a President without a party," though he threw one just before leaving the White House in 1845 to prove them wrong.[12]

In July 1850, Zachary Taylor died of cholera morbus a few days after attending a ceremony for the laying of the cornerstone of the Washington Monument, and Vice President Millard Fillmore was sworn in, in much the same way as John Tyler had been. At a joint meeting of the two houses of Congress, Judge Cranch, on hand again, administered the oath making the New Yorker the thirteenth president of the United States, and a few days later Fillmore sent a message to the two houses that was a kind of inaugural address. In his message, Fillmore lauded "the great man" who "has fallen among us," recommended Congress adopt measures for funeral services, and confessed his own reliance "upon Him who holds in His hands the destinies of nations to endow me with the requisite strength for the task" ahead. The *National Intelligencer* expressed satisfaction with the simple ceremony installing Taylor's successor in office. "The sceptre of the People passed into his hands as quietly and as quickly as a power of attorney could be acknowledged before a justice of the peace."[13]

In Andrew Johnson's case, it was the members of Lincoln's cabinet who took things in hand upon the death of Lincoln in April 1865. "The emergency of the Government," they notified the Tennessean, "demands that you should immediately qualify according to the requirements of the Constitution and enter upon the duties of the President of the United States. If you will please make known your pleasure, such arrangements as you deem proper will be made." Johnson suggested taking the oath in the Kirkwood House, where he had been living since arriving in Washington, and there, at 11 A.M., on Saturday, April 15, the day Lincoln died, Chief Justice Salmon P. Chase administered the presidential oath in the presence of all the members of Lincoln's cabinet except Secretary of State William Seward, who had been wounded in an attempt on his life at the time of Lincoln's assassination. After taking his oath, Johnson made a little speech—mercifully shorter than his vice-presidential harangue—promising to be "governed by the great principles of human rights" as president and adding: "My life, as a public servant has been a laborious one. Duties have been mine; consequences have been God's." His auditors were not impressed; they felt let down because he barely mentioned Lincoln in his remarks, and when he did, not by name.[14]

In 1881, when James A. Garfield died a few weeks after being shot by a disappointed office seeker, the members of his cabinet sent Vice President Chester A. Arthur, then in New York, a telegram advising him to take his oath as president "without delay." Within hours, Justice John R. Brady of the New York Supreme Court administered the office in Arthur's Manhattan home, and the two men signed a statement authenticating their action. But when Arthur got back to Washington, he took the oath again, at the suggestion of Attorney General Wayne MacVeagh, just in case the oath-taking in New York hadn't been perfectly legal. The second ceremony, held in the vice president's office in the Capitol, was more elaborate. Former presidents Grant and Hayes were present, along with members of Garfield's cabinet and some members of Congress. Supreme Court justice Morrison R. Waite administered the oath, and Arthur kissed the Bible on which he had placed his left hand, and then read a short statement he had written praising Garfield. He also took the occasion to emphasize the strength of American institutions in a time of crisis. "No higher or more assuring proof could exist of the strength and permanence of popular government," he said, "than the fact that, though the chosen of the people be struck down, his constitutional successor is peacefully installed without shock or strain except the sorrow which mourns the bereavement."[15]

In 1901, when a young anarchist shot William McKinley in Buffalo, where he was attending a Pan-American Exposition, Vice President Theodore Roosevelt was hiking in New York's Adirondack Mountains with his family. Roosevelt was rushed to Buffalo to be sworn in as president by U.S. District judge John R. Hazel. After signing his name to a document legitimating the swearing in, TR told the cabinet members who had assembled for the emergency: "In this hour of deep and terrible national bereavement, I wish to state that it shall be my intention and endeavor to continue, absolutely unbroken, the policy of President McKinley, for the peace and prosperity and honor of our beloved country." Ohio's conservative Republican senator Mark Hanna was at first horrified by the thought of TR in the White House. "Now," he exclaimed, "that damned cowboy is President of the United States!" A few weeks later, however, he felt reassured. "Mr. Roosevelt," he told the *New York World*, "is an entirely different man today from what he was a few weeks since. He has now acquired all that is needed to round out his character—equipoise and conservatism. The new and great responsibilities so suddenly thrust upon him have brought about this change." But TR had not really changed all that much.[16]

Calvin Coolidge didn't change much, either, when he became president upon the death of Warren Harding in 1923. Coolidge seems to have been one of the few people who didn't mind being vice president; he was glad, he said, after assuming the post, to have "a regular job" again. But a sudden job change came on August 3, 1923, when he was visiting his father's farm near Plymouth, Vermont. Around midnight, a telegram from Washington brought the news that Harding had just died of a heart attack and that Coolidge should make prompt arrangements to be sworn in as president. Soon after, Colonel John C. Coolidge, Coolidge's father, a notary public, administered the oath of office to his fifty-one-year-old son by the light of a kerosene lamp. Attorney General Harry Daugherty had telephoned from Washington with the exact words of the presidential oath. There was a Bible in the room, but Coolidge didn't use it because, he later explained, it wasn't the custom in Vermont to swear on Holy Writ. But he did add the words, "So help me God," as most other presidents had, after completing the oath. He also murmured, "I think I can swing it," when the ceremony, witnessed by some neighbors, newsmen, and the local congressman, was over. Soon after, returning to Washington, however, he took his oath of office for a second time. Attorney General Daugherty questioned the validity of the first oath because Coolidge's father, a state official, was only authorized to swear in officers in the state of Vermont. Justice A. A. Hoehling of the District of Columbia Supreme Court administered the second oath, but "Silent Cal" refrained from delivering himself of any inaugural remarks this time.[17]

Harry Truman's accession to the presidency in April 1945, upon the death of Franklin Roosevelt, came shortly after he presided over an afternoon session of the Senate during which he wrote a letter home. Informed, right after the Senate adjourned, that he should get over to the White House as soon as he could, he raced through the Capitol basement, evading Secret Service guards, boarded his car, and reached the White House in record time. "Harry," said Mrs. Roosevelt, when he was taken to her study, "the President is dead." Stunned by the news, Truman murmured, "Is there anything I can do for you?" Returned Mrs. Roosevelt: "Tell us what we can do. Is there any way we can help you?" Mrs. Roosevelt asked for permission to fly on a government plane to Warm Springs, Georgia, where her husband had died, and Truman, suddenly realizing that he was now the president, promptly granted her request. During his oath-taking, in the White House's Cabinet Room early that evening, "everyone was crying and carrying on," Truman recalled, "None of us could believe that FDR was gone."[18]

As Chief Justice Harlan Fiske Stone administered the oath, Truman's wife, Bess, and daughter, Margaret, stood close by, and members of Congress, cabinet members, newspaper reporters, and photographers attended the ceremony. Truman kissed the Bible on which he had put his hand, after taking his oath, and then discussed funeral arrangements with Steve Early, one of FDR's aides, and authorized Secretary of State Edward R. Stettinius to announce that the conference planned in San Francisco to launch the United Nations Organization would go ahead, as scheduled, on April 25. Truman struck Stettinius as "a simple sincere person, bewildered, but who is trying to do everything in his power to meet this emergency."[19]

Sixteen years later the country faced another presidential emergency: on November 22, 1963, John F. Kennedy was assassinated in Dallas, Texas, where he had planned to give a speech when the motorcade he headed reached the city's Trade Mart. Vice President Lyndon B. Johnson was in one of the cars passing down Commerce Street when Lee Harvey Oswald fired the fatal shots from the Book Depository along the way, and the Secret Service agent in Johnson's car shouted, "Get down!" as soon as he heard the shots, and sat on LBJ's right shoulder until the motorcade reached the hospital, to which it had quickly been diverted.

When the doctors pronounced the popular president dead, LBJ refused to leave Dallas until Mrs. Kennedy and the president's remains were brought aboard *Air Force One* at Love Field for the flight back to Washington. From Washington, Attorney General Robert F. Kennedy, the president's brother, called to say that the oath of office should be administered immediately, before LBJ left for Washington, and that it could be administered by any judicial officer of the United States. The deputy attorney general, Nicholas Katzenbach, called to dictate the wording of the oath to LBJ's secretary. Johnson picked Judge Sarah Hughes, whom JFK had appointed to the U.S. District Court in Dallas, to administer the oath. When Mrs. Kennedy came aboard the plane for the return trip to Washington with her husband's body, LBJ was shocked, he wrote later, "by the sight that confronted me. There stood that beautiful lady, with her white gloves, her pink suit, and her stockings caked with her husband's blood. There was a dazed look in her eyes."[20]

Judge Hughes ran into trouble getting to *Air Force One.* When she arrived at Love Field, the guard refused to let her through at first and yielded only when a bystander identified her. When she finally boarded the plane, a bit breathless, she administered the oath to the new president, with Mrs. Kennedy standing next to him on one side and his wife, Lady Bird, standing on the other side. Johnson kissed both his wife and Mrs. Kennedy after taking his oath.

Soon after Judge Hughes left, the plane departed for Washington, and when it arrived at Andrews Air Force Base, outside of Washington, early that evening, Johnson did not leave the plane until the casket was taken off and Mrs. Kennedy had deplaned. Then he walked down the ramp with his wife, shook hands with some of the people gathered there, and went over to the microphones and made a brief statement. "This is a sad time for all people," he said. "We have suffered a loss that cannot be weighed. For me, it is a deep personal tragedy. I know that the world shares the sorrow that Mrs. Kennedy and her family bear. I will do my best. That is all I can do. I ask for your help— and God's."

Although many of President Kennedy's admirers had difficulty reconciling themselves to his replacement, most observers, including Mrs. Kennedy, thought Johnson had behaved creditably in the crisis. Years later, Jack Valenti, one of LBJ's aides, recalled that Johnson exhibited "a coolness and a calmness and a poise" right after the assassination "that to the rest of us, near hysterical, was almost bewilderingly magic."[21]

NONE of the eight "accidental presidents"—from Tyler to Johnson—had vice presidents waiting in the wings to take over if anything happened to them as they finished the deceased presidents' terms. In 1967, however, the Twenty-fifth Amendment was added to the Constitution providing for the president to fill a vacancy in the vice presidency, subject to congressional approval. Six years later, in October 1973, the amendment went into operation when Vice President Spiro Agnew, charged with income-tax evasion and bribe taking, resigned his office. President Richard Nixon appointed Michigan congressman Gerald R. Ford, a Republican moderate, to fill the post, and both houses of Congress voted to approve the appointment. Chief Justice Warren E. Burger swore Ford in as vice president.

But Nixon's presidency itself came soon to an end. In August 1974, as the House Judiciary Committee, after an extensive investigation, began considering articles of impeachment charging obstruction of justice and abuse of power in the Watergate case, Nixon announced his resignation and Ford was sworn in as president by Chief Justice Burger in the East Room of the White House. "As I waited for the proceedings to begin," Ford wrote later in his memoirs, "I felt a sense of awe. It was different from the feeling I'd had when I took my oath as a member of Congress in 1949 or even as Vice President in 1973. At this historic moment, I was aware of kinships with my predecessors. It was almost as if all of America's past Presidents were praying for me to succeed."[22]

Some two hundred people—friends from Michigan, old congressional friends, cabinet members, military officials, and reporters—watched as Ford took his oath, his hands on a Bible, held by his wife, Betty, which was opened to a passage in Proverbs that he used as a prayer every night: "Trust in the Lord with all thine heart; and lean not into thine own understanding." Afterward, Ford walked over to the podium, "conscious that the world was watching me," and delivered a short speech calling for prayers for Nixon and his family and promising to be president of all the people. "My fellow Americans," he said, "our long national nightmare is over. Our Constitution works. Our great Republic is a government of laws and not of men. Here the people rule."[23]

SWEARING IN THE PRESIDENT

COVERING THE INAUGURATION OF William McKinley in 1897, the widely traveled journalist Richard Harding Davis was impressed by the civilian nature of America's presidential oath-taking ceremony as well as by its simplicity. When the president takes his oath, Davis pointed out, "there is not a single man in uniform to stand between him and his fellow-countrymen, crowded together so close to him that by bending forward he could touch them with his hand."[1] And the ceremony that "makes a President," he added, "lasts less than six minutes, while six hours are required to fasten the crown upon the Czar of Russia and to place the sceptre in his hand." In the twentieth century, to be sure, presidential inaugurations acquired an important military component lacking in earlier times, and they also came to possess a religious flavor that nineteenth-century inaugurations did not have. Still, the heart of the ceremony—the taking of the oath prescribed by the Constitution that made a president out of a president-elect—remained brief and simple. It took only a few seconds.

Until James Monroe's inauguration in 1817 the presidents took their oaths indoors. Washington, it is true, took his first oath on the portico of New York's Federal Hall looking out on Broad and Wall Streets, but from John Adams until James Monroe the oath-taking was an indoor ceremony, taking place most of the time in the Senate or House chambers right after the vice president was sworn in. Monroe broke precedent. He took his oath and delivered his inaugural address on a platform erected outside Congress Hall, the redbrick building where Congress met while the Capitol was being rebuilt after British depredations during the War of 1812. While he was taking the oath, it was reported, some American eagles "flew majestically" above.[2]

Outdoor ceremonies could accommodate far more spectators than the Senate and House chambers, and as the crowds inundating Washington on inauguration day increased steadily during the nineteenth century with improvements in the means of transportation to the nation's capital, the move outside was inevitable. But the outdoor ceremony in 1817 was not initially planned; it was the result of a last-minute decision, forced by a petty quarrel between President Monroe and Henry Clay, the powerful Speaker of the House. Clay was in a bad mood on the eve of Monroe's inauguration. He was disgruntled because the senators had spent so much of the money appropriated for furnishing

Congress Hall on fancy chairs for their own chamber that there was barely enough left to buy plain wooden chairs for the House. He was also miffed because Monroe offered to make him secretary of war instead of secretary of state, the position he really wanted, since in those days it seemed to be the road to the presidency. Not only did he coldly turn down the War Department offer, he also flatly refused to permit the use of the capacious House chamber for inaugural purposes. He balked at letting the senators (housed on the first floor) move their elegant chairs up to the House chamber on the grounds that "the plain democratic chairs of the House were more becoming." He also argued that the House floor wasn't sturdy enough to support all the people expected to attend the inaugural ceremony. "Very well," Monroe shrugged off Clay's opposition, "I'll take my oath of office outdoors."[3]

Four years later, the weather was so bad that Monroe held his second inauguration in the renovated Capitol Building, but after that, outdoor ceremonies (except on stormy days) became the accepted practice. On inauguration morning, the president-elect headed down Pennsylvania Avenue to Capitol Hill, attended the induction into office of the vice president in the Senate chamber, and then led a procession of notables—members of Congress, Supreme Court justices, foreign diplomats, and special guests—out to a platform constructed on the east portico of the Capitol, before which hundreds, then thousands, gathered in the plaza below to watch him take the oath administered by the chief justice of the Supreme Court and to listen to the inaugural address. Most presidents in the nineteenth century delivered their inaugural addresses first, and then took their oaths, but by the twentieth century, the custom had changed and the oath came first. It made more sense for the president-elect to officially become the chief executive before he outlined the plans he had in mind for the nation after he entered the White House.

In 1981, for the first time, the inaugural ceremony took place on a platform erected on the west front of the Capitol rather than on the east portico. Ronald Reagan planned to mention Washington, Jefferson, and Lincoln in his inaugural address that year, and by standing on the western side of the Capitol he could see, as he talked, the Jefferson Memorial, the hills of the Arlington Cemetery on the left, and in front of him, across the Mall and the Reflecting Pool, the Washington Monument, with the Lincoln Memorial far beyond. The western location also enabled television cameras to shift from one memorial to another as Reagan referred to the three presidents in his speech, thus adding a sense of immediacy to the ceremony for millions of televiewers around the world.

By Reagan's time visuals were crucial. For the 1981 inauguration, TV technicians used many cameras, took hundreds of shots from different angles so that people watching the proceedings on television were able to see the ceremony from the inside, the outside, and from on high. "The differences between nature and art all but dissolved as Ronald Reagan became the nation's 40th president," declared the *Washington Post*. "It was a scene as theatrical as any in which Mr. Reagan played in Hollywood—the only thing missing was a sudden shaft of sunlight." But the sun did, in fact, come out during the ceremony, and it became part of the telecast. "Well, the sun has appropriately enough ah come out now," reported one of ABC's correspondents, "and begun to shine once again on this beautiful Capital City. I guess that's ah an indication of how the country feels... about the inauguration of the new president."[4]

Chief Justice Warren E. Burger, who administered Reagan's oaths in 1981 and 1985, was the twelfth chief justice to perform the task, and William Rehnquist, who succeeded him in 1986, performed the twentieth century's three remaining ceremonies. From 1789 to 1997, only thirteen chief justices did the honors, with John Marshall being the busiest (nine inaugurations, from Jefferson to Jackson), followed by Roger Taney (seven inaugurations, from Van Buren to Lincoln). William Howard Taft was the only former president to administer the oath, and the first time he did so, on the occasion of Calvin Coolidge's inauguration in 1925, he delivered the oath slowly and deliberately because he was "fearful lest I might forget it," he said later. But, he added happily, his slow delivery made it so distinct, "that I have heard from many places in the country that they heard every word and recognized my voice." In 1929, when he inducted Herbert Hoover into office, he said "preserve, maintain, and protect," instead of "preserve, protect, and defend," but few people noticed the error. The other twelve chief justices seem to have performed the ceremony without any slips, including Roger Taney, who, at eighty-four, looked like a "galvanized corpse" at his last inauguration in 1861.[5]

Most presidents took the oath with right hand raised and left hand resting on a Bible. Frequently there was something special about the Bible; it might be an old family Bible (like George Bush's), a gift of the president's mother when he was a boy (Cleveland's and Eisenhower's), an inaugural present from some admirers (Polk's), and, on three occasions, it was the very Bible that George Washington had used in 1789. At first the Bible was opened at random for the ceremony, but by the middle of the nineteenth century, presidents were selecting favorite passages or passages relating to themes they intended to explore in their inaugural addresses.

In 1865, Lincoln's Bible was opened to a passage in Isaiah, and after the ceremony Chief Justice Salmon P. Chase presented the Bible to Mrs. Lincoln with the passage carefully marked. In 1905, Theodore Roosevelt's Bible was appropriately opened to the words, "Be ye doers," and as he recited the oath, he stood straight, like a soldier, chin in and chest out, spoke as if he were "biting his words," according to one reporter, "and showed his teeth in the familiar Roosevelt way depicted in cartoons."[6] Herbert Hoover requested the Sermon on the Mount for his induction into office in 1929, but there was a slipup, and the Bible was instead turned back to Proverb 29: "Where there is no vision, the people will perish; but he that keepeth the law, happy is he." John Quincy Adams was the only president not to use a Bible; he swore his allegiance to the Constitution with his hand on a book containing the laws of the United States. Adams was no conventional secularist, but his conscientiousness about reserving the Good Book for strictly religious purposes was unique. Even church-state separationist James Madison took his oath on a Bible.

Franklin D. Roosevelt's scriptural preference was for the passage in First Corinthians about faith, hope, and charity, and he utilized that passage in all four of his inaugurations. *New York Times* reporter F. Raymond Daniell thought that

FDR's oath-taking in 1937, his second, while the rain was falling, was unusually impressive. "The unexpected, the un-scheduled, the more drastic incident took place before the President began his inaugural address," observed the *Times*. "It was indefinable, intangible, and yet it impinged upon the consciousness of almost everyone there, as Lincoln's elo-quence at Gettysburg must have impressed those fortunates who heard it. It came as he repeated after Chief Justice Charles Evans Hughes the traditional oath of office taken by the thirty-one Presidents who have preceded him.

"The President and the Chief Justice were scarcely a yard apart. The Presidential flag crept up the mast slowly and soddenly as the magnified voice of Justice Hughes floated over the crowd.

"Mr. Roosevelt, with his left hand upon the Bible and his right hand upraised, listened intently to the solemn words with which for 150 years the chosen leaders of the people have acknowledged their responsibility to all the nation.

"Then he responded. There was no trace of the famous campaign smile. His strong jaw came out; his strong vibrant voice resounded over the rain-drenched throng and was car-ried resonantly to the far island territories and to ships at sea by the mechanistic miracle of radio.

"Not content was he to say 'I do.' Instead he repeated the oath verbatim, emphasizing by his manner and by his voice the words 'Constitution,' 'preserve, protect and de-fend,' and bearing down hard on the word 'domestic,' as contrasted with foreign enemies.

"It was a moment to be remembered. At the risk of being trite, one might say that it was not what was said but the way in which it was said. The emphasis was not lost upon the crowd. Under the umbrellas men and women turned to one another. They understood."[7]

Whether the conservative Justice Hughes understood is another question. A few days later, Roosevelt told Samuel I. Rosenman, one of his speech advisers, that when Hughes read the oath and came to the words, "support the Constitution of the United States," he felt like saying to him: "Yes, but it's the Constitution as I understand it, flexible enough to meet any new problem of democracy—not the kind of Constitution your Court has raised up as a barrier to progress and democracy." Still, the liberal president and the conservative justice remained on good terms. Four years later, when Hughes swore FDR in as president for a third time, he told the latter afterward: "I had an impish desire to break the solemnity of the occasion by remarking, 'Franklin, don't you think this is getting to be a trifle monotonous?' " Hughes had retired by the time of FDR's fourth inauguration, in 1945, and Chief Justice Harlan Fiske Stone, a good liberal Republican whom FDR had elevated to the chief justiceship, performed the ceremony.[8]

George Washington said "So help me God," after taking his oath in 1789, and kissed the Bible, too, and most of his successors followed his example. In 1909, when Taft kissed the Supreme Court Bible that Chief Justice Melville Fuller brought to the ceremony and cried, "So help me God!", there were loud cheers in the audience and some looks of surprise, for Taft, a Unitarian, had been called an infidel during the presidential campaign the year before. For some reason, Franklin Roosevelt omitted the utterance at his first inauguration in 1933, perhaps because he was eager to get to the address outlining his approach to the economic crisis facing the nation, but in 1937 he did as Washington and the other presidents (except for John Quincy Adams) had done at the end of the oath. In 1941, Hughes said, "So help you God?" when he finished reading the oath, and FDR affirmed, "So help me God," and in 1945 he needed no prompting.[9] In 1961, when John F. Kennedy was taking his oath on a Douay Version of the Bible (an authorized Roman Catholic translation) that had belonged to his grandmother, he inadvertently moved his hand from the Bible to his side, and afterward some people questioned the validity of his oath. But the White House patiently explained that the Constitution didn't prescribe the use of the Bible at the inaugural ceremony and that it was simply a tradition that had begun with George Washington.

At his inauguration in 1949 Harry Truman used two Bibles—the one on which he took his oath right after FDR's death in 1945 and the other a facsimile of the Gutenberg Bible, which friends in his hometown, Independence, Missouri, had given him—and for a time using two Bibles was the vogue. In 1953, Dwight D. Eisenhower used the George Washington Bible, as well as the one his mother gave him when he graduated from West Point; in 1969, Richard Nixon used family Bibles, dated 1828 and 1873; in 1977 Jimmy Carter used the George Washington Bible, as well as a Bible his mother had given him; and in 1989, George Bush used the Washington Bible, as well as a family Bible when he took his oath. Bill Clinton reverted to the one-Bible tradition at his inaugurations in 1993 and 1997.

The wives of the presidents didn't get into the oath-swearing act until the twentieth century, though in 1869, right after taking his oath, Ulysses S. Grant turned to his wife (who was sitting on the inaugural platform near him), took her hand, and exclaimed: "And now, my dear, I hope you're satisfied." In 1913, Woodrow Wilson used a little Bible (opened to a passage in the Psalms) belonging to his wife, Ellen, and she stood by him as he took his oath. In 1921, Warren G. Harding's wife, Florence, didn't stand by her husband as he was sworn in, but according to at least one reporter she came close to participating in the ceremony. "Mrs. Harding's eyes were fixed upon her husband," he wrote; "it seemed that she was repeating the words after him. Her big, gray eyes were shining; her face flushed. She nodded slightly; I felt as if she were confirming her husband's promises."[10]

Not until 1965, when Lyndon Johnson became president, did a presidential wife actually take part in the ceremony. At 12:30 P.M., as cannons across the Potomac boomed a twenty-one-gun salute, Mrs. Johnson took a position between Chief Justice Earl Warren and LBJ, and, gazing into her husband's eyes, held up a dog-eared family Bible Johnson's mother had given him, while Warren started reading the oath. But after Johnson repeated the first phrase of the oath, he suddenly realized that he had forgotten to put his hand on the Bible, so he quickly corrected himself and continued reciting the oath so slowly and softly that he could hardly be heard. After adding, "So help me God," he looked at Lady Bird and she affectionately squeezed his hand, then he turned and began his inaugural address. The wives of Johnson's successors—Pat Nixon, Rosalynn Carter, Nancy Reagan, Barbara Bush, and Hillary Clinton—all participated in the oath-taking ceremony, and Reagan kissed his wife afterward, as did Clinton. (In 1993, Clinton also hugged everyone around him except Chief Justice Rehnquist.) Nancy Reagan was deeply moved as she held the Bible for her husband in 1981. "*My Lord,*" she recalled thinking, "*here I am standing here, doing what I've seen other women do in photographs and on television. And it's me. And it's us. It's really happening.*"[11]

For years the inaugural ceremony began promptly with the vice president's oath and then the president's, and ended with the president's inaugural address, but in the last part of the twentieth century, religious elements were added that lengthened the ceremony whose simplicity Richard Harding Davis had celebrated in 1897. In 1933, Franklin Roosevelt inaugurated the custom of attending a church service in Washington before proceeding to Capitol Hill, and although church attendance was always optional, it became an essential part of the inaugural activities. In 1941, FDR also added a benediction to the oath-taking ceremony, and in 1945, an invocation (by Episcopal minister Angus Dun) as well as a benediction (Catholic priest John A. Ryan). In 1953, Eisenhower added a rabbi (Abba Hillel Silver) to the ceremony, and in 1957, he included four religious leaders— Protestant, Catholic, Jewish, and Greek Orthodox. Not all his successors were that ecumenical. George Bush invited popular evangelist Billy Graham to deliver all the prayers at his swearing in, and in 1997, Bill Clinton included Graham on the program, too. It was Graham's eighth appearance at an inauguration; in all, he had participated in more inaugurations than Justice Taney, but fewer by one than Justice Marshall.

The religious side of America's inaugurations has never, to be sure, approached that of British coronations, which include the sacrament of the Lord's Supper, and the American ceremony has been balanced by the addition of non-religious elements since World War II, including choirs, opera singers, and popular songsters rendering "The Star Spangled Banner" and other patriotic songs for the delectation of the inaugural audience. Opera diva Jessye Norman sang a medley of religious and patriotic songs just before Clinton took his oath in 1997, and after he delivered his address, Santita Jackson, daughter of civil-rights activist Jesse Jackson, sang the national anthem, accompanied by the Resurrection Choir (made up of members of various black churches that had been destroyed by arsonists during the past few months). "Great singing," exclaimed a college student, hurrying off to Pennsylvania Avenue and the afternoon parade afterward, "and I'd say O.K. speech."[12] In an innovation, Kennedy invited poet Robert Frost to appear at his swearing in in 1961, and Clinton, following in his hero's footsteps, had a poet at his inauguration in 1997: Miller Williams, an Arkansas poet who didn't claim to be in the same league with Frost, read a folksy poem, "Of History and Hope," especially written for the occasion, that pleased many people.

THE inaugural ceremonies didn't always go smoothly. Sometimes the presidents were late and the crowds outside the Capitol became restless, particularly in bad weather. At Lincoln's first inauguration a boy fell out of a tree just as Lincoln began speaking, but the lad was uninjured. At Hoover's inauguration in 1929, Mrs. Hoover and Mrs. Coolidge got lost on their way out to the inaugural platform and their husbands waited bewilderedly until they finally appeared and the show could go on. When Bush came to recite his oath in 1989, he was so keyed up that he blurted out, "I do—," just a beat ahead of the moment he was supposed to begin repeating the oath after Chief Justice Rehnquist, but he quickly caught himself, smiled nervously, and began again.[13] But these were minor slipups compared to the two crises that faced Kennedy during his installation into office in 1961.

The first crisis involved Richard Cardinal Cushing of Boston, a friend of the Kennedy family, who gave the invocation. He offered the first of four prayers (representing the Catholic, Protestant, Jewish, and Greek Orthodox faiths) that, as in 1957, formed a part of the inaugural ceremonies. Cardinal Cushing's prayer was by far the longest; it took twenty minutes to deliver. At one point, in fact, as Cushing slowly droned on, Speaker Sam Rayburn's sister became impatient, sat suddenly down, and murmured: "That man should be shot."

But Cushing had his reasons. While he was praying, a trickle of smoke had begun rising from the lectern. When Secret Service Chief U. E. Baughman saw the smoke, his heart, he wrote later, almost stopped; though he had checked the wires underneath the podium before the ceremony, he was now almost sure there was a short circuit, but he wondered whether the firemen (whom he had sent at once into action) could locate the trouble in time to prevent a fire. His first impulse was to clear the inaugural stand at once, and three times he started to give the order, but he resisted each time for fear of starting a panic. Finally, "after an eternity of four minutes," as he put it later, one of the firemen located the short-circuiting wires, disconnected them, and quickly brought the smoldering to an end. The trouble, it turned out, had started in an old electric motor, used, since Franklin Roosevelt's days, to adjust the height of the lectern.[14]

Afterward, Cardinal Cushing revealed that he had seen the smoke and it had occurred to him that it might be coming from a smoldering bomb intended for Kennedy, and for that reason he had decided to recite his prayer as slowly as he could so that if there was an explosion, he, not Kennedy, would take the impact of it. Only a few people seated nearby—including Eisenhower and Kennedy—had noticed the smoke, but they remained calm and relaxed, knowing that the Secret Service had things under control. Reporting the event, *Newsweek* suggested that "some of the onlookers, numbed by the 22-degree cold, looked as though they might be more comfortable if the Capitol had burned down." Some wags, according to the *Washington Times-Herald,* said the smoke "was a sign from God" for the Cardinal "to shut up." Inaugural planners put a time limit on prayers for the next inauguration.[15]

The appearance of poet Robert Frost, at JFK's request, on the 1961 program, right after Vice President Johnson's swearing in, also ran into some trouble. Frost wrote a special poetic preface to "The Gift Outright," a poem he had written in 1930, which he planned to read at the inauguration. He also wrote Kennedy a gracious response to the invitation to appear on the program. "If you can bear at your age the honor of being made president of the United States, I ought to be able at my age to bear the honor of taking some part in your inauguration. I may not be equal to it but I can accept it for my cause—the arts, poetry, now for the first time taken into the affairs of statesmen." The preface he composed for the occasion contained the lines:

> Summoning artists to participate
> In the august occasions of the state
> Seems something artists ought to celebrate.[16]

Unfortunately, when Frost walked over to the lectern and spread out the paper on which he had written his preface, the bright sun blinded him and he found it impossible to read. "I am not having a good light at all here," he murmured, and Vice President Johnson leaped forward to shade Frost's paper with his hat. But it didn't help, and Frost finally told the audience: "This was supposed to be a preface to a poem that I can say to you without seeing it. The poem goes this way...." He then recited "The Gift Outright" from memory. In doing so, he did something unusual for a writer: he changed a word in the last line of the poem to make it fit Kennedy's inauguration. The original phrase, referring to America, was, "Such as she was, such as she would become," but Frost changed the "would" to a "will," because, as he later explained, Kennedy "wants to say 'will' because it is in the four years ahead that he is going to do something here." Recounting Frost's "misadventure" at the podium, *Newsweeek* thought it provided "one of the most moving moments of the ceremony."[17]

GEORGE WASHINGTON'S FIRST INAUGU-
ral address in 1789 was splendid in its sweep, but his second, delivered in 1793, was a tiny little gem. The old hero
was out of sorts when he faced his second inauguration.
Having reluctantly agreed to serve as president for a second term, he was surprised, then grievously wounded, by
the vicious attacks he received in the press for espousing
Hamiltonian rather than Jeffersonian policies for the young
republic. He was particularly upset when his critics blasted
the public celebration of his sixty-second birthday, just
twelve days before the inauguration, as a "monarchical farce."
Washington was no prima donna, but he did enjoy the

recognition he received for his many years of service to his country.

For a time Washington considered the possibility of taking the oath of office in 1793 quietly at home, with only the heads of departments present, but his secretary of war, Henry Knox, convinced him that it was important for him to appear in public for the occasion, since he was the only force holding the young nation together. His secretary of treasury, Alexander Hamilton, and Secretary of State Jefferson agreed with Knox. In the end, Washington decided to go ahead with a swearing-in ceremony in the Senate chamber, with Associate Justice William Cushing administering the oath. But his inaugural address was short and curt: two paragraphs, four sentences, 135 words, the shortest in inaugural history. In the first paragraph Washington declared, "When the occasion proper for it shall arrive, I shall endeavor to express the high sense I entertain of this distinguished honor," and in the second paragraph, referring to the presidential oath, he announced: "If it shall be found during my administration of the government I have in any instance violated willingly or knowingly the injunction thereof, I may (besides incurring constitutional punishment) be subject to the upbraidings of all who are now witnesses of the present solemn ceremony."[1] It's a pity that such long-winded orators as William Henry Harrison didn't take a look at Washington's second inaugural when they were preparing their own speeches.

Harrison's address in 1841 was a disaster. He spoke for an hour and forty minutes, despite the bitter cold and the response of the people on the outdoor platform, who stamped their feet and moved around in an effort to keep warm and whispered to one another while he was speaking. Before the inauguration, Daniel Webster tried to get Old Tippecanoe to use a speech that Webster had written for him, but the latter declined, though he graciously consented to look it over and to let Webster see the address he had already written. Webster was dismayed when he got a look at Harrison's handiwork. He thought it too wordy and too loaded with references to ancient Greece and Rome, and that in general it had "no more to do with the affairs of the American government than a chapter in the Koran." He finally persuaded Harrison to let him edit and revise the manuscript, and he apparently slaved for hours before getting it into what he deemed acceptable shape. When he arrived at his boardinghouse afterward, late for supper, and sank onto the couch, thoroughly exhausted, a friend expressed the fear that something unusual had happened. "You would think something had happened," sighed Webster, "if you knew what I have done. I have killed seventeen Roman pro-consuls as dead as smelts, every one of them." Even so, Harrison's address was excruciatingly long, gangly, repetitious, and platitudinous. But those were the days of effusive oratory, and some people—Horace Greeley, for one, and Missouri senator Thomas Hart Benton, for another—even liked it.[2]

It is only fair to note that Harrison's wasn't the only monumentally boring inaugural address ever delivered. Among the fifty-five inaugural addresses composed between 1789 and 1997, only a handful have achieved distinction and bear reading today (except by historians): Washington's first

(1789), Jefferson's first (1801), Lincoln's first (1861) and second (1865), Wilson's first (1913), Franklin D. Roosevelt's first (1933), and John F. Kennedy's (1961). The very best inaugurals discussed important issues with high seriousness, were written with verve, imagination, and an engaging prose style, and were eminently quotable. Theodore Roosevelt was a good writer, but he did not consider inaugural addresses of prime importance, and the speech he made at his inauguration in 1905 was merely creditable.

Until 1933, when Franklin Roosevelt became president, most presidents wrote their own addresses, but by FDR's time, the pressure of public business and demands for presidential speech-making had become so enormous that presidents were forced to turn to professional speechwriters for help in preparing their inaugurals. Presidents utilizing speech advisers usually worked as hard on their inaugural addresses as presidents who composed their own addresses. Sometimes they wrote first drafts for speechwriters to whip into shape or suggested themes and ideas, and even phrases, sentences, and paragraphs for their advisers to use in preparing the inaugural; and they almost always carefully studied the drafts submitted to them by their advisers to be sure they represented accurately what they wanted to convey to the American people on inauguration day.

Teamwork didn't necessarily mean mediocrity; and presidential authorship didn't guarantee distinction. John Adams wrote his own inaugural address in 1797 and it was wordy and ponderous; one gawky sentence contained over seven hundred words. Adams could be vivid, witty, acerbic, and charming in his private correspondence, but his public papers were frequently snoozers. But FDR and JFK, who worked closely with gifted writers, came up with stunning inaugurals in 1933 and 1961.

Some presidents agonized over their inaugural addresses. Weeks before his inauguration in 1881, James A. Garfield began reading the inaugurals of his predecessors and taking notes on them, but he couldn't seem to find time to start writing one of his own. "I must begin preparations for the inaugural," he reminded himself in an entry in his diary, as inauguration day approached. "I have half a mind to make none. Those of the past except Lincoln's, are dreary reading. Doubtless mine will be also." Finally he got around to organizing his thoughts and starting to write, but almost at once felt "unusual repugnance to writing," and toyed again with the idea of skipping the speech at the inauguration. And so it went, on and off, until the night before the inauguration, when he finally got down to business and at long last completed his speech at 2:30 that morning. It was by no means an outstanding piece of work, but he never claimed it was, and after delivering it he was pleased that the "drift of public comment" turned out to be "far better than I expected."[3]

Garfield's ordeal was unusual. But most presidents sought the advice of their colleagues before feeling satisfied with what they had written. Grover Cleveland read the manuscript of the speech he had prepared for his second inauguration in 1893 to a close friend, and only when the friend pronounced it excellent did he commit it to memory. (Cleveland and Pierce were the only presidents to deliver their addresses without manuscripts or notes.) In 1953, Dwight Eisenhower insisted on discussing his inaugural speech in some detail at a conference with the people he had picked for his cabinet, soliciting criticism, not praise, before putting it into final shape.

ABRAHAM Lincoln, the greatest writer of them all, worked hard on the address for his first inauguration in 1861. With the country headed for civil war, he was eager to be conciliatory toward the South as well as to make clear his determination to uphold the Union. He wrote the first draft of the address in Springfield, Illinois, read it to his wife (who seems to have made no suggestions), and then showed it to his friend Judge David Davis (who proposed a few minor changes), just before leaving for Washington. When he reached Indianapolis, he asked his friend O. H. Browning to look it over, and Browning persuaded him to soften one of the statements in the address directed to the South.

Then came an unexpected crisis. When the presidential party reached Harrisburg, Lincoln decided to do more work on the address, but, to his chagrin, he ran into trouble locating the printed copies of the address, which he had put into a "grip-sack" and entrusted to his oldest son, Robert, for safekeeping. "When we reached Harrisburg and had washed up," Lincoln recalled, "I asked Bob where the message was, and was taken aback by his confession that in the excitement caused by the enthusiastic reception [in Harrisburg], he believed he had let a waiter take the grip-sack. My heart went into my mouth, and I started downstairs, where I was told that if a waiter had taken the article, I should probably find it in the baggage-room. Hastening to that apartment, I saw an immense pile of grip-sacks and other baggage, and thought I discovered mine. The key fitted it, but on opening there was nothing inside but a few paper collars and a flask of whiskey. Tumbling the bags right and left, in a few moments I espied my lost treasure, and in it the all-important document, all right . . . !"[4]

His precious document retrieved, Lincoln presumably kept it close by him after that, and when he reached Washington, he showed it to Francis P. Blair, who liked it immensely and proposed no revisions. But William H. Seward, Lincoln's choice for secretary of state, to whom he gave a copy soon after reaching Washington, took Lincoln's request for comments quite seriously, and wrote him a long letter the following day, making several major suggestions for improving the speech. Like Browning, Seward favored toning the speech down in order not to antagonize the South; he also wanted Lincoln to be more conciliatory, especially at the very end.

Seward liked most of what Lincoln had written. He thought Lincoln's arguments against secession and for preserving the Union were "strong and conclusive, and ought not to be in any way abridged or modified." But he thought that "something besides or in addition to argument" was "needful—to meet and remove prejudice and passion in the South, and despondency and fear in the East. Some words of affection," he believed, "some of calm and cheerful confidence" at the close of the address, might help reduce the tensions gripping the nation. For the purpose, he submitted the following paragraph for Lincoln's approval:

I close. We are not we must not be aliens or enemies but fellow countrymen and brethren. Although passion has strained our bonds of affection too hardly they must not, I am sure they will not be broken. The mystic chords which proceeding from so many battle fields and so many patriot graves pass through all the hearts and all the hearths in this broad continent of ours will yet again harmonize in their ancient music when breathed upon by the guardian angel of the nation.

Lincoln decided to follow Seward's suggestion for some conciliatory remarks at the end of the address, but he transmuted the wordy paragraph Seward sent him into a short, but more moving statement, containing, as so often with Lincoln, a touch of poetry:

I am loath to close. We are not enemies, but friends. We must not be enemies. Though passion may have strained, it must not break our bonds of affection. The mystic chords of memory, stretching from every battlefield and patriot grave to every living heart and hearthstone, all over this broad land, will yet swell the chorus of the Union, when again touched, as surely they will be, by the better angels of our nature.[5]

Lincoln's address came first on the program in 1861 (as it did with several other presidents in the nineteenth century), and after Republican senator E. D. Baker of Oregon introduced him to the crowd, Lincoln stepped up to the front of the inaugural platform, put the manuscript of his address on a little table, slipped his new gold-headed cane under the table, and then stood uncertainly for a moment wondering what to do with his tall silk hat. In a famous gesture, Democratic senator Stephen A. Douglas of Illinois (who had beaten Lincoln in a run for the Senate in 1858 and had run against him for president in 1860) leaned forward to relieve him of the burden. ("Well, if I can't be President," he told friends later, "at least I can hold the President's hat.") To the surprise of the spectators, Lincoln took out a pair of steel-bowed spectacles and placed them on his nose before beginning his address. "Take off them spectacles," cried one fellow, "we want to see your eyes." Another man called out: "I didn't know he wore glasses, they ain't in the picture." About this time a man with fiery red whiskers, who had climbed a tree to do some haranguing, started in again and was shushed by people around him before being rushed off to the guardhouse by police.[6]

When Lincoln started reading his address, he seemed a bit nervous, but he soon hit his stride and was speaking in a firm, clear voice. "Never was there a more solemn spectacle," recalled L. A. Gobright. "The thirty thousand auditors who listened attentively to his words, were evidently most deeply impressed with the momentous character of the occasion. There was no noise, no confusion, no thoughtlessness nor indecent scenes of applause or disapprobation. All seemed to be moved with the deep conviction, that their own fate and that of their country, depended on the developments of that memorable day."[7]

Unlike Lincoln, some presidents merely mumbled when delivering their inaugurals. In 1805, Jefferson spoke "in so low a voice," according to John Quincy Adams, "that not half of it was heard by any part of the crowded auditory." Madison also spoke in a voice "so low" in 1813, recalled Sarah Seaton, that "scarcely a word could be distinguished as he spoke." But even presidents who read their addresses loudly and clearly were usually heard by only the people sitting near them on the inaugural platform, leaving the crowd standing below to depend on broadsides reproducing the speech or on newspaper reports to find out what the president had said at his inauguration.[8]

In 1909, when bad weather forced Taft to give his address in the Senate chamber, the *New York Times* rejoiced that for a change the president could be heard by everyone. "Not a word was missed," exulted the editors. "For the first time in a century every handclap that was given represented the honest enthusiasm of the men and women who actually heard the President's words. Those familiar with inauguration ceremonies could hardly believe their eyes and ears. There was no pretense, no humbug, nothing slipshod or ridiculous; the whole was so dignified, so effective, so impressive, that it seemed not like an inauguration, but like something really important."[9]

But it was back to the old ways with Woodrow Wilson, Taft's successor in 1913, and the *New York Times* was moved to complain again. Wilson spoke clearly and confidently at his second inauguration in 1917, on the east portico of the Capitol, but the cold wind carried his words away and it is doubtful that anyone heard him except the chief justice and Mrs. Wilson, who stood by his side. The *New York Times* couldn't help wondering again whether large outdoor ceremonies were worth the trouble and expense, when most people couldn't hear what the president was saying. "It is this feature of inaugurations," said the editors, "which has made many an old-timer wonder whether this particular way of installing our Presidents might not be changed to some way more dignified and impressive, for no President's address has ever been heard by more than fifty people, since present conditions began to prevail, except that of President Taft, which had to be delivered indoors because of a blizzard."[10]

Four years later the problem was solved. When Warren G. Harding took his oath in 1921, an amplifier was used, for the first time, making it possible for everybody on the inaugural platform and all the people in the plaza below to hear his inaugural address. Harding's forty-minute speech was interrupted by applause several times, but one fellow, standing in front of the crowd below, got tired of Harding's lengthy lucubrations and finally exclaimed to a neighbor: "The amplifier is very well, but what Harding needs is a condenser!"[11] In 1925, Calvin Coolidge's speech was broadcast by radio, and in 1929, Herbert Hoover's was captured by "talking pictures." Harry Truman's inaugural was seen on television by a few viewers in 1949 and Dwight Eisenhower's second inaugural by millions in 1957. After that, presidential inaugurations gradually developed into big media events. "Reagan's medium is television," said one of President Reagan's aides in 1981, "and his inaugural speech is precisely designed for a TV audience."[12]

INAUGURAL addresses aren't really an art form. There are passages in Jefferson's and Lincoln's addresses, to be sure, that transcend their historical contexts and speak to us today, but most inaugurals are forgettable. Except in times of crisis—wars and depressions—the presidents' utterances on inauguration day tended to be bland and conventional. They did, of course, deal with the issues of the day, but even in tumultuous times some presidents tried to evade or defang serious issues, such as slavery before the Civil War or the misery of the masses after the war, in order to say things they hoped would achieve consensus by stilling the doubts of some people and quieting the discontents of others.

In the pre–Civil War period some presidents went so far in their inaugural enthusiasm as to declare that the United States was rapidly approaching perfection. Monroe was confident, he said, that the United States "will soon attain the highest degree of perfection of which human institutions are capable" (1821); Van Buren called America "the chosen spot" of the world (1837); Polk dubbed the country "the noblest structure of human wisdom" (1845); and Buchanan, on the eve of the Civil War, pronounced America's "the most perfect form of government and union ever devised by man" (1857).[13] In the twentieth century, presidents stopped talking about perfection, but they continued to hoist the flag and pronounce the United States "the greatest country in the world." During the cold war, they rang the changes on the superiority of American institutions to those of the communist police states.

Some inaugurals were full of froth. Harding's speech in 1929, sighed one observer, was in "the big bow wow style of oratory."[14] But others were quiet and low-key, and still others merely formulaic. The formula went like this: first came the president's gratitude for being elevated to high office, then expressions of humility about his abilities, then a promise to work hard to serve the people, and finally an invitation to all Americans (especially members of Congress) to help him do his best. It was considered good taste, too, from the very beginning, to say a few kind words about the president's immediate predecessor, even if he belonged to the other party, but not all presidents were able to bring themselves to go that far in their search for consensus. Over the years, many presidents have invoked the Constitution and praised the republican form of government, in order to associate their own policies with the basic principles of the American system. Presidents have rarely become personal in their speeches. Ulysses Grant was the only president to confess openly (in his second inaugural in 1873) his bitterness over the attacks on his administration during his first term. Washington handled the same issue more delicately in 1793.

Humor was off limits. Even Lincoln refrained from including a light touch in his inaugural addresses, though in less stressful times he might well have sneaked an ironic little quip into his remarks. In 1837, though, Van Buren inadvertently produced a great deal of mirth by the awkward way he reminded his audience that he was the first president who did not belong to the venerable Revolutionary generation. "Unlike all who have preceded me," he said, "the Revolution that gave us existence as one people was achieved at the period of my birth; and whilst I contemplate with grateful reverence *that memorable event* [emphasis added], I feel I belong to a later age."[15] What was the "memorable event" Van Buren mentioned in his speech, his political enemies wanted to know. His birth? No way! They had a lot of fun with Van Buren's clumsy sentence. But except for occasional gaffes like Van Buren's, whatever humor came out of a president's remarks on inauguration day was postinaugural and bitterly partisan. The Democrats got a lot of rough mileage out of Hoover's inaugural statement, just before the Great Crash, in 1929, "I have no fears for the future of America. It is bright with hope."

As with many speakers on solemn occasions, some presidents chose to beef up their addresses with quotations from eminent sources. Jackson quoted from Washington's Farewell Address in 1833; Polk referred to Jefferson's first inaugural in 1845; FDR made use of Washington's first inaugural in 1941; and Nixon quoted both Lincoln and FDR in 1969. The favorite source for authoritative admonitions, however, has been the Scriptures. Presidents as diverse as Lincoln, Harding, Lyndon Johnson, and Jimmy Carter have turned to the Bible for passages they thought threw light on America's predicament at the time. And a few presidents even introduced prayers into their inaugural speeches. In 1945, FDR read a short prayer at the end of his address, and in 1953, Eisenhower dashed off a prayer of his own just before proceeding to Capitol Hill. After taking his oath as president, he requested permission to offer his prayer before commencing his address. Years later, George Bush did as Ike had; just before beginning his address in 1989, he read a little prayer he had written, calling on God to help Americans use their power "to help people."[16]

Religion has been as much a part of the inaugural address as it has been of the oath-taking ceremony itself. At some point in the address, usually at the very end, all the presidents, beginning with Washington, non–church members as well as communicants, Deists as well as Christians, Unitarians as well as Baptists, appealed to a Higher Power for aid in the tasks facing the nation. The invocations were almost legion: Beneficent Creator, Divine Being, Almighty

Ruler of the Universe, Lord Most High, Giver of Good, Fountain of Justice, Supreme Author of All Good, Divine Being. Jefferson, whose heterodox views led the orthodox to call him "a howling atheist," referred to "that infinite Power which rules the destinies of the universe" in his first inaugural and to "that Being in whose hands we are" in his second. And, in 1909, Taft, criticized for his Unitarianism, called for "the aid of Almighty God in the discharge of my duties."[17] Interestingly, Woodrow Wilson, a devout Presbyterian, and Jimmy Carter, a born-again Baptist, made only passing mention of a Supreme Being in their inaugurals, possibly because they did not feel they needed public reassurance for their personal faith.

Despite the religiosity, even the devoutest presidents carefully avoided sectarianism on inauguration day. The name of Jesus appears in none of the addresses delivered thus far, and there are only three references to the Christian religion in any of the addresses. In 1841, William Henry Harrison, an Episcopalian, expressed "a profound reverence for the Christian religion"; in 1857, Buchanan recommended a "spirit of Christian benevolence towards our fellow-men"; and in 1861, Lincoln declared that "intelligence, patriotism, Christianity, and a firm reliance on Him who has never yet forsaken this favored land are still competent to adjust in the best way all our present difficulty."[18]

Lincoln was not a church member, and was much criticized by pious people for that fact, but he was thoroughly at home with the Bible, particularly the Old Testament, and there is no question but that the Scriptures had a profound influence on his way of looking at things. His second inaugural address, delivered as the Civil War was ending, is astonishing in its concentration on a serious, rather than conventional, examination of the relation between the United States and the Almighty. He wrote the speech in February 1865, and a week or so before the inauguration, he walked into his office one evening holding the manuscript under his arm and announced to some friends: "Lots of wisdom in that document, I suspect. It is what will be called my 'second inaugural,' containing about six hundred words. I will put it away in this drawer until I want it."[19] The address was short—four paragraphs, twenty-six sentences, fewer than seven hundred words—and took only five minutes to deliver.

The speech began matter-of-factly. Lincoln explained that there was "less occasion for an extended address" at his second oath-taking than at his first. The "progress of our arms, upon which all else chiefly depends," he noted, "is as well known to the public as to myself, and it is, I trust, reasonably satisfactory and encouraging to all." He expressed "high hope for the future," and went on to comment on the entirely different situation that faced the country at the time of his first inauguration. "While the inaugural address was being delivered from this place, devoted altogether to *saving* the Union without war," in 1861, he recalled, "insurgent agents were in the city seeking to *destroy* it without war—seeking to dissolve the Union and divide effects by negotiation. Both parties deprecated war, but one of them would *make* war rather than let the nation survive, and the other would *accept* war rather than let it perish, and the war came."

There was a cry of approval when Lincoln read the words, "the other would *accept* war rather than let it perish," and he paused for a moment before finishing the sentence: "and the war came."[20]

The third and lengthiest paragraph in the second inaugural contained the heart of Lincoln's message to the American people in 1865. In it, Lincoln declared that slavery was the cause of the sectional conflict that had turned out to be so horrendous. "One-eighth of the whole population were colored slaves," he pointed out, "not distributed generally over the Union, but localized in the southern part of it. These slaves constituted a peculiar and powerful interest. All knew that this interest was somehow the cause of the war. To strengthen, perpetuate, and extend this interest was the object for which the insurgents would rend the Union even by war, while the government claimed no right to do more than to restrict the territorial enlargement of it." Lincoln went on to call attention to the unexpected consequences for everyone concerned of the resort to arms four years before. "Neither party expected for the war the magnitude or the duration which it has already attained," he observed. "Neither anticipated that the *cause* of the conflict might cease with or even before the conflict itself should cease. Each looked for an easier triumph, and a result less fundamental and astounding."

For Lincoln, there were profound ironies as well as unintended developments in the bloody war over slavery. In a remarkable passage in the inaugural placing the Civil War in a religious setting, he had this to say about the warring sections: "Both read the same Bible and pray to the same God, and each invokes His aid against the other. It may seem strange," he went on, "that any man should dare ask a just God's assistance in wringing their bread from the sweat of other men's faces, but,"—rejecting self-righteousness, he added at once—"let us judge not, that we be not judged." He then noted: "The prayers of both could not be answered. That of neither has been answered fully." And then came his grand conclusion: "The Almighty has His own purposes."

Still, Lincoln couldn't help probing for fundamental reasons and causes. Years of pondering moral and religious questions had led him to develop a providential theory of history that gave transcendent meaning and purposes to the terrible war over which he had presided after his first inauguration. By the time of his second inauguration, he had come to look on history as a perpetual struggle between freedom and slavery, during which the human race advanced steadily, despite frequent setbacks, toward the final goal of freedom for all people everywhere. A devoted Bible-reader, Lincoln looked to the Scriptures for enlightenment, and he came up with a passage from Matthew 18:7, which he thought shed light on America's predicament during the Civil War: "Woe unto the world because of offenses; for it must needs be that offenses come, but woe to that man by whom the offense cometh." Slavery was surely a grave offense in the eyes of God, and perhaps, Lincoln suggested, the terrible suffering of the Civil War came as the "woe unto the world because of offenses" mentioned in the Bible. "If we shall suppose," said Lincoln, "that American slavery is one of those offenses which, in the providence of God, must needs come, but which, having continued through His appointed time, He now wills to remove, and that He gives to both North and South this terrible war as the woe due to those by whom the offense came, shall we discern therein any departure from those divine attributes which the believers in a living God always ascribe to Him?"

The time had come, Lincoln hoped, for an end to the war over the offense of slavery. "Fondly do we hope, fervently do we pray," he exclaimed, "that this mighty scourge of war may speedily pass away." But slavery, Lincoln reminded Americans, was so unjust that it was entirely possible that the "woe due to those by whom the offense came" was not yet completed. As he put it: "Yet, if God wills that it continue until all the wealth piled by the bondsman's 250 years of unrequited toil shall be sunk, and until every drop of blood drawn with the lash shall be paid by another drawn with the sword, as was said three thousand years ago, so still it must be said 'the judgments of the Lord are true and righteous altogether.'" This passage was one of the most powerful indictments of slavery ever made—Paul Berman called it "a titanic invocation of God's wrath over slavery"—and its power rested upon its grounding in the very nature of things. Like his mentor Jefferson, Lincoln lived in a moral universe that was to seem antiquated to many people a century later.[21]

Lincoln ended his speech on a softer note. In the final (and most famous) paragraph of his inaugural, he looked forward to the end of the war and the development of a truly free society. "With malice toward none, with charity for all, with firmness in the right as God gives us to see the right, let us strive on to finish the work we are in, to bind up the nation's wounds, to care for him who shall have borne the battle and for his widow and his orphan, to do all which may achieve and cherish a just and lasting peace among ourselves and with all nations." Lincoln's words seem to

have reached more people than usual in outdoor ceremonies, for reporter Noah Brooks wrote that there were
tears in the eyes of some of the people in the audience, as
Lincoln read his final words. There was a "profound silence" at the end.[22]

A few days after the inauguration, New York's Republican leader Thurlow Weed sent Lincoln some words of praise
for the address, and Lincoln wrote back to say, "Everyone
likes a compliment." Then he added that he expected the
address "to wear as well as—perhaps better than—anything I
have produced; but I believe it is not immediately popular.
Men are not flattered by being shown that there has been a
difference of purpose between the Almighty and them. To
deny it, however, in this case, is to deny that there is a God
governing the world. It is a truth which I thought needed to
be told, and, as whatever of humiliation there is in it falls
most directly on myself, I thought others might afford for
me to tell it."[23]

The reaction to Lincoln's address was mostly favorable,
though not overwhelmingly so, but few commentators had
anything to say about the religious dimension of the speech,
which Lincoln had regarded as crucial. The *New York Herald*
thought well of what "this remarkable rail-splitter" had said
but expressed disappointment that he failed to outline peace
terms for the South. The *Washington Chronicle* confined its remarks to saying that Lincoln's second inaugural was better
than his first, which had been "deprecatory, apologetic, ex-
planatory," while this one was "solemnly affirmative." The
New York Times was more appreciative. "The extreme simplicity of this address, its calmness, its modesty, its reserve,"
the editors pointed out, were "in complete contrast with the

'sound and fury' with which the rebel ruler has recently spoken." *Harper's Weekly* also thought Lincoln's address was "characteristically simple and solemn," but went on to add that it contained "a certain grand and quaint vigor, unprecedented in modern politics." The reception in Britain seems to have been even more favorable than in the United States. "No statesman," said the *Spectator,* "ever uttered words stamped at once with the seal of so deep a wisdom and so true a simplicity." The Duke of Argyll wrote to congratulate his friend, Massachusetts senator Charles Sumner, "on the remarkable speech of your President. It was a noble speech, just and true, and solemn. I think it has produced a great effect in England."[24]

But Charles Francis Adams, Jr., probably said it best. "What think you of the inaugural?" he asked his father in a letter soon after the inauguration. "That rail-splitting lawyer is one of the wonders of the day," he declared. "Once at Gettysburg and now again on a greater occasion he has shown a capacity for rising to the demands of the hour which we should not expect from orators or men of the schools. This inaugural strikes me in its grand simplicity and directness as being for all time the historical keynote of this war; in it a people seemed to speak in the sublimely simple utterance of ruder times. What will Europe think of this utterance of the rude ruler, of whom they have nourished so lofty a contempt? Not a prince or minister in all Europe could have risen to such an equality with the occasion."[25]

RECEPTIONS

10

FOR THE FIRST FEW INAUGURATIONS
nothing fancy was scheduled to follow the oath-taking ceremony. Some presidents, like Adams and Jefferson, simply
returned to their boardinghouses after taking their oaths,
ate lunch with the other boarders, and then chatted a bit
with the friends and officials who dropped by that afternoon to congratulate them. When Jefferson got back to his
lodgings after his first inauguration, he found a stranger at
the foot of the table where he usually sat. One of the women
at the table offered the new president her place, but he accepted it only after she assured him she had finished eating.
Not until the President's House, as it was called, was completed and in good shape, did presidents begin holding siz-

able receptions right after the inaugural ceremony. Madison, Monroe, and John Quincy Adams stood patiently for hours, shaking hands and exchanging pleasantries. They also provided their well-wishers with wine, punch, and "ice creams and bonbons."

Andrew Jackson's reception after his first inauguration in 1829 was the first big one. Unfortunately, it turned into a near riot. Jackson had opened the White House doors to the democratic masses, and they overran the place. The rambunctiousness had begun at the Capitol, when, as soon as Old Hickory took his oath, the crowd below rushed up to the inaugural platform, broke through the chain in front, and mobbed their hero, offering cheers and congratulations. After shaking hands with hundreds, Jackson managed to escape with the help of some marshals, mounted a white horse awaiting him outside the Capitol, and trotted off to the Executive Mansion followed by a mob. "The President was literally pursued by a motley concourse of people," reported Margaret Bayard Smith disapprovingly, "running helter-skelter, striving who should first gain admittance into the Executive mansion, where it was understood that refreshments were to be distributed."[1]

Mrs. Smith was even more shocked when she reached the President's House that afternoon. In the East Room she found people in muddy boots standing on the elegant furniture, straining to get a glimpse of Jackson. Even worse, men were getting into fistfights over the refreshments and, in the process, breaking china, tearing down draperies, and dumping food all over. When waiters entered the room at one point with tubs of orange punch, there was a general rush toward them that ended in punch (and waiters) spilling all over the fine carpets. Jackson kept calm through it all, showing "great courtesy" to "both high and low, rich and poor," before escaping, with the help of friends, through one of the windows and returning to his lodgings at Gadsby's Tavern. He behaved, said one observer, like a "servant in the presence of the Sovereign, the People." Only when the butlers lugged tubs of punch to the lawn outside, followed by thirsty Jacksonians, did the commotion inside subside.[2]

Justice Joseph Story was as shocked by the inaugural brawl as Mrs. Smith was. "The reign of King MOB seemed triumphant," he exclaimed. The *Washington City Chronicle* was similarly censorious. "We regret to say that the President's hospitality on this occasion was in some measure misapplied," declared the editors. "The disorder was considerable, as many were admitted, perhaps unavoidably, that certainly ought not to have been there. There is something due to the character of the nation, on such occasions, and the Marshals should have seen the necessity of excluding such as were guilty of absolute rudeness and vulgarity."[3]

Senator James Hamilton, Jr., took a more indulgent view of the raucous reception. While acknowledging that Jackson's admirers "had a regular Saturnalia" that afternoon, he assured Jackson's friend Martin Van Buren that no great harm was done. "Notwithstanding the row Demos kicked up," he told him, "the whole matter went off very well." Washington's *National Intelligencer* agreed. "What particularly gratifies us, and does credit to the character of our People," declared the editor, "is, that, amidst all the excitement and bustle of the occasion, the whole day and night of the Inauguration passed off without the slightest interruption of the public peace and order, that we have heard of. At the mansion of the President, the Sovereign People were a little up-roarious, indeed, but it was any thing but a malicious spirit." Even Mrs. Smith admitted, with a touch of irony, "It was the People's day, the People's President, and the People would rule!" But polite society remained unreconciled.[4]

At Van Buren's reception in 1837, no refreshments were served and with plenty of policemen on hand to preserve order, things went off nicely. But the new president committed a terrible gaffe. In welcoming the foreign diplomats to the White House, he referred to the diplomatic corps (all the men representing monarchies) as the "democratic corps," and had to apologize and start over. William Henry Harrison's reception in 1841 was without mishaps, but after an hour of handshaking, his hand was so sore and swollen that he decided to suspend the courtesy and merely nod and say hello as his well-wishers passed. By the time of James Buchanan, the inaugural receptions had become smooth and decorous and a bit on the dull side. "Everything passed off pleasantly," reported the *National Intelligencer* of Old Buck's reception in 1857, "the thousands in attendance being agreeably impressed with the dignity and gracefulness with which, under free institutions, the reins of Government can be peacefully transferred from one set of administrators to another." But 1857's "dignity and gracefulness" was short-lived. In 1865 came a reception after Abraham Lincoln's second oath-taking that came close to being as unruly as Andrew Jackson's in 1829.[5]

LINCOLN's reception in 1865 began peacefully enough. At 6 P.M. the Lincolns greeted the special guests—government

officials, military and naval officers, and foreign dignitaries—
for whom a buffet had been set up in the Green Room.
Then, at 8 P.M., the White House was opened to the general
public, and in no time the place was overrun by people who
had been waiting impatiently outside for hours to greet the
president. The White House guards had erected a platform
to allow the orderly entrance and departure of guests
through the French windows in front, but the enthusiastic
crowd simply ignored it. They streamed into the East Room,
pushing the special guests who were still there against the
wall, and pressed onward to the president who, for the next
three hours, gamely shook hands with an estimated six
thousand people. But when some of the guests heard about
the buffet, they made a rush for the Green Room, seized the
food still remaining on the table, and made short work of it.
They also helped themselves to souvenirs: silverware, glass-
ware, candlesticks, china, punch bowls, cups. Some people
even cut off large pieces of the brocade draperies and lace
curtains to take home with them. It took a rush call for
additional policemen and soldiers to restore order. But by
then, according to William Crook, the president's body-
guard, the White House looked as if a "regiment of rebel
troops had been quartered there—with permission to for-
age." When Lincoln saw the carnage at the end of the
evening, he was heartsick. "Why should they do it?" he
sighed. "How can they?"[6]

Walt Whitman rather enjoyed the rumpus. "Never was
such a compact jam in front of the White House—," he recalled, "all the grounds fill'd, and away out to the spacious
sidewalks. I was...in the rush inside with the crowd—
surged along the passage-ways, the blue and other rooms,

and through the great east room. Crowds of country people, some very funny. Fine music from the Marine band, off in a side place. I saw Mr. Lincoln, drest all in black, with white kid gloves and a claw-hammer coat, receiving, as in duty bound, shaking hands, looking very disconsolate, and as if he would give anything to be somewhere else." But Lincoln's eyes lit up when he saw a young lieutenant (who had lost his leg at Petersburg) on a crutch in the reception crowd, pushed his way over to the fellow, took the lieutenant's hand in both of his and, eyes moist, cried out: "God bless you, my boy!" As he returned to his place, the lieutenant told a friend with him: "Oh, I'd lose another leg for a man like that!"[7]

Frederick Douglass, the great abolitionist leader who had escaped from slavery as a youth in Maryland, was not a special guest that evening, but after attending the inaugural ceremony and hearing the "brief but weighty" inaugural address, he decided to join the crowd at the White House after 8 P.M. to pay his respects to the Civil War president. Several months earlier, he had conferred with Lincoln, at the latter's request, about emancipation policy, and he had come to the conclusion that "Mr. Lincoln was not only a great President, but a *great man*—too great to be small in anything. In his company I was never in any way reminded of my humble origin, or of my unpopular color." Douglass wanted some of his black friends to accompany him to the reception, but they all begged off, fearing the usual rebuffs. Convinced that "someone must lead the way, and that if the colored man would have his rights, he must take them," Douglass went with a white friend to the reception. On reaching the White House entrance, however, to his dismay, two policemen stationed there ordered him to leave, informing him they had orders to refuse admittance to blacks. Douglass was indignant. "I told the officers I was quite sure there must be some mistake, for no such order would have emanated from President Lincoln, and that if he knew I was at the door he would desire my admission." The policemen then seemed to relent and offered to conduct him to the reception line. "We followed their lead," Douglass later wrote, "and soon found ourselves walking some planks out of a window, which had been arranged as a temporary passage for the exit of visitors." Douglass halted as soon as he saw the trick and reproached the officers. "You have deceived me. I shall not go out of this building till I see President Lincoln."[8]

Fortunately, at that point, Douglass saw a white man he knew in the crowd who was acquainted with Lincoln, so he sought him out and explained his plight. "Be so kind," he said, "to say to Mr. Lincoln that Frederick Douglass is detained by officers at the door." The man quickly relayed the message to Lincoln, and Douglass soon found himself in the East Room, where the president stood, like "a mountain pine high above all others," receiving guests. When Lincoln saw Douglass, he cried out: "Here comes my friend Douglass," stepped forward, took Douglass's hand, and exclaimed: "I am glad to see you. I saw you in the crowd today, listening to my inaugural address; how did you like it?" "Mr. Lincoln," returned Douglass, "I must not detain you with my poor opinion, when there are thousands waiting to shake hands with you." "No, no," persisted Lincoln, "you must stop a little, Douglass; there is no man in the country whose opinion I value more than yours. I want to know what you think of it." Replied Douglass: "Mr. Lincoln, that was a sacred effort." Lincoln seemed pleased. "I am glad you liked it!" he exclaimed, smiling.[9]

Later on, Douglass learned that the policemen at the White House hadn't received orders from Lincoln or anyone else to exclude blacks from the reception. When he told his black friends about his cordial reception by the president, they "were well pleased with what had seemed to them a doubtful experiment, and I believe were encouraged by its success to follow my example." But Douglass was too realistic to suppose that the Thirteenth Amendment freeing the slaves (which was ratified by the requisite number of states by the end of the year) would eliminate prejudice as well as slavery.[10]

FOUR years later, the grand reception, following Ulysses Grant's first inauguration in 1869, started off nicely, but ended in chaos as well. It was held in the evening, for it supposedly replaced the customary inaugural ball, and it took place in the newly completed Treasury Building instead of in the White House. There was no liquor (to spare the guests drunken scenes) and no handshaking (to spare Grant bursitis). There was dancing in some of the rooms, but it was downplayed, since the sponsors of the event were eager to avoid criticism for holding a Republican Party celebration in a nonpartisan building belonging to all of the taxpayers. It was a reception, they insisted, not a ball, though it had all the accoutrements of inaugural balls: fancy decorations, beautiful flowers, handsome gowns. In any case, the fine marble dust permeating the new building from the recent stonecutting discouraged dancing. As people danced, according to Mary Clemmer Ames, they felt as if they were "taking with every breath a myriad of homeopathic doses of desiccated grindstone.... There are mortals who still curse, and swear, and sigh at the thought of it."[11]

But the reception went swimmingly. "President Grant made an excellent impression by his unpretending simplicity," reported Washington's *Evening Star,* "leaning lightly forward by his finger ends upon the little marble table before him and bowing his acknowledgments to the salutations of the visitors. Mrs. Grant, ladylike and unaffected, and her children's frank and unassuming style showed that they had been trained by a good mother."[12] There were no black Republican officeholders at the reception. Local black leaders, who had remained uninvited, tactfully indicated beforehand that they did not plan to attend, thus solving a problem that had been worrying the organizers of the event.

At midnight came supper. The Grants (as well as Vice President Schuyler Colfax and his wife) and their honored guests dined in private rooms upstairs and departed soon after. And then, despite careful planning, things went wrong. As soon as supper was announced for the other guests, there was a general rush down to the supper room, with people emptying the tables as fast as the waiters could bring out the food, and then a stampede into the kitchen where a hefty woman cook repelled the invaders by hurling dishcloths at them. There was chaos, too, when the party ended, as the guests sought the coats and hats they had checked in the cloakroom and then looked for the carriages they had parked outside. "Picture it!" wrote Mrs. Ames afterward, almost in disbelief. "Six or more thousand people clamoring for their clothes! In the end they were all tumbled out 'promiscuous' on the floor. Then came the siege! Few seized their own, but many snatched other people's garments—anything, something, to protect them from the pitiless morning, whose wind came down like the bite of death. Delicate women, too sensitive to take the property of others, crouched in corners, and wept on window ledges; and there the daylight found them. Carriages, also, had fled out of the scourging blast, and the men and women who emerged from the marble halls, with very little to wear, found that they must 'foot it' to their habitations. One gentleman walked to Capitol Hill, nearly two miles, in dancing pumps and bare-headed; another performed the same exploit, wrapped in a lady's sontag. Poor Horace Greeley, after expending his wrath on the stairs and cursing Washington anew as a place that should be immediately booted out of the universe, strode to his hotel hatless. The next day and the next week were consumed by people searching for their lost clothes."[13]

Harper's Bazaar, however, took a more benign view of Grant's inaugural night than Mrs. Ames did. "Every kind of intoxicating liquor had been excluded, and all precautions taken to insure propriety," the editor reminded its readers; "and in these respects the efforts of the managers were crowned with complete success. That people were jostled, dresses torn, wrappings lost and carriages missed here and there did not detract from the general good-humor, and the guests laughed instead of grumbled at these trifling mishaps, and only echoed the words of the great chief, 'Let us have Peace.'"14

GRANT'S reception in 1869 was the last of the rowdy ones. In 1877, Rutherford B. Hayes greeted a delegation of a thousand people from Ohio, his home state, in the White House, right after his swearing in, and when hundreds of people who had gathered outside complained of favoritism, he invited them all in and spent the next two hours politely shaking hands and exchanging greetings. After this, the receptions following the inaugural ceremonies fell into desuetude, largely because the afternoon parade developed into one of inauguration day's major events, and presidents began lingering in the Capitol for lunch before riding back to the White House to commence reviewing the parade. In 1897, the newly installed president, William McKinley, had a corned beef sandwich, some salad, and a cup of coffee with members of Congress in one of the Senate's committee rooms and then headed to the stand erected in front of the White House to review the parade.

Some presidents ate lunch in the White House rather than in the Capitol; they hosted buffet luncheons for special guests after the inaugural ceremony and then entered the reviewing stand to watch the afternoon parade. Most of the buffets were small, but in 1933 Franklin and Eleanor Roosevelt entertained a thousand guests for lunch after FDR's swearing in and broke a few precedents, too, while they were at it. Old-timers on the household staff were startled by the way both Roosevelts casually departed from the customary White House proprieties. For one thing, Roosevelt escorted his mother, rather than his wife, to the table, and, for another, Mrs. Roosevelt helped the butlers serve the guests. "The First Lady didn't try to bring any discipline into the proceedings," recalled Lillian Rogers Parks, a member of the household staff. "The butlers couldn't believe their eyes or their ears—the President was not served first, but had to take his turn like everyone else."[15]

But Mrs. Roosevelt was the real iconoclast in 1933. She did something unprecedented for a president's wife just before the luncheon: she agreed to give an interview to Associated Press reporter Lorena Hickok about the inaugural ceremony and her own plans for the future. "It was very, very solemn and a little terrifying," she told Hickok. "The crowds were so tremendous, and you felt that they would do anything, if only someone told them what to do. No one at all close to people in public life today can fail to realize that we are all of us facing extremely critical times. No woman entering the White House, if she accepts the fact that it belongs to the people and therefore must be representative of whatever conditions the people are facing, can light-heartedly take up residence here. One has a feeling of going it blindly because we're in a tremendous stream and none of us know where we're going to land. The important thing, it seems to me, is our attitude toward whatever may happen. It must be willingness to accept and share with others whatever may come and to meet the future courageously, with a cheerful spirit." She added that she hoped that while she was in the White House she could serve as the eyes and ears of her husband, by meeting as many people as she could, and letting him know what they were saying and thinking. She did all of that, and more, in the years to come, as the nation struggled to pull itself out of the Great Depression.[16]

In 1945, the Roosevelts entertained a thousand people at a buffet luncheon once again, right after the "back porch" inauguration—FDR's fourth—on the south portico of the White House. It took the East Room, the State Dining Room, and the basement corridor to accommodate them all. For the menu, Roosevelt recommended serving chicken à la king, but the Executive Mansion's housekeeper, Henrietta Nesbitt, opted for wartime austerity: cold chicken salad, rolls without butter, unfrosted pound cake, and coffee.

Just before Roosevelt put in an appearance at the buffet, he took his son James aside. FDR was thoroughly chilled from the outdoor ceremony and experiencing some pain. "You know, Jimmy," he confided, "I have to go to a reception now and shake hands with a thousand people, and I don't think I can do it." "Then don't do it," James told him. "I have to do it," insisted FDR. "It would look bad to bow out. I don't dare to shake the faith of the people. That's why I ran again, Jimmy. The people elected me their leader, and I can't quit in the middle of a war." He sighed, and then said: "There's a bottle of bourbon up in my room. If you'll go up and sneak it down to me and I can get some inside of me, I think I can get through this."

James went up, got the bottle, smuggled it back under his coat, and poured a tumbler half full of whiskey. His father, he recalled, drank it as if it were medicine, and then went to the buffet for a few minutes without anyone but his son knowing how bad he felt. "I was deeply disturbed," James wrote later. "Before returning to the Philippines I ran around like a chicken with its head cut off, trying to get one of his physicians or someone close to him to tell me what was wrong with Pa. The only person who would admit to me that he thought Father was a sick man was Lieutenant-Commander George A. Fox, U.S.N., Father's physical therapist."[17]

FDR didn't spend much time at the luncheon. He left Eleanor and Mrs. Truman to do the honors there and went to the Red Room to receive a few close friends in a more relaxed setting. Before leaving the State Dining Room, however, he had a brief encounter with Vice President Truman, whom he hardly knew. Truman had resigned from the Senate the day before and had been officially unemployed until he'd taken his oath as vice president that morning. "So I'm on the payroll once more," he remarked, producing a grin from Roosevelt. A few weeks later Roosevelt died of a cerebral hemorrhage and Truman became president.[18]

FDR's was the last of the big buffets. Four years later, Harry Truman had lunch in the Senate after being sworn in as president, and so did all of his successors, from Eisenhower to Clinton. But the postinaugural luncheons in the Capitol soon turned into little inaugural events of their own, at which the president and congressional leaders promised to work lovingly together for the good of the country. By Ronald Reagan's time the inaugural luncheon was being attended by over two hundred people, meeting in the Capitol's Statuary Hall in the Rotunda, and being televised for the world to watch. At the luncheon in 1985 Reagan was presented with a symbolic key to the House of Representatives, and in 1993 Clinton received a letter opener to "cut through the tangle of legislative challenges."[19]

And on the occasion of Clinton's second inauguration in 1997, Republican leaders, now controlling Congress, drank champagne toasts to the president, called it a "joyous occasion," and presented Clinton with the flags that had flown over the Capitol that morning. "For today," responded Clinton, "I think we should all enjoy being Americans. Enjoy the parade. Enjoy the balls. But most of all, enjoy the great gift of American citizenship."[20]

THE INAUGURAL PARADES

11

FOR MANY AMERICANS, THE PARADE UP
Pennsylvania Avenue to the White House after the inaugural ceremony at the Capitol has been the high point of the
day's activities. It is not only the "most consistently colorful
event of all," wrote Don Oberdorfer, a *New York Times* inauguration observer, in 1965, but also probably "the most
history-laden parade in the Western hemisphere, and sometimes one of the most bizarre." Some people even leave the
Capitol ceremony before the president finishes his inaugural
address in order to get choice positions on the sidewalks
and in the bleachers along the Grand Avenue for watching
the afternoon parade.[1]

Like so many of the inaugural activities, the afternoon parade has been a gradual development, not a deliberate creation. It grew out of the morning procession from the White House to the Capitol and back and quickly superseded the former as one of the main events of the day. The morning procession is mainly practical; it involves getting the president-elect to the Capitol for the swearing in and back to the White House afterward in a dignified and decorous fashion. The afternoon parade, which took form after the Civil War, is more spectacular; it involves more participants, takes more time, and allows the president to watch the marchers pass as he stands in a special reviewing stand erected in front of the White House.

The first inaugural parade took place in 1873, on the occasion of Ulysses Grant's second inauguration. After being sworn in at 12:30 P.M., Grant headed the usual procession back to the White House, and then took his place in a special pavilion set up in Lafayette Square across from the White House to review the troops (including West Point cadets and Annapolis midshipmen). The temperature was cruel, and a few cadets passed out from the cold, but one observer, Mary Clemmer Ames, pronounced the parade a smashing success. "The entire body of soldiers march and mass," she wrote, "till as far as the eyes can reach through the glittering sunshine, one only sees gleaming helmets, flashing bayonets, glancing sabers, the Cadets on double quick, the Middies firing their howitzers, officers displaying fine horses and uniforms, drum-majors tossing their batons, bands playing, and cannon thundering."[2]

There was no parade in 1877, when Rutherford Hayes took office, but in 1881, the new president, James A. Garfield, stood patiently for two and a half hours watching more than fifteen thousand men in line march jauntily by the White House.

The Garfield parade, which was the most impressive military display in Washington since the Grand Review of the Union Army at the end of the Civil War, featured Generals William Sherman, Philip Sheridan, and Winfield Hancock, and included the U.S. Marine Band, led by John Philip Sousa, who had composed a special inaugural march for the event. There were a few unscheduled participants: minstrels from a show playing in the National Theater, who sneaked into the parade for the fun of it; some men wearing Confederate uniforms (but, to Garfield's relief, waving a Union flag); and a hearse that went astray and somehow ended up in the procession. But despite the mishaps, the parade received warm accolades, and after 1881, the morning procession declined rapidly in importance, and the afternoon parade became a major inaugural event.

The military components of the parades—army, navy, marine, and, in the twentieth century, air force units—continued to be important, but after 1881, civilian organizations began joining the ranks and soon came to overshadow the servicemen most of the time. Some civilians became standard: state governors, members of political clubs and civic organizations, college students, hometown bands, and veterans. From time to time, Native Americans in tribal costumes joined the ranks, and, in 1893, for the first time, a few woman marched proudly in the parade for Grover Cleveland's second inauguration.

The 1893 parade also featured fancy floats and lively stunts, replicas of the War of 1812's famous frigate, *Constitution*, trained seals, dancing horses, dog acts, and G.O.P. elephants. Some Engineer Corps officers released a dozen carrier pigeons as they saluted the president, and the birds rose in the air, circled about, and then flew north carrying messages about the inauguration to Philadelphia and other cities. In the same parade one man carried a live bantam rooster, and when he reached the White House, the rooster got loose and ended up spending the night with the Clevelands.

Some observers deplored the frivolous side of the parades, even suggesting that military professionals take over the whole show. Writing in *Harper's Weekly* in 1897, right after William McKinley's inauguration, Henry Loomis Nelson insisted that the parade that year was successful largely because "there was a large and important part of regular troops in it." Loomis went on to belittle the other elements in the parade: the "little boy-soldier companies" of militiamen "playing soldier" clumsily, and the "visiting clubs" of silk-hatted men in neat overcoats, carrying canes on their shoulders. Nelson suggested dumping the militiamen, as well as the civilians, and turning the parades over to professional military men. "Why can we not stop the parade when the real parade is over?" he wanted to know. "Why is it necessary to give a place to every command that applies, no matter how grotesque it may be?" The *Washington Post* disagreed. "As this republic," wrote the editors, "makes no pretension to the maintenance of a standing army in the sense in which the term is understood in Europe, we wisely avoid any attempt at a great military display." Still, the *Post* couldn't help chortling over the fact that "the solid soldiers who paraded yesterday were a fine illustration of what we might do in that line if necessity required a rallying round the flag." Most inaugural celebrants felt as the *Post* did.[3]

The afternoon parades were usually tailored to some extent to the president whose accession to office they were celebrating. In 1889, political clubs carried life-size pictures of Benjamin Harrison (grandson of William Henry Harrison) with the caption, BIG CHIP OFF THE OLD BLOCK. In the parade for Theodore Roosevelt in 1905, there were plenty of cowboys and Rough Riders cavorting around, though his daughter Alice's proposal to include Judge Alton B. Parker (TR's opponent in the 1904 election) and some prominent Democrats marching in chains was, of course, rejected. Woodrow Wilson, former president of Princeton, had plenty of Princetonians giving college yells for him in 1913; FDR listened delightedly to bands playing "The Franklin Delano Roosevelt March," composed by William H. Woodin, his treasury secretary, in 1933; and Harry Truman danced a little jig in 1949 when he heard an old-fashioned calliope come down the street tooting out "I'm Just Wild About Harry." For Dwight D. Eisenhower in 1953 there were ten floats from Texas (where he was born) dramatizing the various stages of his life: his birth in Denison; his first job as a lad in a dairy; his years as a cadet at West Point; his marriage; his career in the army, especially during World War II; his position as president of Columbia University after the war; and his election as president of the United States.[4]

Among the press corps covering the 1953 parade was a twenty-four-year-old society girl turned reporter, Jacqueline L. Bouvier, who had been working at a weekly salary of $42.50 as the "Inquiring Camera Girl" for the *Washington*

Times-Herald since graduating from college. Her story and sketches of the 1953 parade appeared the next morning under the headline, "Picnic Lunches Help Crowd Wait for Inaugural Parade." She described the parade as "one of the most colorful spectacles ever to tumble down Pennsylvania Avenue" and went on to report that Mrs. Eisenhower "jumped up and clapped when the West Point cadets went by," the president "beamed when the Kansas cowboys, his home state contingent passed," and that there were "floats of every color and description," including Georgia's "simulating Mr. Eisenhower playing golf" and Indiana's, with a choir singing, "Mamie, the First Lady of the Land." Eight years later, the young Jacqueline, now married, sat in the reviewing stand herself, with the new president, John F. Kennedy, at her side.[5]

Unlike the presidential oath-taking ceremony, the inaugural parade for the most part lacks a religious dimension. From time to time, it is true, clergymen participate in the parade, but they do so as citizens, like the politicians, club members, businessmen, and students, not as official representatives of their faiths. In 1953, however, the Eisenhower parade featured an elaborate structure called "God's Float," on which rested a place of worship (nondenominational of course), inscribed with two slogans: IN GOD WE TRUST and FREEDOM OF WORSHIP. Intended to represent Eisenhower's oft-stated belief that there is a need everywhere for "a *deeply felt* religion" and that "the Almighty takes a definite and direct interest day by day in the progress of this nation," God's Float led the editor of an Episcopalian journal to comment wryly: "Standing for all religions, it had the symbols of none, and it looked like nothing whatsoever in Heaven above, or in the earth beneath, except possibly an oversized model of a deformed molar left over from some dental exhibit." *New York Times* columnist Anne O'Hare McCormick reported that the float had been added at the last minute "to show that this is a nation that believes in God." But, she added, "the piety was incidental. Everybody came for a party, and a party it was."[6]

THE souvenirs and trinkets offered by vendors (called "fakirs" in the nineteenth century) along Pennsylvania Avenue, where crowds gathered to see the parade, were adapted, like the parade itself, to the presidents being honored. In 1897, not only were pictures of William McKinley, the doughty defender of the gold standard, available for customers; there were also plenty of goldbugs, varying in size from that of a fly to that of a bullfrog. For those celebrating Theodore Roosevelt's inauguration in 1905, there were Rough Rider hats, kerosene oil cans with TR's picture on them, little brown bears wound up to dance, and pieces of wood bound together, called "Teddy's Big Stick." (A clothing store on the Avenue also announced, DE-LIGHT-ED—Roosevelt's favorite ejaculation—in bright electric lights.) William Howard Taft's big smile was celebrated in 1909 with badges, worn by thousands containing the admonition, "Smile, Smile, Smile." Woodrow Wilson's parade in 1913 inspired sheet music for the song, "Woody's a Jolly Good Fellow"; big sticks modeled after the professor's blackboard pointer; and yardsticks labeled "Wilson's rule," bearing the words A FULL MEASURE OF PROSPERITY FOR ALL. One shop along the way announced in letters three feet high, WHITE HOUSE LUNCHES LIKE MRS. WILSON WILL COOK THEM FOR FIFTY CENTS. In 1965, Lyndon Johnson's face appeared on dozens of souvenirs: inaugural medals, bracelets, plates, plaques, and ashtrays. In 1977 Jimmy Carter, a former peanut farmer, inspired a peanut logo, inscribed on inaugural buttons, key chains, scarves, lapels, and tiepins; and at the same time restaurants in the vicinity offered peanut punch, fancy peanut-butter sandwiches, and an "inaugural crêpe," made of ice cream, peanut-caramel sauce, and chopped peanuts. 1997's inaugural offerings included medallions and pens with Bill Clinton's face on them, as well as license plates emblazoned with a promise to "build a bridge to the future" (Clinton's favorite catchphrase).[7]

THE number of people flocking to Washington for presidential inaugurations rose steadily as the means of transportation—railroads, automobiles, buses, planes—multiplied over the years, and the crowds lining Pennsylvania Avenue for the afternoon parade grew from hundreds right after the Civil War to thousands by the end of the nineteenth century to hundreds of thousands during the twentieth century. On fair days, the bleachers along the avenue were packed with people (at roughly five to twenty dollars a seat), the sidewalks jammed, and the windows of buildings along the way filled with spectators. The number of paraders varied considerably, sometimes less than ten thousand, but on occasion more than thirty thousand. Most parades lasted about three hours, but a few went on for five, with the final units not reaching the White House until nightfall.

In 1953, Eisenhower met with some of his associates to discuss ways of shortening or speeding up the afternoon parade so that "the poor devils who march" wouldn't have to wait on the side streets in the cold for the parade to get started and then reach the White House so late in the afternoon that they could hardly be seen. But the 1953 parade, scheduled to last three hours, ended up taking five. Mamie Eisenhower stood stoically in the White House stand beside her husband, watching the paraders, but she was finally forced to seek relief for her aching feet. She found a chair toward the rear of the stand, sat down, slipped off her shoes, reached down, and began rubbing her arches. When news photographers spotted her and rushed over to get some pictures, she told them she didn't mind. Every woman in the country, she said, would sympathize with her, though, she added, with a wink at her mother standing nearby, perhaps she shouldn't be caught "giving aid and comfort to her arch-enemies."[8]

Eisenhower stayed conscientiously to the end of the parade in 1953, anxious to make it clear to those bringing up the rear that he deeply appreciated their efforts. He realized that the inauguration committee, headed by Styles Bridges, a Republican senator from New Hampshire, found it impossible to refuse any group that wanted to participate in the lengthy parade. "The result was," Ike wrote in his memoirs, "that I had to remain in the stand long after the hour set for the end of the parade; not until nearly seven o'clock did the last two elephants go by." But he seems to have enjoyed the parade. To the dismay of the Secret Service, he leaned out of the stand to shake hands with some of the governors passing by in cars, and from time to time he invited old friends (who had not been cleared by security) into the stand, apparently not realizing the possible dangers to which he was exposing himself. When a cowboy from California came by on horseback and lassoed the new president, with a whoop and a holler, it was with the permission of the Secret Service. The spectators were enormously amused by the stunt. Ike was not. He flashed his famous grin, but his son later revealed that he was irked, not amused, by the tomfoolery.[9]

Most parades moved along smoothly on inauguration afternoon, but on occasion there were minor crises. In 1949, when President Truman stood gleefully with Vice President Alben Barkley in the glass-enclosed reviewing stand, watching soldiers, sailors, cowboys, Native Americans, pretty girls on floats, and Missouri mules pass by, there was a sudden uproar in the crowd near the president, and Secret Service agents rushed over to see what was going on. It turned out to be Broadway star Tallulah Bankhead (daughter of William Bankhead, late Speaker of the House) making the commotion. A devoted Truman fan, she didn't have a ticket and got into a noisy argument with a policeman blocking her way. Fortunately, one of the Secret Service men recognized the actress and let her join the president in the reviewing stand. A little later, when Strom Thurmond, Truman's Dixiecrat segregationist opponent in the 1948 election, passed the stand with a delegation of South Carolinians, Bankhead let out a series of loud boos, leading Mrs. Truman to tell a friend nearby, "I wish I had nerve enough to do that." Truman himself simply turned his back on Thurmond, and when Chief Justice Fred Vinson, a Kentuckian, was about to raise his hand in greeting, he reached out and pulled Vinson's hand down. When Herman Talmadge, Georgia's Dixiecrat governor, rode by, Truman gave him the cold shoulder, too.[10]

In 1969, Richard Nixon ran into hostile demonstrations as he and his wife left the Capitol after the oath-taking and headed the procession down Pennsylvania Avenue toward the White House reviewing stand. When the presidential motorcade reached the National Theater near Thirteenth Street, a crowd of youthful anti–Vietnam War protesters assembled there began waving Vietcong flags, flourishing a poster proclaiming, NIXON'S THE ONE—THE NUMBER 1 WAR CRIMINAL, burning little American flags that Boy Scouts had distributed for the parade, and chanting, "Ho, Ho, Ho Chi Minh, the NLF (National Liberation Front) is going to win!" They also began hurling rocks, beer cans, pennies, sticks, and, of course, the conventional obscenities, at the president's limousine. There were more than four hundred anti-war militants in the demonstration, and they regarded peaceful protests against the Vietnam War as largely futile.[11]

The leaders of the National Mobilization Committee to End the War in Vietnam had planned a nonviolent "counter-inaugural" demonstration against the war for January 20, and they disavowed the militants as "crazies" (though they were not entirely unsympathetic to them). But the ultra-militants created an "anxious moment" (as it was called) for the Secret Service, when they tossed what appeared to be a bomb at the president's car. The missile turned out to be a harmless ball of tinfoil, but when the Secret Service man at the wheel of the limo first saw it, he instinctively accelerated the car from about four to seven miles an hour. Through it all, the Nixons remained seemingly unperturbed, and two blocks later, when they had left the protesters behind, Nixon rolled back the bulletproof glass top of the limousine so that he and the First Lady could stand in the rear of the closed car, head and shoulders well above the open roof, and return the greetings of their well-wishers along the avenue. The "crazies" soon headed for other parts of the city to continue their demonstrations, and by nightfall the police had arrested eighty-one of them for disorderly conduct.[12]

For the rest of the afternoon Nixon was in a gay mood. He joked with his companions in the bullet-proof reviewing stand, smiled almost constantly, and waved energetically to the floats passing by. He was especially enthusiastic about the band from his old high school in Whittier, California, but he applauded the other dedicated marchers in the gray cold, too. The states, lined up alphabetically, followed by the territories, emphasized different themes in their floats. The state of Washington featured the aircraft industry; Colorado, a ski slope and ski jump; New Jersey, black-and-white horses pulling a globe; Georgia, pretty girls, formally dressed, on a curving stairway; Ohio, a thirteen-year-old girl holding a poster saying BRING US TOGETHER (1969's inauguration theme); and Puerto Rico, advertisements for the island's tourist attractions. There were army, navy, and air force units in the parade, as usual, as well as West Point cadets and Annapolis midshipmen. Mamie Eisenhower ("America's Queen Mother") drew cheers from the crowd as her car passed, while California governor Ronald Reagan received "Oohs," and New York governor Nelson Rockefeller elicited "wows." In the final minutes of the parade, Nixon gave the Secret Service another scare by stepping down from the reviewing stand to shake hands with some of the spectators. "Don't crowd, folks, don't crowd," he cried, flashing a big smile, as agents moved in cautiously to ease him back to the White House grounds. *Time* called "the triumphal parade" a "box office success."[13]

Not all the presidents enjoyed the afternoon parade the way Nixon did, though most of them behaved as though they did. Calvin Coolidge, however, could not disguise the fact that he found the parade following his inauguration in 1925 an ordeal, not a moment of glory. "He was solemn and undemonstrative for the most part," reported the *New York Times,* "during the fifty minutes the parade was passing." The parade itself was no great shakes. It had been pared down to less than an hour and a *Washington Evening Star* columnist complained that if the pageantry accompanying presidential inaugurations was slimmed down much more, the ceremony itself might disappear. There were no political or civic groups in the parade, and except for some Sioux and some state governors (including Wyoming's Nellie Ross, the nation's first woman governor, who received great applause), conventional military units—army, navy, marine—dominated the procession. The parade was a half hour late in getting started, and Silent Cal asked two or three times about the delay, but after the parade started, he had nothing more to say. "A review in silence," some people called it, and the marchers themselves seemed to lack enthusiasm. "Why?" wondered Ike Hoover, the White House's chief usher, afterward. "The only cause I can assign is the apparent lack of appreciation of the President for such demonstrations. The people certainly like to be noticed and the President could not or would not warm up to them." Coolidge, reported Kansas editor William Allen White, "looked silently down his nose" at the marchers, "with his own peculiar petrified grimace on his face" and took the heart out of the procession. "It takes two to wake up the hurrahs of a crowd," observed White, "the hurrahers and the hurrahees. That fine, fair Coolidge day the hurrahee's emotions—never tenacious—were spent by four o'clock." As soon as the parade ended, Coolidge returned to the White House, had a bite to eat, and then "threw himself across the bed, worn and weary." It was Ike Hoover's impression that Coolidge would have preferred an inauguration in which he simply walked to the Capitol, took his oath, and then re- turned to the White House for his nap.[14]

Coolidge was an exception. Most presidents were at least mildly interested in the parades organized in their honor on inauguration day. And some of them, like Theodore Roo- sevelt, came close to being in ecstasy as they stood in review in front of the White House after taking their oaths in the Capitol. As more than thirty thousand men, representing hundreds of civil and military organizations paraded past TR in 1905, he smiled, laughed, shouted, yelled, clapped his hands, swayed to the rhythm of the bands, and came close at times to dancing around the reviewing stand. He loved the band music: the Sousa marches, the ragtime ren- ditions, the patriotic songs ("Star Spangled Banner" and "America, the Beautiful"), and the popular tunes, like "Dixie" ("That is one of the best tunes in the lot"), and, especially, "There'll Be a Hot Time in the Old Town Tonight," a fa- vorite of the Rough Riders whom he led in Cuba during the Spanish-American War. He also enjoyed the signs and banners passing by: THE PRESIDENT'S NEIGHBORS (carried by people from Oyster Bay, Long Island), ALL I ASK IS A SQUARE DEAL FOR EVERY MAN (flourished by a political club). He particularly enjoyed the banner presented by some coal miners, wearing overalls, with lamps on their caps, celebrating his help in settling the anthracite coal strike in 1902: "WE HONOR THE MAN WHO SETTLED OUR STRIKE."[15]

Adoring, as he did, things military, Roosevelt stood tall when the army and navy units saluted him as they passed the White House. "Those are the boys," he told his associates, as the West Point cadets and Annapolis midshipmen appeared. "They're superb." When the Seventh Cavalry came by, its band playing "Garry Owen," he remarked: "That is a bully fighting tune, and this is Custer's old regiment, one of the finest in the service." He applauded the "jackies" from some of the navy's war vessels with great gusto, explaining to his companions in the stand, "Those are the men who will help to avert the danger of an international war." As a squadron of the Ninth Regular Cavalry, a black regiment, went by, he exclaimed: "Ah, they were with me at Santiago!" The Rough Riders, of course, gave him special pleasure, and he got a big kick out of seeing one of the men lasso a spectator and carry him along in the march for a minute or two.[16]

TR made a big point of applauding the soldiers in the parade who came from the "Territories" (Puerto Rico and the Philippines), acquired during the Spanish-American War, for he regarded anti-imperialistic critics of the war as narrow-minded "isolationists" who were blind to America's world responsibilities. When some Puerto Rican militiamen came by, he turned to Georgia senator Augustus O. Bacon, a prominent anti-expansionist, and chortled: "They look pretty well for an oppressed people, eh, Senator?" The appearance of some Filipino scouts (with their band playing, for some reason, "The Irish Washerwoman") led him to lean far over the railing of the stand and clap his hands vigorously. "The wretched serfs disguise their feelings admirably," he teased Senator Bacon. A few minutes later he turned to Senator Henry Cabot Lodge (who shared his expansionist views) and remarked in a voice loud enough for Bacon to hear: "You should have seen Bacon hide his face when the Filipinos went by. The 'slaves' were rejoicing in their shackles!" Bacon refrained from reminding TR of the tremendous loss of life in the U.S. campaign to quell the Filipino insurrection that broke out after the United States took over the Philippine Islands from Spain in 1898.[17]

The cowboys in the 1905 parade practically sent TR into orbit. When fifty or so of them, led by his friend Seth Bullock, came dashing up Pennsylvania Avenue waving their sombreros and cheering lustily, Roosevelt waved his hat frantically in response. One cowboy put spurs on his steed and raced toward Roosevelt at such speed that he almost fell over the railing, but, to TR's delight, at the last minute he wheeled his horse and rejoined his companions. Then, as T.R. watched with a big smile, the cowboys rolled merrily away, yelling and hollering, and snaring unwary bystanders with their lariats.[18]

The appearance, soon after, of six famous Native American leaders, in war paint, and carrying spears and tomahawks, produced hearty greetings from the president. Headed by the old Apache warrior Geronimo, and including Quanah Parker (Comanche), Little Plume (Nez Perce), Buckskin Charley (Ute), Hollow Horn (Sioux), and American Horse (Sioux), the six men turned snappily in their saddles as they rode by, uttering whoops and hollers for "the Great White Father" (according to reporters). The commissioner of Indian affairs, who arranged for their participation in the parade, had seen to it that a corps of cadets from the Carlisle Indian School in Pennsylvania, representing the "new Indians," marched that day, too. There were also some Harvard undergraduates, in cap and gown, in the parade, and as they passed, they gave the Harvard yell ("Harvard, Harvard, Harvard, rah, rah, rah, rah!"), and TR, a Harvard man, leaned over and told the cheerleader, "I want you boys to come over to the White House tonight. Mrs. Roosevelt and I want to shake hands with you."[19]

At the end, when the last of the marchers had passed by, TR exclaimed: "It was a great success. Bully. And did you note that bunch of cowboys? Oh, they are the boys who can ride! It was all superb. It really touched me to the heart." The *New York Times* also pronounced the 1905 parade a great success. "Old timers agree," wrote the editors, "that in point of picturesqueness, variety, and general interest, no inaugural procession in many years has approached that which, to the music of many bands, the rattle of thousands of horses' hoofs, and the steady tramp of thousands of feet, swept from the Capitol up Pennsylvania Avenue and between the silent figures of the Court of History to where the President, backed by the flower of official Washington, stood waiting to review it." There were comments afterward about the president's ordeal, standing so long that afternoon, with only a brief rest now and then, during halts in the parade, but Mike Donovan, TR's former boxing instructor, averred: "It would take something more than a little bantam-weight stunt like that to feaze [sic] a heavyweight like the President!"[20]

The afternoon parades didn't faze TR's successors, either—except for Coolidge—and the marchers for Franklin Roosevelt in 1933 and for John F. Kennedy in 1961 were especially impressive. For FDR's first inauguration, three hundred members of the electoral college marched in the parade, at the president's request, for he wanted to remind people of the role that electoral votes, as well as popular votes, played in electing American presidents. In 1933, some movie stars also joined the parade for the first time, and Tom Mix, the celebrated Western star, turned out to be one of the most popular figures in the FDR parade. The Kennedy parade in 1961 boasted 32,000 participants—including forty bands, thousands of troops, and forty huge floats—and lasted three and a half hours. Mrs. Kennedy left long before it was over, but JFK stayed to the very end. "I'll stay if it takes all night," he vowed. "I'm not leaving until the last man has passed." His favorite float featured a PT boat, painted to represent PT 109, the one he commanded during World War II, carrying members of his wartime crew who gave him snappy salutes as they passed the reviewing stand.[21]

Snappy salutes were a big thing with Ronald Reagan. On the occasion of his first inauguration in 1981, he was fascinated by the way the soldiers and sailors in the inaugural parade executed an eyes right and a brisk salute as they passed the presidential reviewing stand. "Is it appropriate for me to return their salute?" he finally asked an army general near him in the stand. "It is appropriate, sir," replied the general, "if your head is covered." Since he was hatless, Reagan simply nodded, his hand placed over his heart, in response to the salutes, but later he told his friend Michael Deaver, "I really felt uncomfortable not returning those salutes the men gave me, just standing there, motionless." Exclaimed Deaver: "Mr. President, you are the commander in chief now, you can do whatever you want." Reagan's eyes lit up, Deaver wrote later, "and to this day, he salutes everything that moves."[22]

In 1989, Reagan's successor, George Bush, returned the salutes of military personnel the way Reagan had, but in 1993, when Bill Clinton reviewed the parade after his first inauguration, he at first omitted the military gesture. At one point, the reporters covering the parade for the *New York Times,* looking for gaffes, were delighted when an army officer walked over to Clinton and saluted him, and the new president "froze for a few seconds before he realized that his new status as Commander in Chief required him to salute back." But like the *Times* reporters, Clinton probably didn't know that most presidents, including Clinton's hero, JFK, deliberately refrained from returning military salutes in kind, because, as civilian commanders of America's armed forces, they were not in uniform, and they symbolized the principle of civil supremacy over the military in the American system. For them, a smile, wave, nod, or friendly hello replaced the military propriety, and any of those gestures would have been just right for Clinton.[23]

Clinton saluted, of course, when his second inauguration rolled around in 1997, though not with the panache of Reagan, as reporters dutifully noted, and he expressed the same boyish glee at the afternoon parade as he had in 1993 (and TR had shown in 1905). There were eighty-four units in the twentieth century's last inaugural parade, with some six thousand participants, including the usual military, naval, and air force units, high school bands, and floats from all fifty states, as well as special acts such as jugglers, jump ropers, stilt walkers, unicyclists, metal-hoop marchers, and tumblers—the usual "mishmash," as one reporter put it, "of patriotism, pride, and silliness." But 1997's parade offered some special features for the second-term president's enjoyment: the marching band from the University of Arkansas; Irene, the Democratic donkey, just in from Alabama, accompanied by a handler named Doc and a mule called Bill; an elementary school chorus from rural Washington State mouthing the recorded words of a song "If It Takes a Village," written by their teacher, which was based on one of Mrs. Clinton's books; and Rope Warrior, a jump roper from Chicago who jumped rope while in a sitting position (he called it his "tush-up"). "This is a celebration of the American civil religion," observed Marvin W. Kranz, an American history specialist for the Library of Congress. "It shows the diversity and the oneness of the nation. There's a certain amount of hokiness to it, after all. But so what?"[24]

For polka lovers in the country (and there were many), the highlight of the 1997 parade was the appearance of Frank Yankovic, the King of American polkadom. Crowned the polka king in 1948, the eighty-one-year-old accordionist and his wife, Ida, arrived in Washington the day before the inauguration with a contingent of polka dancers from Milwaukee to take part in the parade. "He is an icon; he is a legend," a Wisconsin Polka Hall of Fame spokesman told reporters. "He is to polka what Elvis Presley was to rock-and-roll." In the parade for Clinton, Yankovic sat on a throne attached to the Hall of Fame float, as all around him musicians played and dancers performed the polka. The float's featured song was "The White House Polka," sung by Barbara Lane, the polka queen of Milwaukee, who wrote it for the inauguration. It went in part:

> *We're on our way to the White House,*
> *Pennsylvania Avenue.*
> *We're on our way to the White House,*
> *And we're proud of our red, white, and blue.*
> *The polka is our state dance,*
> *A dance that sets the pace.*
> *It's great to play for the President.*
> *But Wisconsin's our home base.*[25]

Clinton seems to have enjoyed the tribute, but it is not on record that he did any polka dancing himself at the inaugural balls that night. He wasn't exactly the polka type.

The Inaugural Balls

12

COVERING WILLIAM McKINLEY'S SEC-
ond inauguration for *Harper's Weekly* in 1901, reporter Francis Leupp found the festivities increasingly wearisome as
the day wore on, and he seems to have resented the fact that
he still had an inaugural ball to attend that night. "We
Americans," he grumped, "are perhaps the only people who
do not feel that we have had a good time unless we are thoroughly tired at the end of it; so, giving themselves and their
most honored public servants a bare chance for a mouthful
of dinner, the festival-makers of Washington don their gala
raiment and repair to the inaugural ball."[1]

Leupp's views were not common. Henry Adams called
inaugurals balls a "melancholy occasion," but for most in-

augural celebrants the evening ball was inauguration day's pièce de résistance: it was a chance to see the president and his wife, elegantly attired, up close, and the women attending enjoyed doing some fancy dressing of their own. The music and dancing and, in the nineteenth century, the lavish refreshments, added to the excitement, and so did the possibility of getting to shake hands with the newly installed president and perhaps hear him make a little speech. "The inaugural ball is always the climax of the day," the *Washington Post* observed in 1897. "To the minds of many there is nothing comparable to it."[2]

There was the inevitable snob appeal. "Anyone who is anyone is there," sniffed Theodore Roosevelt's high-flying daughter Alice, "and a lot of people who are no one try to get in as well."[3] Some observers, to be sure, minimized the exclusiveness. The "most humble citizens, having the price of a ticket," insisted *Harper's Weekly* in 1909 (when William Howard Taft became president), "may, in theory, meet upon a social plane the incoming head of the nation" at the inaugural ball.[4] But it was only a theory. Few humble citizens could, in fact, afford the tickets: five dollars and ten dollars in the nineteenth century and over one hundred dollars in the late twentieth century. Nor could they handle the cost of the exquisite gowns, designed and planned months in advance, that were sine qua non for the women attending the ball, as well as for the First Lady. One observer succinctly summed up the appeal of the inaugural ball that climaxed Grover Cleveland's first inauguration in 1885: "one of the finest displays of beauty, health and wealth ever congregated in America."[5]

Some presidents, like Jimmy Carter in 1977, substituted

parties for the traditional ball; these parties were intended to be more accessible to the ordinary citizen, but the effort at democratization failed to catch on. Though the thousands who waltzed, fox-trotted, and jitterbugged at the Carter parties seem to have enjoyed themselves, *Newsweek*'s Pete Axthelm was frankly scornful. He called the Carter gatherings "sterile, low-budget affairs that seldom ventured beyond political homilies," and warned: "A few more such 'people's parties' could bring back snobbery."[6] The fancy balls returned, sure enough, with Ronald Reagan, Carter's successor, in 1981, and continued to the end of the twentieth century.

The first official inaugural ball, open to the public, took place in 1809, with the accession of James Madison to the presidency. There were balls for George Washington's two inaugurations, to be sure, but they were private affairs, one given by the French minister a few days after Washington took his oath in 1789, and the other by Philadelphia's Dancing Assembly in 1793. Washington, who loved dancing, took to the dance floor to do the minuet on both occasions, but his immediate successors, John Adams and Thomas Jefferson, had fireworks, not balls, for the last event in their inaugurations, and went to bed early on the night of their oath-taking ceremonies. But Jefferson turned up for his friend and successor Madison's swearing in, in 1809, and also appeared at the evening ball.

The grand inaugural ball for Madison, held at Long's Hotel, across from the Capitol, was called "the most brilliant and crowded in Washington" (though the Federal City was still fairly primitive in those days), and four hundred guests turned up for the occasion. Jefferson, now "the plain, unassuming citizen," arrived at Long's before Madison did, and the band greeted him with the tune, "Jefferson's March," composed in his honor. Soon after, Madison appeared, with his wife, Dolley, and his sister-in-law, Anna Cutts, in tow, to the accompaniment of "President Madison's March." Observer Margaret Bayard Smith thought the new president's wife looked like a queen. "It would be *absolutely impossible* for anyone to behave with more propriety," she said of Dolley, "unassuming dignity, sweetness, grace. It seems to me that such manners would disarm envy itself and conciliate enemies." Mrs. Smith's heart "beat with pleasure," she confessed, when she exchanged a few remarks with Jefferson, and she enjoyed her chat, a little later, with President Madison. Madison walked over to her, she recalled, made "some of his old kind and mischievous allusions," and then asked how things were going with the well she was having dug at her place in the country. "'Truth is at the bottom of a well,' is the old saying," he reminded her, "and I expect when you get to the bottom of yours, you will discover most important truths. I hope you will at least find water."[7]

As the ballroom became crowded, Jefferson decided to leave, but Madison lingered, and to Mrs. Smith he seemed "spiritless and exhausted," worn out by the day's activities. "While he was standing by me," she remembered, "I said, 'I wish with all my heart that I had a little bit of seat to offer you.' 'I wish so too,' said he, with a most woe-begone face, and looking as if he could scarcely stand,—the manager came up to ask him to stay to supper, he assented, and turned to me, 'but I would much rather be in bed.'" By this time, she added, the ballroom was a "moving mass" through which "it was scarcely possible to elbow your way," and "poor Mrs. Madison was almost pressed to death" by people pushing forward to get a look at her.[8]

When it came time to dine, the French minister, General Turreau, led Mrs. Madison to the supper table, while the British minister, David Erskine, escorted her sister, Mrs. Cutts. Mrs. Madison stationed herself between the two foreign ministers (to keep the peace, some people whispered) at the center of the long, crescent-shaped dining table, with Madison facing her directly across the way. For Mrs. Smith, Dolley Madison "really, in manner and appearance, answered all my ideas of royalty. She was so equally gracious to both French and English, and so affable to all."[9]

When the dancing commenced, Thomas Tingey, one of the sponsors of the ball, presented Mrs. Madison with the cotillion's first number. "What shall I do with it?" she murmured. "I don't dance." "Give it to a neighbor," suggested Tingey. "Oh, no," protested Mrs. Madison, "it will look like a partiality." "Then I will," decided Tingey, and he passed it on to Mrs. Cutts. Wrote Mrs. Smith later: "I really admired this in Mrs. Madison." Then she added, a bit cryptically: "Ah, why does she not in all things act with the same propriety? She would be too much beloved if she added all the virtues to all the graces." Mrs. Smith never made clear her reservations about Mrs. Madison; perhaps she thought Dolley's sociability bordered at times on flirtation.[10]

As the dancing continued, the air in the ballroom turned stale, and at length several people fainted and had to be carried outside. Efforts to open the windows were fruitless; the painted window sashes were stuck tight. In desperation, some of the guests started smashing the windows, and, as cold air came pouring in, the ballroom quickly became tolerable again. The dancing continued until midnight, but long before that, the Madisons had left. John Quincy Adams took a jaundiced view of the evening. "The crowd was excessive," he wrote in his diary that night, "the heat oppressive, and the entertainment bad."[11]

Despite JQA's strictures, the Madison ball was judged a great success, and for Madison's second inauguration in 1813 there was another ball, this time in Davis's Hotel on Pennsylvania Avenue that won plaudits as "a most lovely assemblage of the lovely ones of our district."[12]

After Madison, the inaugural ball became a regular, and increasingly elaborate, part of the inauguration day's activities. Presidents hardly ever missed them and they rarely omitted them from the inaugural schedule unless they were in mourning or the country was at war. Until the late twentieth century, however, the presidents refrained from taking to the dance floor themselves. William Henry Harrison was an exception; he was the first president, after George Washington, to do some dancing at an inaugural ball. For his inauguration in 1841 there were three balls (to accommodate all the people pouring into Washington by train and clamoring to participate in the festivities), and Harrison danced with the wives of prominent Whigs at all three, since his wife was still in Ohio. After Harrison, no president appeared on the dance floor until Lyndon Johnson in 1965, and after that presidential dancing became customary. By then, the puritanic disapproval of dancing among middle-class Americans had long since withered away.

If the president didn't dance, what did he do in the old days at the balls held in his honor? A routine soon developed. An hour or so after the ball commenced, the president appeared in the ballroom, with his wife and an escort, to the tune of "Hail to the Chief," marched through an opening made by the dancers on the dance floor to the other side of the room, took his position on a platform stationed there, and spent an hour or two chatting with his associates and greeting guests who came by to congratulate him. In time, the hotels and government buildings hosting the balls provided rooms for the president and his entourage on the second floor, where he could chat with friends and greet well-wishers, and from which he could venture out onto a balcony nearby to watch the dancers below do the best they could in the jam-packed room below. The president and his party got to dine first, later in the evening, and usually left soon after.

Decorations for the inaugural ballrooms were usually lavish; there were flower displays; huge representations of the presidential seal on the walls; red, white, and blue bunting; and, on at least one occasion, a huge statue of the Goddess of Liberty illuminated with electric lights (then a novelty), greeted the guests as they entered the ballroom. Sometimes the decorations were tailored to the new president; for William McKinley, the celebrated champion of the gold standard, the color scheme at both his inaugurations was conspicuously yellow. Sometimes the music fit the president, too. In 1881, the German Orchestra of Philadelphia played some of James A. Garfield's favorite tunes from Gilbert and Sullivan between dances; and in 1889, John Philip Sousa, conducting the U.S. Marine Band, played a piece entitled "Presidential Polonaise" that he had composed in honor of Benjamin Harrison. In the 1930s, big names in popular music played at the inaugural balls: Rudy

Vallee, Guy Lombardo, Benny Goodman, Xavier Cugat, Lawrence Welk, Lionel Hampton. In the 1970s rock bands and singers appeared at the balls.

But the "presence of the fair sex," as a chronicler put it in 1837, was, from the beginning, "a brilliant feature of the assembly," and received extensive space in the newspapers covering the inauguration. "The multitude of recherché dresses worn by ladies of distinction it would be impossible to enumerate," wrote the *New York Times* of 1861's inaugural ball. "Many ladies who wore velvets, moires, and heavier silks dispensed with hoops altogether, thereby displaying their good taste as well as their regard for the appreciation of some approximation to the female form which still inheres or lingers in the mind of man." But the *Times* wasn't entirely pleased. "Some ladies," it complained, "displayed the bad taste of wearing their rings over their gloves."[13]

The president's wife was invariably the center of attention at the inaugural balls. Newspapers were ecstatic about the satin gown worn by Grover Cleveland's young wife, Frances, in 1893; and in 1897, women waved their handkerchiefs and men clapped their hands when Ida McKinley appeared in the ballroom in a gown of white satin, brocaded in rich design, with diamond earrings, a diamond brooch, and diamond side combs. The gown worn by Theodore Roosevelt's wife, Edith, in 1905, an American creation, also elicited much praise. Before inauguration night, Mrs. Roosevelt asked the designer to destroy the cloth and the pattern in order to avoid any publicity about the dress, but the designer talked to the press anyway, and soon received a curt note from Mrs. Roosevelt: "Greatly annoyed by your advertisement of my gown to the New York

Sun. . . . Fear this makes it impossible for me to employ you again."[14]

Mrs. Roosevelt's gown was heavy, so the inaugural committee shorted the promenade across the dance floor to five minutes and offered to enlist "two powdered youths to act as train bearers," but Mrs. Roosevelt turned down the offer and managed nicely by herself at the ball. Four years later, the gown worn by Mrs. Taft was hailed as one of the handsomest gowns ever seen in Washington, and after the inauguration she decided to present it to the Smithsonian Institution. It was the first contribution the Smithsonian received for its collection of First Ladies' gowns.[15]

In 1969, to the despair of Mark Evans, the inaugural ball chairman, as a concession to the times, there were pressures for more informal attire at the balls planned for Richard Nixon's inauguration. "This is pageantry," he said of the inaugural balls. "It's the only pomp and circumstance we've got in this country. We want everyone to go dressed to the ultimate. We want every husband to complain for years about the cost of his wife's dress and hair-do." In the end, though, there was some relaxation in the rules: white tie preferred for men, but black tie (even turtleneck shirts) permissible, while for women, pants suits were acceptable. "Women," wheezed Evans resignedly, "will be admitted in their formal drawers." But Mrs. Nixon appeared attractively gowned on inaugural night, and four years later she glittered, according to *Time,* "in a long-sleeve turquoise ballgown designed by Adele Simpson."[16]

In 1977, despite Jimmy Carter's preference for informality, his wife, Rosalynn, took seriously her opportunity to shine sartorially at the "parties" her husband scheduled to

replace the customary balls. With Ronald Reagan in the
White House in 1981, things were back on track. In 1985,
Nancy Reagan wore a $22,500 white Galanos gown loaned
to her for the occasion and made the rounds of the balls
with her husband in about three and a half hours.

THE inaugural balls didn't always go off as scheduled.
Sometimes the president arrived later than expected or left
too early, and frequently the dance floor became too crowded
for comfort. At several balls in the middle of the nineteenth
century, moreover, the announcement later in the evening
that dinner was served transformed the guests into a horde
of frenetic food gatherers, who threw all propriety to the
winds in their eagerness to get at the food. In 1845, at the
ball for James K. Polk, when refreshments were served,
there was a near-stampede toward the tables bearing food
and drinks.

The guests were even more ravenous, if anything, at
Zachary Taylor's ball in 1849. When dinner was announced, there was a general rush toward the tables, as
though, sniffed a British visitor, "these people had not eaten
for days. Men tore the meat off turkey skeletons—women
dug jeweled hands into cakes—champagne drenched gowns
and suits." Both men and women fainted in the crush that
night, it was reported, and had to be lugged outside where
the snow was beginning to fall. Taylor managed to get away
by one in the morning, but the party went on until four. By
that time, all the servants had left and the guests discovered
their hats and coats in a big pile in the middle of the nearby
City Hall lobby. There was a general scramble for the wraps,

but it soon became clear that the only hope was to "try on till you got a coat to fit." Young Abraham Lincoln, who had just finished a term as congressman, never did locate his hat, and he finally left bareheaded. "It would be hard," wrote one of the guests, "to forget the sight of that tall and slim man, with his short cloak thrown over his shoulders," setting out on a long walk home in the snow without a hat.[17]

The ball for James Buchanan in 1857 was no more successful. Held in the Grand Saloon, a huge structure erected for the occasion in Judiciary Square, and attended by six thousand people, the Buchanan shindig was almost as disorderly as Congress was in the years leading up to the Civil War. Despite careful planning, hot wax from the candles in the chandeliers dripped down on the dancers, gradually dimming the luster of their fine clothes. "One man," wrote a society reporter, "danced elegantly in such good time to Gungle's exquisite strains that the drops of candle and grease falling on his coat looked like notes of music properly arranged!" If so, they were the only thing properly arranged that evening. Soon after Buchanan departed, the dining room was thrown open to the other guests, and, reported the *New York Times:* "Then came that Balaklava charge, which characterizes the onslaught at every festive scene, when the doors of the supper room are opened. Onward they rushed!" By 4 A.M., when the party ended, the celebrants had gone through 400 gallons of oysters, 500 quarts of chicken salad, 1,200 quarts of ice cream, 500 quarts of jellies, 60 saddles of mutton, 4 saddles of venison, 8 rounds of beef, 75 hams, 125 tongues, and patés of every description, plus several barrels of chilled champagne, and, it was calculated, 3,000 dollars' worth of wine. Some congressmen got so drunk during the melee they had to be trundled off to City Hall to keep from producing a riot.[18]

Equally rowdy was the National Inaugural Ball accompanying Abraham Lincoln's second inauguration in 1865. Attended by four thousand people, it began promisingly, with Lincoln sitting on a platform greeting guests while the dancers gracefully performed quadrilles, waltzes, galops, schottisches, and polkas. But when suppertime arrived, shortly after midnight, the party fell apart. The long supper table was able to accommodate about four hundred people, and the organizers of the meal planned to move people, four hundred at a time, into the supper room, in an orderly fashion, after the Lincolns finished eating. Unfortunately, their plans went awry. When the doors were opened to the guests, just before the Lincolns left, the sudden rush of people flooding from the ballroom quickly reduced the supper room to shambles. "It looks like a scramble," cried Mrs. Lincoln, as she and her husband jumped up to get out of the way. "Well," returned Lincoln, "it appears to be a very systematic scramble." There was no way the Lincolns could get through the mob and out the front door, so they left by a side door, weaving through a labyrinth of alcoves and back stairs to their carriage outside. No one seems to have noticed their hasty departure. Reporter Noah Brooks thought the "wildness" of the crowd that night was "similar to some of the antics of the Paris commune."[19]

Fortunately there was no more wildness after 1865. Subsequent balls were better organized and the amount of food dispensed was considerably reduced. (By 1953, only tiny sandwiches and weak punch were available.) From Ulysses Grant (1869) to William Howard Taft (1909) the parties went off without a hitch. After Taft, however, came a large lacuna in the procession of balls that had entertained the inaugural crowds ever since Madison's day. Democratic president Woodrow Wilson dispensed with the customary ball in both 1913 and 1917, and his Republican successors— Warren G. Harding, Calvin Coolidge, and Herbert Hoover— also did without them. In 1933, the Democrats scheduled a ball to celebrate Franklin Roosevelt's first inauguration, but when FDR indicated he would not attend, there were hundreds of ticket cancellations, only to be rescinded when Mrs. Roosevelt announced her intention to put in an appearance. But FDR omitted the balls for his next three inaugurations, and not until 1949 was the tradition, begun in 1809, finally resumed.

In 1949, Harry Truman, formally attired, with his wife, Bess, looking "regal" in her ball gown, shook hands with hundreds of guests gathered in the National Guard Armory, and watched the dancers, including daughter, Margaret, from a balcony above the dance floor. But the Truman ball wasn't entirely traditional. For one thing, blacks were welcome at the party; Truman had decreed integration for his inauguration. For another, he took time out to make some informal remarks to the crowd, and even do a little teasing, before leaving at the end of the evening. Throughout the night, Margaret recalled, her father's face was "shining like a moon," for, she said, "this had been his day of days."

For Eisenhower four years later, there were two balls, to accommodate the crowds, and in 1957, four of them. At one of the 1957 balls a writer for the *New Yorker* observed the "President having marvelous time—beaming, waving, bowing. Mamie looked great. I smiled at President, saluted.

President smiled back, saluted, President and Mrs. Eisenhower departed, smiling, waving."[20]

But the presidents still didn't take to the dance floor the way George Washington and William Henry Harrison had done years before. Even the youthful John F. Kennedy refrained from dancing as he and his wife, Jacqueline, appeared at the inaugural balls held in his honor in 1961. JFK teased about it at the crowded Statler-Hilton Hotel. "There's only one feature of this ball I don't like," he told the dancers. "The minute I arrive the music stops and I never get a chance to dance." At this, many of the women in the ballroom raised their hands and volunteered: "Me, me!" But Kennedy took his position with his wife in the presidential box overlooking the ballroom to watch the dancing, as so many of his predecessors had done. After a while, though, he slipped away and went upstairs to visit a private party thrown by Frank Sinatra, which included Hollywood beauties Angie Dickinson, Janet Leigh, and Kim Novak. When he returned a half hour or so later, looking sheepish, with a *Washington Post* under his arm (looking as if he had stepped out to buy a paper), "his knowing wife," recalled one of his friends, "gave him a rather chilly look."[21]

Finally in 1965, Lyndon B. Johnson integrated the president himself into the inaugural dancing. There were five balls that year, with more than 28,000 people paying twenty-five dollars each to attend the dances, and, as LBJ quipped, when he saw the crowded ballrooms: "Never before have so many paid so much to dance so little!" Making the rounds that night, Johnson really "had a ball," as *Time* put it. At the Mayflower Hotel, he changed partners nine times in thirteen minutes, flushed and sweating, but supremely happy. One of his partners was Margaret Truman (who represented her ailing father at the inauguration). Spying her in a box with her husband, he hoisted her over the railing, and, to the delight of the crowd, twirled her over to the dance floor as the orchestra played "I've Got the World on a String."[22]

Wherever Johnson went that giddy night, he got in a good word for the Great Society, his beloved social program. At the Shoreham Hotel he had a bit of advice for the dancers: "Now, I want y'all to get to bed early tonight so we can all get to work early tomorrow for the Great Society." At the Sheraton Park Hotel, crammed with seven thousand guests, mostly Texans (LBJ called it the "Sheraton-Texas"), he crowed: "One thing you can say for the Great Society, it sure is crowded!" Once settled in the presidential box, he reeled off a series of witticisms that *Time* thought sounded a little like discards from comedian Bob Hope's routines. "The Secretary of Labor is in charge of finding you a job," he told the guests, "the Secretary of the Treasury is in charge of taking half of your money away from you, and the Attorney General is in charge of suing you for the other half." Then, as the Texans flocked around him, he took to the dance floor with his wife, Lady Bird, and, *Newsweek* reported, "glided off like a well-heeled old grad and his wife at a college homecoming tour routine." The Sheraton Park was his last stop, and just before leaving he told the revelers: "Don't stay up late. There's work to be done. We're on our way to the Great Society!"[23]

After Johnson, dancing and teasing the crowds became part of the president's agenda when visiting the balls on inauguration night. "I thought this was supposed to be a ball," cried Richard Nixon mock-seriously, as he surveyed one of the six overcrowded balls he and his wife, Pat, attended in 1969. At one of the six balls he visited in 1973, as he began his second term, he told the dancers that reporters were always looking for "firsts," and that he had a "first" of his own for them. "This is my fourth Inaugural Ball," he went on to say, "and the first one at which I have danced." At the Sheraton Park, he and his wife fox-trotted, cheek to cheek, while Lionel Hampton played "People Will Say We're in Love."[24]

For Ronald and Nancy Reagan there were nine inaugural balls in 1981. Some forty thousand people bought tickets to the various white-tie affairs, and while going from one place to another, Reagan not only took to the dance floor with his wife; he also made a few informal remarks that delighted the Republican celebrants. "There isn't anything we can't do," cried Reagan triumphantly at one of the balls, "and together we're going to do it!" The planners of Reagan's first inauguration spent $15 million to transmit scenes of the balls in Washington via satellite to eighty-seven "mini-balls" being held around the country to celebrate the day, but ticket sales paid for the expense, and the money raised at the "satellite balls" (in places like Hastings, Montana, and Pocatello, Idaho) went to local charities. "Here we are on the first night," exalted Reagan at one of the balls, "and there are communities that are keeping their money at home. We're going to do our best to see that the idea catches on."[25]

Reagan made little speeches wherever he went, but at the Air and Space Museum he turned to his wife after some brief remarks and said, "I think now I'll dance with my best lady." And to the delight of the guests, he did just that, to the tune of "You'll Never Know How Much I Love You." His quips pleased the crowd, too. After having his picture taken against the backdrop of the Wright Brothers' biplane hanging from the ceiling, he turned back to the crowd and exclaimed: "No matter what they say, it isn't true that I flew that." He enjoyed teasing about his age, and the Grand Old Partyers loved it. There were nine balls (and 140,000 guests) in 1985, and the Reagans appeared at all of them and danced at all but two.[26]

When George Bush succeeded Reagan as president in 1989, there were eleven balls, nine for black-tie guests, paying $175 each, and two for the younger set, costing $35. Mrs. Bush suggested that her husband was "a bit of a deadbeat on the dance floor," but the two of them fox-trotted their way through the balls until after midnight. A few days before, the inaugural planners had asked Bush what his favorite tune was so bandleaders would know what to play when he and his wife appeared. When he referred the question to his wife, Barbara, she suggested a song from *My Fair Lady,* one of their favorite shows, entitled, "I Could Have Danced All Night." But Bush protested. "Don't say that song," he exclaimed; he was afraid the title would be taken literally. So he and Barbara agreed to pick another tune, "On the Street Where You Live," from the same musical. Something went wrong, however, and when the Bushes arrived at the Union Station party for their first dance of the evening, around 9:30, the band at once broke into "I Could Have Danced All Night." Bush looked surprised and betrayed, and his wife shook her head disapprovingly at the players. But Bush gamely twirled Barbara about on the dance floor for a few seconds, then stopped abruptly, announcing, "OK," and dragged her off as she shrugged her shoulders. Cried the president as they left: "You can say you saw here first a lousy dancer trying to dance the first dance with the First Lady of the United States of America."[27]

There were thirteen balls for Bill Clinton in 1993, as well as scores of unofficial parties and celebrations, at which seventy thousand Democrats, it was estimated, partied until dawn. As the "new King of Rock and Roll" (the nickname some celebrants gave the president) visited the balls with his wife, he played the saxophone, hugged people, whooped, swayed, and danced with Hillary, while the crowds screamed, swooned, danced, rocked, and rolled. Clinton looked handsome in black tie, according to reporters, and his wife looked splendid in a sparkling purple ball gown, with her head tossed back "and laughing like a prom date" when they took to the dance floor. At the MTV ball in the Convention Center, rock star Tabitha Soren escorted the two of them across the stage, but their daughter got bigger shrieks than they did: "Chelsea! Chelsea! Chelsea!"[28]

In a little talk at the MTV ball, Clinton told the crowd, "What I am most proud of is that a lot of young people turned out in record numbers to vote." At the Arkansas ball he announced: "I'm going to pull my new prerogative and let Hillary speak first." Mrs. Clinton then thanked the Arkansans for "the friendship, love, prayer, and your consistency over the long months." After her remarks, the "saxman-in-chief," as a *Washington Post* writer dubbed the new president, picked up a saxophone and did a couple of choruses from "Your Mama Don't Dance," while his mother, along for the fun, listened proudly. At one of the balls a reporter called out: "Would you rather be playing your sax or working on your economic plan?" Responded Clinton: "Tonight I would rather play my saxophone, but tomorrow

I'd rather work on my economic plan." The *Post*'s Jacqueline Trescott summed up the Clintons' inaugural evening: "Thirteen balls, 12 choruses of 'Hail to the Chief,' 11 dances, 5 sax breaks, a hundred pointed fingers, unaccountable hugs. And home almost on time. It truly is a new day."[29]

ON JANUARY 20, 2001, GEORGE W. Bush, former governor of Texas, became the first president's son to take the presidential oath since John Quincy Adams in 1825. He was also the first since Benjamin Harrison in 1888 to win the presidency with fewer popular votes than his opponent. And he was the first to become president after the U.S. Supreme Court intervened in a dispute over returns from Florida, called a halt to the recounting, and, in effect, handed the victory to Bush by a small majority of electoral votes. "Someday, son," a proud father tells his boy in a newspaper cartoon appearing after a bitterly divided Court gave Bush the nod, "you might grow up and get picked by the Supreme Court to be president!" Some people called Bush "the president-select."[1]

The quarrel over Florida's ballots—the confusing butter-fly-looking ballots in one county and punch-hole ballots elsewhere that produced pieces of cardboard called "chads" that didn't always fall out when pressed by voters—led one wag (aware that there was a Green Party candidate) to propose an inaugural banquet for the victor consisting of "chad roe, butterfly shrimp on wilted Green, mixed word salad, and, as their just dessert, humble pie."[2]

Delay in picking the president meant delay in inaugural planning; Washington's hostesses, caterers, party planners, calligraphers, and equipment rental companies were "in list hell," as one event planner put it, until the bitterly divided Supreme Court disposed of the Florida farrago. But Republican inaugural planners went quickly into action and explained they were organizing "a celebration of democracy in action rather than a victory." When Bush "raises his right hand...to become our next president," announced Connecticut's Democratic senator Christopher Dodd, "we'll watch not as Democrats and Republicans but as Americans." Despite protest demonstrations on inauguration day, most Americans seemed to feel as Dodd did.[3]

The inauguration of Bush *fils* in 2001 turned out to be as lavish as that of Bush *père* in 1989. Centered on the theme, "Celebrating America's Spirit Together," it lasted four days and included fund-raising candlelight dinners (at $2,500 a ticket), tributes to America's writers, veterans, and youth, a parade containing high school and college bands from Texas, and eight balls, plus a Black Tie and Boots Inaugural Ball on inauguration eve, featuring Texana. There was open house at the Executive Mansion on the day after the inauguration, as in 1989.

The Texas touch ("Texification") was pronounced. "Everybody who's anybody in Texas will be in Washington next week," crowed a Fort Worth newspaper columnist just before the inauguration. That included Bevo, the University of Texas at Austin's longhorn mascot; Old Pete, a life-size mule statue from Muleshoe, a tiny Texas town; and Reveille, the collie mascot of Texas A & M University. On display at the Black Tie and Boots Inaugural Ball, moreover, were creatures from the Fort Worth Zoo indigenous to the Lone Star State: a Harris hawk, an American alligator, an armadillo, a roadrunner, a screech owl, and a barn owl. "You can't have a party without cuddly creatures," explained a spokesman for the ball. "You can pet the alligator, cuddle with an armadillo, sit on the bull, and do the two step all in one place."[4]

Just before leaving Midland, his boyhood home, for Washington, George W. exclaimed: "I'm going to take a lot of Midland and a lot of Texas with me up there."[5] But some Texans—mainly Democrats—disparaged the Texas baggage Bush promised to take to the capital: "Like his *alleged* ranch in Crawford," said one Texan (who secretly voted for Democratic candidate Al Gore). "They've got some cows, but that's farm country. It used to be impolite in Texas society to ask, 'How many head of cattle are you running?'—that's like saying, 'How much money have you got in your pocketbook?'—but it's not impolite in Crawford, because that's not cattle country. This is not the LBJ ranch we're talking, O.K.? I don't even think he has a truck." But most Bushies acknowledged that in recent years Texas had come to be more like the rest of the country. "You're not going to see Bush wearing string ties," said one Texan. "I'm not expecting what somebody thinks of as Texas culture," insisted another Texan, "I'm expecting just plain old American culture." Still, for many people Bush's West Texas twang gave his inauguration a cowboy flavor. One Texas Democrat, who likes Tex-Mex cuisine, observed that "the one good thing that might come out of all of this is that D.C. might finally get a good Mexican restaurant and not one where you have to have four margaritas and then after your tastebuds are completely dulled say, 'Not bad for Washington.'"[6]

Inauguration day was dark and drizzly, but Bush recited his oath confidently and delivered his address briskly, with his parents watching proudly, and then reviewed the parade and attended the balls with his wife, Laura. Like his father in 1989, he deprecated his dancing skills. "I confess I'm not the world's greatest dancer," he announced at one of the balls, "but you're going to have to suffer through it." At another ball, he joked about his dancing and then "reluctantly, awkwardly sashayed with his wife for periods ranging from 29 to 67 seconds (as actually timed by Associated Press reporters)." But even people who hadn't voted for him counted on his performance as president to outshine his performance on the dance floor.[7]

INAUGURAL VIGNETTES

Lachrimosity (1797)

Looking back on his oath-taking in 1797, John Adams seems to have been impressed mainly by the inaugural day's lachrimosity. He wrote his wife, Abigail, that "there was more weeping" at the inauguration "than there has ever been at the representation of any tragedy." Everyone, he said, "talks of the tears, the full eyes, the streaming eyes, the trickling eyes." He realized the moisture was for his predecessor, George Washington, for, as he put it, "the sight of the sun setting full orbed and another rising less splendid was a novelty." But he rejoiced at the peaceful passing of the torch after the political animosities of the past few years. "A Solemn Scene it was indeed," he wrote, "and it was made

more affecting to me by the presence of the General, whose
countenance was as serene and unclouded as the day."
Then he added wryly: "He seem'd to me to enjoy a triumph over me. Methought I heard him think ay! I am fairly
out and you fairly in! See which of us will be the happiest."[1]

Federalist Regrets (1801)

In 1801, the Federalists dreaded the inauguration of
Jefferson (whom they excoriated as a "democrat"). In one
town, a devout Federalist removed the clapper from a church
bell, so Jeffersonians wouldn't have the pleasure of hearing
it ring for Jefferson on inauguration day. In Boston, the
Columbian Centinel, a Federalist newspaper, printed an obitu-
ary, not a congratulatory statement, on the replacement of
Adams (who left town without attending Jefferson's inauguration) by Jefferson on March 4:

YESTERDAY EXPIRED
Deeply regretted by MILLIONS of grateful Americans
And by *all* GOOD MEN,
THE FEDERAL ADMINISTRATION
of the
GOVERNMENT of the *United States*
animated by
a WASHINGTON, an ADAMS—a HAMILTON, KNOX,
STODDERT AND DEXTER
Aet. 12 years[2]

Jefferson and Marshall (1801)

Just before his inauguration, Jefferson wrote John Marshall, the Federalist whom Adams had made chief justice of

the Supreme Court, asking him to administer the oath on March 4. "I shall with much pleasure attend to administer the oath of office," Marshall replied, and "shall make a point of being punctual."

On inauguration morning, Marshall started a letter to his old friend, South Carolina's Charles Cotesworth Pinckney. "Today a new political year commences. The new order of things begins," he reminded his friend. "Mr. Adams I believe left the city at 4 o'clock in the morning and Mr. Jefferson will be inaugurated at 12. There are some appearances which surprise me. I wish however more than I hope that the public prosperity and happiness may sustain no diminution under democratic guidance." Then he had this to say about the incoming president: "The democrats are divided into speculative theorists and absolute terrorists. With the latter I am not disposed to class Mr. Jefferson." He went on to say that if Jefferson aligned himself with the "terrorists," it was "not difficult to foresee that much calamity is in store for our country," but if he did not align himself with them, "they will soon become his enemies and calumniators." At this point, he broke off the letter and hurried to the Capitol so he could arrive punctually, as he had promised, for the inaugural ceremony. The swearing in went smoothly; Jefferson was the first of nine presidents Marshall was to swear in.

After the ceremony, Marshall returned to his lodgings and finished his letter to Pinckney. "I have administered the oath to the President," he wrote. "You will before this reaches you see his inauguration speech. It is in general well judged and conciliatory. It is in direct terms giving the lie to the violent party declamation which has elected him; but it is strongly characteristic of the general cast of his political theory." Marshall wasn't the only Federalist who was reassured by the words, appearing early in Jefferson's inaugural address: "We are all Republicans; we are all Federalists."[3]

Jackson's Spectacles (1829)

When Andrew Jackson arrived in the Capitol for his first inauguration, one Washingtonian noticed that as he walked "down the aisle with a quick, large step, as though he proposed to storm the Capitol," he was wearing two pairs of spectacles: one for reading and the other for seeing at a distance, with the pair not in use lying across his head. "On this occasion," reported the observer, "the pair on his head reflected the light; and some of the rural admirers of the old hero were firmly persuaded that they were two plates of metal let into his head to close up the holes made by British bullets at New Orleans."[4]

JQA and Jackson (1829)

When Jackson arrived in Washington for his inauguration in 1829, he was still fuming over the attacks on his wife, Rachel, during the recent presidential campaign, and he blamed John Quincy Adams for not restraining his supporters during the contest. Still, he was all set to pay a courtesy call on the president until his friends talked him out of it. Adams was hurt by the slight, and Adams's friends were indignant. "It was such a mark of indignity," declared one newspaper editor, "that self-respect forbids Mr. Adams to overlook it."

But JQA tried to be courteous himself. He sent a messenger to tell Jackson he would be out of the Executive

Mansion by inauguration day so the new president could "receive his visits of congratulations" there after the inaugural ceremony. Jackson sent a message back begging Adams not to inconvenience himself, but he refrained from inviting him to the ceremony. JQA consulted members of his administration, and all but one opposed attending it. In the end, Adams's family moved to a house on Meridian Hill, north of Washington, the day before the inauguration, and Adams followed them, on foot, a little later, unrecognized by Washingtonians. He also put a notice in the newspapers requesting citizens who planned to call on him, as was the custom, "to dispense with the formality."[5]

Zachary Taylor's Welcome (1849)

General Taylor arrived in Washington on February 23, the anniversary of Buena Vista (one of his victories in the Mexican War) and was greeted noisily by thousands of people who had waited for hours at the station. "Well, old Zach has come at last," a young man in the crowd wrote his sister the following day, "and I suppose no one ever met with a more cordial reception than our citizens gave him last night. I hurried over my supper and started out of the door, and directly I was out of it I heard a hum all around me, as of a great many people. I hurried on to Pennsylvania Avenue and saw thousands of persons hurrying to one spot, viz, the depot; I of course joined in and such hurrahing, and pushing and knocking down, I never saw before. We at last arrived at the depot and there we saw every description of fireworks, and firearms waiting for the whistle of the cars, to be left off."

An hour or two later, when the train pulled into the station, Taylor and his party were greeted with cannons,

Roman candles, and skyrockets, and it took Old Rough and Ready an hour to get through the cheering multitudes to his carriage and drive to the Willard Hotel. After resting a bit, he appeared on the hotel balcony to greet his adoring admirers. Reporters praised his looks: well-shaped head, kindly and intelligent face, dignified bearing. He was, though, somewhat stouter than they had expected.

Taylor took it easy over the weekend, then called on President Polk and began receiving visitors. "We have reason to believe," declared the *National Intelligencer,* "that the impression made on the numerous persons . . . who called on the General yesterday, scarcely one of whom had ever seen him before, was highly favorable. The blended urbanity and dignity of his demeanor, his kindness . . . and benevolence . . . are calculated to win . . . esteem. We . . . were pleased to observe the alertness and vigor which mark his movements after . . . many years of hard . . . and wearing service." Whig leader William H. Seward thought Taylor was "the most gentle-looking and amiable of men," and that everything he said and did "indicated sincerity of heart, even to guilelessness." When Michigan senator Lewis Cass, his Democratic opponent in the 1848 presidential race, dropped by to congratulate him, Taylor got up, held out his hand, and exclaimed: "Good morning, General, how do you do?" "Very well indeed, General Taylor," returned Cass. "This is the second time I follow your route, but you got twice ahead of me." Smiled Taylor: "The race is not always to the swift, nor the battle to the strong."[6]

Buchanan's Health (1857)

James Buchanan was feeling queasy when he took his oath as president in 1857. It wasn't the crisis over slavery that bothered him; it was the state of his health. He was suffering from some kind of gastrointestinal infection and hadn't eaten any solid food for several days. Some people called his ailment the "National Hotel disease," for he contracted it (as did several other people) after attending a banquet in his honor at the hotel. When he tried subsisting on rum for a time, punsters said he was having a "rum go" (an odd event) on his way to the presidency.

When he called on President Pierce to discuss moving into the White House, Old Buck politely declined Pierce's invitation to dinner, just to be on the safe side. And when he took his oath and delivered his address the following day, he was medicated by his doctor as well as fortified with brandy; nonetheless, he succeeded in getting through the ceremony without mishap. Soon after moving into the White House Buchanan installed his own cook in the kitchen and recovered his health.[7]

Volcano (1857)

Though still feeling under the weather, Buchanan put in a brief appearance at the inaugural ball with his niece, Harriet Lane, who was to be the hostess while he was in the White House. Despite the "terpsichorean gaiety" and the bountiful refreshments (including a huge cake, four feet high, topped by a flag bearing the arms of every state in the Union), the foreign guests were keenly aware of the crisis over slavery tearing the nation apart (which Buchanan tried to solve by appeasing the slave interest in his inaugural address). At some point that evening, the Russian minister, Baron de Stoeckl, dancing with the wife of the French minister, was reported to have remarked that the ball reminded him of the ball he attended in Paris just before the Revolution of 1830, at which Talleyrand, passing Louis Philippe during a quadrille, whispered: "Sire, we are dancing on a volcano."[8]

Fashion Show (1861)

During the nineteenth century, newspapers spent a great deal of space on the gowns worn by the president's wife and other prominent women at the inaugural balls. The *New York Times* report in 1861 was typical. "Mrs. Lincoln looked extremely well," the *Times* declared, "and was attired in the most elegant manner; her dress was made of white satin very ample and rich, but almost entirely covered by a tunic, or rather skirt, of the finest point appliqué. Her corsage, which was low, and the short sleeves, were ornamented richly by a pericle made of the same material, and the shawl, also of the same rich lace, was most exquisite. Passementerie of narrow fluted satin ribbon completed the dress. Her jewels were of the rarest pearls, necklace, ear-rings, brooch, and bracelets. Her hair, which was put plainly back from her face, was ornamented with trailing jessamine and clustering violets most gracefully."

As to some of the other women, the *Times* continued, "Mrs. Secretary Welles, a lady of rather petite figure, was dressed in a mode-coloured silk, with black lace shawl. Mrs. Secretary Usher, of about the same stature, wore a rich dress of garnet satin, very plain but richly made. Mrs. Postmaster General Dennison, who is a very fine-looking lady, wore a most becoming dress of heavy black velvet, brilliant jewels and hair plainly dressed. Her daughter was in white muslin, embroidered with black. Mrs. Fred Seward, wife of the Assistant Secretary of State, was attired in a pretty rose-colored silk, handsomely trimmed. Mrs. Senator Harris, who has the appearance of a well-preserved English lady, wore a most elegant dress of corn-coloured silk, trimmed with point appliqué. One of the most elaborate and rich dresses in the room was worn by Mrs. George Francis Train. It was a very finely plaited blue silk, trimmed with a flounce of thread lace, almost as deep as her skirt, and other laces to match. Her hair was powdered with gold."[9]

A Story for Lincoln (1861)

At the inaugural ball in 1861, Lincoln shook hands with people for over two hours and, according to Henry Adams, looked as though "no man living needed so much education as the new President, but all the education he could get would not be enough." During the evening Vice President Hannibal Hamlin introduced Colonel James Dunning of Bangor, Maine, to the president, and Dunning, to Lincoln's delight, turned out to be a good storyteller. He told Lincoln about a soldier who was court-martialed for pointing his gun at a man and forcing him to eat a crow. Asked at the trial whether he recognized the complainant, the soldier cried: "Do I recognize this gentleman? Why, yes, he's the gentleman who dined with me yesterday!" Lincoln shook with laughter and told Dunning: "Come up to the house some night next week and tell me some more of your stories."[10]

Kindhearted (1877)

When President Hayes took his oath in 1877, the chief clerk of the Supreme Court held the Bible for him. Afterward, the clerk marked the passage on which Hayes had rested his hand with a lead pencil and sent the Bible to Mrs.

Hayes. The passage was Psalms 118:12–"They compassed me about like bees; they are quenched as the fire of thorns; for in the name of the Lord I will destroy them." When Mrs. Hayes saw it, she laughed and said her husband was too kindhearted to destroy anything.[11]

We Shall Return (1889)

On March 4, 1889, when Benjamin Harrison became president, Jerry Smith, one of the White House servants, escorted Mrs. Cleveland to her carriage and said good-bye. "Now, Jerry," she said, as she entered the carriage, "I want you to take good care of all the furniture and ornaments in the house, and not let any of them get lost or broken, for I want to find everything just as it is now, when we come back again." Astonished, Jerry cried: "Excuse meh, Mis' Cleveland, but jus' when does you-all expec' to come back, please,–so I can have everything ready, I mean?" Mrs. Cleveland smiled. "We are coming back just four years from today," she told him. And they did just that.[12]

Weather Wager

About ten days before Benjamin Harrison's inauguration in 1889, five treasury officials made a pool on the weather for inauguration day. Each chipped in five dollars and put five slips of paper in a hat with the following inscriptions: (1) cloudy weather; (2) rain; (3) snow; (4) clear, with temperature above 50 degrees; (5) clear, with temperature below 50.

A day or so later another treasury official who heard of the pool asked to be included. But there was no other possibility, they told him. "We've covered all possible conditions . . . unless the heavens rain frogs." But the man persisted, so they finally told him if he thought up "some weird kind of weather," they would let him in. "Tell you what," said he, after thinking it over. "I'll chuck my little five on the proposition that it both rains and snows on inauguration day." So they let him throw five dollars into the pool.

It turned out to be a "soaking, depressing, sloppy day" for Harrison's inauguration, so by the time of the procession to the Capitol the men who had originated the scheme were ready to give the pot to the man who had picked rain. But the rain-and-snow man wasn't ready to concede. "Well," he said, "you haven't exactly won the $30 yet, you know. Day's long yet—it's only noon now—and it may be that you're just packing that good money around for me." No sooner had he spoken, one of the men recalled, than "huge wet flakes of snow began to fall with the rain," and the rain-snow combination continued for some time after that. With the first fall of snow, the rain man resignedly reached into his pocket, pulled out the thirty dollars and handed it to the rain-and-snow man.

"Well, you never heard such an insufferable brute in all your born days as that man was," one of the treasury men remembered. "He was positively unendurable, that's what he was. Didn't gloat loudly or boisterously, but for the whole of the afternoon, and far into the night . . . he'd let out cracks about sure-thing players . . . and all that sort of thing that sure did have a twisty effect upon our nerves." Four years later, when the winner proposed another weather pool, there were no takers in the Treasury Department.[13]

Cleveland's Tryout (1893)

In late February 1893, Dr. Wilton M. Smith, a Presbyterian minister, visited Cleveland, who was president-elect for the second time, at his home in Lakewood, New Jersey. "Come into my den," said Cleveland after dinner. "I want to read you my inaugural address."

Cleveland read it through to its conclusion, an appeal to the "Supreme Being who rules the affairs of men," and awaited the minister's response. Dr. Smith told him: "I like it immensely and its conclusion best of all."

Smith never forgot the way Cleveland paced up and down the floor after finishing his address, and then blurted out: "Doctor, I suppose at times you will not approve many things I do, but I want you to know that I am trying to do what is right. I have a hungry party behind me, and they say I am not grateful. Sometimes the pressure is almost overwhelming, and a President cannot always get at the exact truth, but I want you to know, and all my friends to know, that I am trying to do what is right."

The president had tears in his eyes as he began pacing the floor again, and blew his nose to conceal his feelings. Smith's approval seemed to reassure Cleveland, and he went on to commit his address to memory, so that on March 4 he was able to speak, just as he had in 1885, without manuscript or notes.[14]

Damned Glad (1897)

Like most presidents, Cleveland was happy to retire at the end of his second term, and he was in a good mood as he prepared to attend McKinley's inauguration in 1897. "I was glad when Mr. McKinley came to Washington to be inaugurated . . . ," he recalled years later, "and I took a drink of rye whiskey with him in the White House and shook hands with him and put my hat on my head and walked out a private citizen."

It was not, of course, as simple as that. On the morning of the inauguration Cleveland rode to the Capitol with McKinley and then retired to the President's Room in the Capitol, as was the custom, to await the adjournment of Congress and the commencement of the inaugural ceremonies. While he was there, chatting with members of his cabinet, some congressmen came by to press him to sign a bill just passed, but he firmly refused. A little later two senators and one member of the lower house arrived to announce that the two houses of Congress had completed their work and desired to know whether the president had any further communication to make. "Tender my congratulations to the two Houses on the performance of their work," responded Cleveland, "and say to them I have nothing further to communicate." After they left, Cleveland told his associates about a governor who had a "very wild legislature" to deal with, and when a committee finally came to announce they had ended their work, he exclaimed: "Tell them, that I am damned glad to hear it."[15]

Preinaugural Filibuster (1901)

On the eve of McKinley's second inauguration in 1901, Montana Republican senator Thomas H. Carter decided that a rivers and harbors bill adopted by both houses and awaiting final touches was wasteful and should be defeated. So about midnight, March 3, he looked at the Senate clock and announced his determination to talk the bill to death, even if it meant talking until noon, the hour set for McKinley's second inauguration on March 4. "This bill cannot become a law," he declared, "unless my strength fails between this time and twelve o'clock on the 4th of March." Then he launched his talkathon. A Maryland senator spelled him briefly while he got something to eat, and, toward dawn, a quorum disappeared for a time and he was able to get a little rest. But with only a few interruptions after that, he continued to pour forth a stream of words and soon came close to beating all records in the Senate up to that time for filibustering.

Inauguration morning, workmen swept the Senate chamber, rearranged the furniture, and got things ready for the inaugural ceremony while Carter talked on. Senators favoring the bill shifted impatiently in their seats, muttered curses, and some even took to the floor to criticize Carter, but this only helped him. Carter was still talking when the gallery doors were opened and the inaugural guests began filling the seats in the gallery. "The spectacle which met their eyes," wrote one reporter, "was one never seen before on a similar occasion. Here was the sombre Senate chamber prepared for the inauguration of the President and Vice President, with seats arranged for the President and his Cabinet, the Supreme Court of the United States, the Diplomatic Corps, the officers of the army and navy, the House of Representatives and other distinguished guests. Some of the Senators were grouped upon one side of the chamber and there, near the front row of desks, stood Carter denouncing the rivers and harbors bill." Fortunately, when the time came to start the inaugural proceedings, Carter ceased talking and the ceremonies could begin. But Carter had achieved his objective; he had talked the bill to death.[16]

Presidential Shaving (1901)

Soap companies, as well as souvenir vendors, sometimes moved in for the kill at inauguration time. On the occasion of McKinley's second inauguration in 1901, Williams'
Soap Company placed the following advertisement in
Harper's Weekly:

IF YOU ASPIRE TO BE PRESIDENT, SHAVE!
It is a curious fact that nearly every President of the
United States has shaved. About every President
during the past sixty years has used Williams' Shaving
Soap. It might almost be said that no one can hope to
be President who does not use Williams' Shaving
Soap.... You may never be President, but you can feel
like a king every time you use Williams' Shaving
Soap.[17]

Preinaugural Dinner at the White House (1909)

A few days before Taft's inauguration, Theodore Roosevelt invited him and his wife, Helen, to dinner at the
White House. Roosevelt regarded Taft, his former secretary
of war, as one of his best friends, looked upon him as his
political heir, and hoped his friendly gesture would scotch
rumors in Washington of a rift between the two men. "People
have attempted to represent that you and I were in some
ways at odds during the last three months," Taft wrote back,
"whereas you and I know that there has not been the slightest difference between us, and I welcome the opportunity to
stay the last night of your administration under the White
House roof to make as emphatic as possible the refutation

of any such suggestion." He signed the letter: "With love and affection, my dear Theodore." TR wrote back at once. "Your letter," he told Taft, "is so very nice—nice isn't anything like a strong enough word, but at the moment to use words as strong as I feel would look sloppy—that I must send you this line of warm personal thanks and acknowledgment." He added: "You put in the right way to address me at the end!"

Unfortunately, the dinner party was a bust. TR and Taft managed their usual jovial exchanges well enough, but the tension between their wives was clear to the other guests. Mrs. Roosevelt was cool and distant all evening. She was offended by the changes Mrs. Taft planned to make in running the White House; she also resented a remark Mrs. Taft made, during a tour of the White House a few days before, about the position of a table in one of the rooms. She was in low spirits, moreover, at the thought of leaving the White House, and worried, too—or so Mrs. Taft thought—about TR's plan to go big-game hunting in Africa right after leaving the presidency. "The President and Mr. Taft, seconded by other guests," Mrs. Taft recalled, "did their best...to lighten the occasion, but their efforts were not entirely successful."

Elihu Root, newly elected senator from New York, was one of the guests, and he tried to liven things up at the dinner party, but he was too mournful over TR's imminent departure to be of much help. Archie Butt, Taft's military aide, another guest, thought he saw Root's tears spilling into the soup, and TR's daughter Alice also noticed his tears. Years later, Taft recalled with a shudder the "dreadful dinner the Roosevelts gave us," with "Root trying to make things bright and Mrs. Roosevelt teary and distraught."

In 1913, when someone suggested that he invite his own successor, Woodrow Wilson, to a similar inauguration-eve dinner, Taft told Mabel Boardman (a friend who was also at the dinner): "Nellie is dead set against it because of her memory of the Roosevelt dinner to me. You were at that funeral."

Only Alice, TR's mischievous daughter, seems to have enjoyed the fiasco. Having taken a dislike to Mrs. Taft, she sneaked out into the garden after dinner and buried "a bad little idol" there which she hoped would bring bad luck to the Tafts when they replaced the Roosevelts in the White House.[18]

The Tune They Dared Not Play (1913)

On the day before Woodrow Wilson's first inauguration, the military and civic bands in town for the inaugural parade were busy "blowing themselves thirsty," as the *New York Times* put it, and "beating Washington deaf all day." They played "every tune under the singing stars," the *Times* went on, but "tomorrow there is one they dare not play— any band but one. In past years it was customary for each band in the parade, as it came abreast of the President's reviewing stand, to blare forth 'Hail to the Chief!' The bands enjoyed this well-meant expression of their allegiance immensely, but they took no thought of the President and those with him on the stand. To these, the entire inaugural parade came to be one single long-drawn-out agony of 'Hail to the Chief!'" To save the president and his associates this kind of musical torment in 1913, the inaugural committee on arrangements decreed that only one band could play "Hail to the Chief" in 1913; all the others were instructed to omit the tune from their repertoires.[19]

The Frightened Horse (1913)

While Wilson was returning to the White House after his inauguration in 1913, a cavalryman's horse suddenly plunged toward the president's carriage and looked as though he would plant his forefeet in it. A dozen troopers frantically rushed over to grasp the bridle, while Wilson himself leaned calmly out of the carriage and patted the frightened horse on the neck.[20]

"Let the People Come Forward!" (1913)

After Wilson took his oath and stepped up to the rostrum to deliver his inaugural address, he suddenly noticed that the police had cleared a large area in front of the inaugural stand to keep the crowd on the plaza from getting too close. Somewhat surprised, he instructed the guard to take the rope down. "Let the people come forward!" he cried, and they did so in short order. His admirers quoted his words as evidence that the new administration intended to be closer to the people than most of Wilson's predecessors.[21]

Spry as a Schoolgirl (1913)

Promptly at 1:35 P.M., when Chief Justice Edward D. White got up to swear Wilson into office, "the most human touch in the picture of the day asserted itself," according to the *New York Times*. Ellen Wilson, the president's wife, found she couldn't see her husband well from where she was seated, so, as "spryly as a schoolgirl," said the *Times,* she moved her chair up to the side of the rostrum and stood on her seat, grasping the railing as she gazed at the president while he took his oath and kissed the Bible. She remained standing there until he finished his inaugural address.[22]

Ex-President Taft Lingers (1913)

Unlike TR, who left for home right after Taft delivered his inaugural address in 1909, Taft himself insisted on riding back to the White House with Wilson after the latter's address in 1913. When the carriage containing Wilson and Taft reached the White House, they both got out, walked rapidly through the entrance door, and paused uncertainly, a little embarrassed. Wilson seemed more comfortable than Taft, but neither appeared to know just what to do next.

Presently one of the ushers went over to tell Wilson that the guests at the luncheon party he had scheduled were assembled in the dining room and waiting for him to join them.

Wilson turned to Taft and invited him to lunch, but instead of declining, as Wilson expected, Taft accepted the invitation and said there was surely time enough for him to eat a sandwich before joining Mrs. Taft for his departure from Washington.

"And the way he said it!" recalled Ike Hoover, the White House's chief usher. "No one who heard it but whose sympathy was excited. He said it in such a sad way, as if to convey the idea either that he was actually hungry or else just wanted to eat once more within those portals that had been so dear to him for the four years past."

When the two entered the dining room, the guests crowded around Wilson to congratulate him on his inaugural address, and Taft was left standing alone. "It was really sad to observe Mr. Taft," wrote Hoover later. "No one appeared to pay any attention to him." Finally the former president got some salad and a sandwich and was starting to nibble at his food when someone reminded him there wasn't much time left to pick up his wife and get to Union Station. "This had the desired effect," Hoover noticed, "and he was practically dragged away from the scene of his former achievements."[23]

Wilson and the Suffragists (1917)

On Sunday, March 4, 1917, the day before Wilson's second inauguration, five hundred women, representing the National Woman's Party and the Congressional Union for Woman Suffrage, put on a demonstration around the White House, hoping to induce the president to support a women's suffrage amendment to the Constitution. Every woman carried a banner containing the insignia of a state on it, as well as some suffragist slogans and the party's tricolor (purple, white, and gold). In order to carry the banners, the demonstrators had to leave umbrellas behind and expose themselves to the cold rain that was drenching Washington that day. For three hours the suffragists marched slowly around the president's home, hoping that whoever looked out of the White House windows would see a wall of banners everywhere.

Before commencing the march, a delegation of suffragists requested a meeting with President Wilson, but the police sergeant on duty at the White House entrance insisted he had instructions not to leave his post for any reason whatsoever and was unable to transmit their request. While they were arguing with him, the eastern exit to the White House grounds was thrown open and president and Mrs. Wilson drove out in their automobile, headed to the Capitol for Wilson's private Sunday oath-taking.

"The marchers formed a line between which the machine passed," reported the *New York Times,* "but President Wilson gave no evidence that he saw the dripping banner bearers. He looked straight before him and did not accord them any form of salutation, and Mrs. Wilson appeared equally ignorant of their presence."

Frustrated, the women had to settle for a promise from the police sergeant that he would eventually get their resolutions on behalf of women's suffrage to the president. After that, they moved four times around the White House and then returned to their headquarters across the way in Lafayette Park.

Policemen seemed to outnumber the demonstrators, but the police were there partly to protect the suffragists from their enemies in the crowds lining Pennsylvania Avenue, and for this the women were grateful. Women of all ages (twenty-two to eighty-two) and from all forty-eight states participated in the demonstration. "One lone man marched stolidly with the women," according to the *Times,* "and looked neither to the left nor right as other men applauded or jeered him in passing."

The day's demonstration ended with a mass meeting of suffragists in the National Theater at which one woman sang "The Women's Marseillaise." Afterward, they announced they would make no effort to disturb Wilson's inauguration on Monday. And they were as good as their word, though many of them turned up for the ceremony. It was only with reluctance that Wilson came to accept a federal amendment for women's right to vote.[24]

Mrs. Wilson and Mrs. Harding (1921)

A week or so before Warren Harding's inauguration, Mrs. Wilson, learning that the Hardings were in town, invited Mrs. Harding to tea with the idea of introducing her to Elizabeth Jaffray, the housekeeper, and arranging a guided tour of the White House so she could make plans for the day she and her husband took over the place. "She arrived on time," Mrs. Wilson recalled, "wearing a dark dress, a hat with blue feathers, and her cheeks highly rouged. Her manner was so effusive, so voluble, that after a half-hour over the tea cups I could hardly stem the torrent of words to suggest I send for the housekeeper so she could talk over her desires as to the House."

But to Mrs. Wilson's distress, when Mrs. Jaffray appeared, Mrs. Harding didn't shake hands with her, but "gazed at her through eyeglasses which she put on over a black mesh veil fastened tightly about her face." Mrs. Wilson excused herself at this point and left for an appointment in town. When she returned several hours later, she found Mrs. Harding still there, talking noisily to the cook, and, to Mrs. Wilson's dismay, she didn't leave until eight o'clock.

The second encounter, the day before the inauguration, went no better. Mrs. Harding wore the same hat, which Mrs. Wilson disliked, though a different dress, and President-elect Harding sat in an armchair chatting with the president, one leg thrown over the arm of the chair. "We tried to make things go," Mrs. Wilson insisted in her memoirs, "but they both seemed ill at ease and did not stay long." Wilson was easier on Harding than his wife was. "I really like him," he told a friend after seeing the president-elect again on inauguration day.[25]

Coolidge Ponders (1925)

On the morning of his inauguration in 1925, Calvin Coolidge led a motorcade with a military escort to the Capitol where he proceeded directly to the President's Room near the Senate Chamber and went to work on a pile of bills passed by the Sixty-eighth Congress just before it adjourned. There were seventy-seven bills in all. Coolidge signed seventy-six of them without any hesitation, and then lingered over the seventy-seventh.

That bill raised the salaries of congressmen, cabinet members, and the vice president. Coolidge knew they deserved the raises, but he also knew he intended to stress government economy in his inaugural address, so his ruminations on the bill were, according to Kansas publisher William Allen White, lengthy and intense. "He gazed vacantly around at the walls," reported White, "took off his glasses, wiped them with his new, clean handkerchief, put them on again, began to twirl them nervously. He beckoned Budget Director Lord, traced his finger over three lines of the bill and asked in a whispered voice a short question. Still the President hesitated. Minutes passed. He drank the glass of water which McKenna, the doorman, had brought him, looked up at the wall clock. He saw that he had been debating with himself ten minutes. He fidgeted a moment, went to the toilet, came back again, looked at the clock. It was 11:56. He settled down, put on his glasses, sighed a little short sigh and signed the bill, the last official act of the accidental President."

Relieved that his work was finished, Coolidge went over to the Senate to listen with what some observers thought was barely concealed indifference to Charles Dawes take his oath as vice president. And after his own swearing in, Silent Cal called for economy in government just as he had planned. "I favor the policy of economy," he said, "not because I wish to save money, but because I wish to save people. The men and women of this country who toil are the ones who bear the cost of the government. Every dollar that we carelessly waste means that their life will be so much the more meager. Every dollar that we prudently save means that their life will be so much the more abundant. Economy is idealism in its most practical form."[26]

Antarctic Congratulations (1929)

On the day of Herbert Hoover's inauguration, Commander Richard E. Byrd of the Antarctica Expedition, isolated for the South Polar winter on the Ice Barrier of Antarctica, sent the following congratulatory message to Washington: "Little America, Antarctica, March 4, President Hoover, via Secretary of the Navy, Washington, D.C.: The members of the most distant American unit at Little America, Antarctica, send you heartiest congratulations and best wishes. Richard E. Byrd."[27]

Coolidge Leaves with a Smile (1929)

On his last day as president, just before attending Hoover's swearing in, Coolidge signed a bill, first suggested by the *St. Louis Post-Dispatch,* creating a weekend home for the president. "The bill appropriating $48,000 to approve Mount Weather for a Presidential refuge is just being signed by me," he notified the *Post-Dispatch*. "I congratulate you on the success of the campaign, first broached in your newspaper, and almost unanimously approved by the press of the nation. The Congress has shown an inclination to treat a President with the same kind of consideration it extends to our birds and other wild life."[28]

Preinaugural Panic (1933)

By the time of FDR's first inauguration, the Great Depression touched off by the stock market crash of 1929 had reached its nadir: production was grinding to a halt, with unemployment widespread, agriculture foundering, and the nation's financial structure crumbling. "World literally rocking beneath our feet," wrote Agnes Meyers, wife of the Federal Reserve Board head. "Hard on H[oover] to go out of office to the sound of crashing banks. Like the tragic end of a tragic story....H's administration is Greek in its fatality."

In the days just before FDR took his oath, panic hit the country, as one bank after another closed its doors in cities, towns, and villages across the land. On the morning of March 4, the *New York Sun* carried a disturbing report on the situation in the nation's capital just hours before the inaugural ceremony: "CAPITOL CROWD IN WILD RUSH TO FIND CASH....The thousands of men and women visitors who left their hotels and rooming houses today to attend the inaugural ceremony went to Capitol Hill with worried faces....Women in brilliant evening frocks and men in evening clothes scurried from bank to bank and from hotel to hotel, seeking any amount of cash to carry them on.

They were too late.... Shortly after 2 A.M., a wave of anxiety swept from hotel to hotel as the words of the impending events were whispered and telephoned and shouted." It was the considered opinion of financial titan J. P. Morgan, Jr., that "the emergency could not be greater."

FDR's promise, in his inaugural address on March 4, to take "action, and action now" to save the American system from collapse received an enthusiastic response. "It was very, very solemn, and a little terrifying," said Mrs. Roosevelt afterward. "The crowds were so tremendous, and you felt that they would do anything—if only someone would tell them what to do."29

Breaking Precedents (1933)

FDR enjoyed breaking precedents. He picked Frances Perkins (a social worker on his staff when he was governor of New York) as his secretary of labor, the first woman to serve as a cabinet member; he invited the members of his cabinet and their families to attend church with him before the inaugural ceremony; and he arranged for his cabinet to take the oath of office in the Oval Room of the White House right after the inaugural parade. "No Cabinet has ever been sworn in just this way," he gloated to Jim Farley (former Democratic National Chairman and now Postmaster-General in the cabinet), explaining that "it gives the families of the new Cabinet an opportunity to see the ceremony." He went on to say that it was his "intention to inaugurate precedents like this from time to time." Wrote Farley in his memoirs years later: "The last remark was something of an understatement. No President so shattered tradition and no President set so many precedents."

Eleanor Roosevelt broke some precedents, too; she shared her husband's distaste for excessive formality. When Mrs. Hoover invited her for a tour of the White House a few days before the inauguration, the First Lady offered her successor an official car and a military aide (either in uniform or civilian attire), to accompany her to the White House. But Mrs. Roosevelt declined the courtesy; she liked to walk, and decided to stroll over from her hotel, about a half mile away. "But, Eleanor, darling, you can't do that!" wailed Warren Delano Robbins, FDR's cousin, the State Department's chief of protocol. "People will recognize you! You'll be mobbed!" But Mrs. Roosevelt persisted, and after touring the White House with Mrs. Hoover, she again refused a White House car and instead hailed a passing taxi for the return trip.

After seeing Mrs. Roosevelt in action, the White House's chief usher, Ike Hoover, realized that with the Roosevelts in the White House, things were going to be "quite different from what we had known before." He wasn't really surprised that when the time came, Mrs. Roosevelt pitched in to help the movers arrange the furniture, and she unpacked books and carried them to the bookcases by herself. On inauguration day, she served hot dogs at the inaugural luncheon, gave an interview to a newspaper reporter right after the ceremony, and stood in for her husband at the ball that night, instead of letting the vice president perform the function, as the Hoovers had in 1929. The *Nashville Tennessean,* for one, approved the unpredictable First Lady. Recalling Theodore Roosevelt's lively daughter Alice, the editors declared: "It begins to look as if Anna Eleanor Roosevelt is going to make Alice Roosevelt Longworth look like Alice-Sit-by-the-Fire."[30]

Adjusting His Hat (1933)

After FDR delivered his inaugural address and left the platform, Tom Beck, a New York publisher, was fascinated as he watched the president come down the ramp on his son James's arm, with his cane and hat in the other hand. FDR had picked up his hat after the speech in such a way that if he put it on his head it would be on backward. He couldn't free his hands to turn the hat around or give it to his son to do so, Beck noticed, so, as he moved down the ramp, his left hand worked laboriously on the rim of the hat until he had moved it around so he could put it on with the front forward.[31]

Inaugural Invitations (1937, 1953)

A few days before FDR's second inauguration, a handsomely engraved invitation from Rear Admiral Cary T. Grayson, Grand Master of Ceremonies, appeared on Roosevelt's desk. FDR let out a roar of delight, seized a pen, and scrawled a note across the bottom to W. E. Rockwell of the White House Bureau: "Please regret this invitation. I will be too busy." From Rockwell came a sheet of White House stationery on which Adrian Tolley (the White House's veteran penman) had written the following message in Roosevelt's spidery handwriting: "President regrets that because of rush of official business, he is unable to accept the courteous invitation to be present at the ceremonies attending the Inauguration of the President of the United States, January twentieth, nineteen hundred thirty-seven." Once again exploding with laughter, FDR grabbed a pen and scrawled another note to Grayson across the bottom: "I have rearranged my engagements and work and I think I may be able to go. Will know definitely Jan. 19. FDR."

Four inaugurations later, just before the 1953 ceremony, Mrs. Eisenhower received a beautiful embossed invitation to the inaugural ball. "What should we do about this?" she asked Ike. "Turn it down," he advised, with a straight face. "Tell them we've got another engagement."[32]

After the Inauguration (1937)

After his first inauguration, FDR spent the night with his advisers toiling over measures to cope with the banking crisis. Four years later there was still much to do but less urgency. On inauguration night, FDR's mother, wife, and children joined a sparse audience for an inaugural concert at Constitution Hall, but Roosevelt repaired to his upstairs study. Around 9:30 P.M., Stephen Early, the presidential secretary, telephoned the president. FDR asked Early to guess what he was doing. "Stamps?" ventured Early. "That's right," chuckled Roosevelt, a devoted philatelist.[33]

FDR's Slip of the Tongue (1941)

FDR delivered his third inaugural address at a time when the United States was becoming increasingly involved in Britain's war against Nazi Germany and China's resistance to Japanese aggression. Early in the speech he made a slip of the tongue, which was unusual for him. "To us there has come a time," he said, "in the midst of swift happenings, to pause for a moment and take stock—to recall what our place in history has been, and to rediscover what we are and what we may be. If we do not, we risk the real peril of inaction." He misread the last word as "isolation," but quickly added, "the real peril of inaction." After the inauguration, he underlined the word *inaction* on the reading copy of his speech, and wrote: "I misread this word as 'isolation,' then added 'and inaction.' All of which improved it!"[34]

"Special Musicale by Negro Artists" (1941)

On the night of FDR's third inauguration, Eleanor Roosevelt attended a "special musicale by Negro artists," held in the Departmental Auditorium. The musicale was meant to be a counterpoise to the concert held in Constitutional Hall the day before, from which blacks had been excluded. Attended by sixteen hundred people, half black and half white, the "Negro gala" presented a program of popular and classical music that ended with everyone singing Irving Berlin's recently composed "God Bless America."

During the course of the evening, Emory B. Smith, one of the event's planners, expressed faith in the principles enunciated by the president on inauguration day, and, looking pointedly at Mrs. Roosevelt, declared that "there should be no misconception on the part of anyone concerning our loyalty to our Nation and our devotion to our God." Former ambassador to Russia, Joseph Davies, chairman of 1941's inauguration committee, attended the gala, too, and after it was over, he declared: "I have had a real thrill in attending this charming, delightful concert, the last of the events connected with the Inaugural. The atmosphere here tonight is typical of the devotion to idealism, democracy, human freedom, liberty and the Christian religion which has animated the people all over this land of ours today."[35]

Without Fuss (1945)

When FDR delivered his fourth inaugural address in 1945, only 559 words long, he was not feeling well. As he began speaking, he experienced a sudden pain, which caused his entire body to shake, and his son James, standing behind him, was afraid he might be unable to proceed with the speech. But FDR quickly recovered and went on to complete his manuscript without any further difficulties. "Roosevelt was a man who knew his duty," wrote one of his admirers years later. "As a boy he had learned to bear his pain 'without fuss.' He did so now. He read his speech quietly and with a gentle dignity. It was a simple homily of the sort Dr. Peabody, his headmaster at Groton, had often preached."

Samuel Rosenman, FDR's speech adviser, was also impressed with the president's performance that day. "It was deeply moving to watch him standing there in the cold winter air," he observed, "without overcoat or hat, delivering these simple words. Oblivious of the people in front of him or the people all over the world who were listening to him, he seemed to me to be offering a prayer. It was a prayer... that all the peoples of the world, and their leaders, be endowed with the patience and faith that could abolish war."[36]

Carnival Time in Washington (1949)

Though Harry Truman was a man of simple tastes, the Democrats were determined to celebrate his surprise victory over Thomas E. Dewey in the 1948 election with joy and abandon, and his inauguration turned out to be the most lavish up to that time. It was "carnival time in Washington," *Newsweek* reported; there was "an uproar of parties all week." *Time* (Republican-leaning) grumped that it was a "costly carnival," adding that the thirteen-hundred-member inaugural committee "toiled feverishly to make the four-day show the biggest, most expensive Presidential Inauguration in history." But Henry R. Luce's newsweekly tried to be understanding about it: "After all, it was the nearest thing the U.S. had to a coronation, a rare chance for the republic's leaders to turn out in top hat."

Ironically, the Republicans themselves contributed generously, though unintentionally, to the jubilee. Expecting a Dewey victory, the Republican-controlled Congress, normally parsimonious, voted $80,000 (an ample sum in those days) for inaugural purposes, and the Democrats gratefully—and gleefully—put the money to good use. Just before election day in November, Republican senator C. Wayland ("Curley") Brooks of Illinois, chairman of the Senate-House Inaugural Committee, had announced that the 1949 inauguration was going to be "the biggest damn inaugural in modern times," and the Democrats did all they could to make it so. As Vice President–elect Alben Barkley of Kentucky (soon to be called "the Veep") put it: "we Democrats tried to show the proper appreciation by always referring to the ample and lavish grandstands along the parade route as the 'Curley Brooks Memorial Stadium.'"[37]

Color-Blind (1949)

If the 1949 inauguration was lavish, it was also color-blind. President Truman insisted that blacks be invited to all the major social events of the week, and as a result his inauguration turned out to be (as his daughter, Margaret, proudly noted years later) "the first integrated inauguration in our nation's history."

When a delegation of Democrats from New York checked into a hotel in Washington where they had reservations, the clerks found rooms for the whites but refused to accommodate the blacks. New York City's Deputy Commissioner of Housing, J. Raymond Jones, one of the group, was indignant. He made it clear that all the delegates, or none of them, were to stay at the hotel, and the manager reluctantly gave way. But soon after the New Yorkers were assigned rooms, the telephones in the rooms housing the blacks went on the blink. Commissioner Jones was equal to the occasion. Aware that the owners of the Washington hotel also controlled some hotels in New York City, he let it be known that "a reinspection" of the Manhattan hotels was under way. It wasn't long before the New York blacks found the telephones in their rooms back in working order.

NAACP head, Walter White, recalling Truman's order desegregating the armed forces in 1947, was heartened by the Truman policy. The Truman administration's attack on racial segregation, he declared, "seemed part and parcel of an Inauguration which had about it a special tone of recognizing the new place of all ordinary Americans." *Newsweek* filled in the details. "From the moment the whiskey started flowing Monday afternoon until the hang-overs exploded Saturday morning, there was no racial segregation. Negroes and whites sat elbow to elbow in the stands as they watched the inaugural ceremonies and the parade. Negroes attended the inaugural gala at the Armory Wednesday night; they danced at the inaugural ball there on Thursday.... In the Army units which paraded . . . , Negro and white soldiers marched side by side. A Negro sergeant barked orders at white troops, just as white sergeants barked orders at Negroes."[38]

Outdoes Alexander! (1953)

Congress planned and paid for the swearing-in ceremonies on Capitol Hill, appointing a joint House-Senate committee to make the arrangements. But it took a huge committee of volunteers, headed by a chairman appointed by the president-elect, to plan and raise money to cover the expenses of the parties, receptions, parades, and fancy balls that came to be an integral part of the inaugural celebrations. For Eisenhower's inauguration in 1953, over two thousand volunteers, working long hours, labored for weeks in six different buildings on the scores of committees, subcommittees, and sub-subcommittees required to get the job done. "Even Ike," observed Joseph McCarraghy, the grand chairman that year, "may never know how many chairmen were required to gavel how many meetings in order that he might become President of the United States." Usher L. Burdick, Republican House member from North Dakota, exclaimed: "This outdoes Alexander, Hannibal, Caesar, and Napoleon!" But subsequent inaugurations were even more opulent than Eisenhower's. Proceeds from souvenirs, concessions, and the sale of tickets to various events paid for the expense of inaugural festivities, and whenever there was a surplus, the money went to charitable causes.[39]

Black Marshal (1957)

In 1957, E. Frederick Morrow became the first black marshal to participate in an inaugural parade and to be invited to sit with his fiancée in the president's reviewing stand after the division he led passed the White House. He was also invited to attend the preinaugural service at the Presbyterian church to which the Eisenhowers belonged before attending Ike's swearing in.

The usher in the church "was obviously in a dither," Morrow recalled, when he arrived at the church with his fiancée, and refused to seat the two until he had consulted with the chief usher. When the two left at the end of the service, moreover, they couldn't help overhearing a member of the church tell her friend: "He must be a high Government official, because if he were not, he would never *dare* enter *our* church." But the parade that afternoon went off nicely. "I rode down the historic parade route in an open car," Morrow wrote in his memoirs. "The thousands of Negroes along the route were particularly enthusiastic, and I was pleased that my being there gave them a lift and a feeling of belonging. When we passed the presidential box, I raised my hat in tribute to the President and Mrs. Eisenhower, and he gave me an enthusiastic wave, as did the Vice-President." Morrow and his bride-to-be also attended the inaugural ball that night and enjoyed themselves thoroughly.[40]

Interested (1961)

The day before his inauguration, JFK was asked by a reporter, "Are you excited?" Kennedy thought for a moment and then said: "Interested." After he took his oath the following day, he glanced at his wife, and, according to the *New York Times,* she gave him a "'you-did-all-right' smile." The balls that night "might well have daunted—or at least wilted—a less dedicated or attractive couple than the new

President and his first lady," observed *Life* magazine in its coverage of the inauguration. "But wherever he turned up during the long day's festivities Jack Kennedy managed to look both as handsome and as serious as a storybook President should. Jacqueline Kennedy, decked out in a white sheath gown, captivatingly contrived to resemble both a fair princess at a fancy dress ball and a little girl enjoying her first party." The 1961 inauguration brought Mrs. Kennedy's "first constant exposure to the media as a bona fide public figure," reported Carl S. Anthony in the *Washington Post*. "The daily attention to her clothing became unprecedented. Double-stranded pearls, bouffant hairstyles, simple sheath dresses, off-the-shoulder gowns, bulky sweaters and—yes—pillbox hats became the fashion of the early '60s."[41]

Resting Up (1961)

Long before the afternoon parade ended, Mrs. Kennedy left the reviewing stand and returned to the White House to rest up a bit. She had a "Reception for Members of the President and Mrs. Kennedy's Families" to attend, following the parade, and five inaugural balls to take in that night. But she never made it to the Kennedy-Lee-Bouvier-Auchincloss reception.

Mrs. Kennedy's relatives and in-laws arrived at the White House late that afternoon and waited for her to make an appearance. After a while they became restless, and her mother, Janet Auchincloss, explained that her daughter was "up in the Queen's bedroom, trying to relax." When JFK came in around seven, after the parade ended, he cried: "Where's Jackie?" "Oh, she's upstairs resting," Mrs. Auchincloss told him. "Well," said JFK, "I guess I better go on up there too," and he left. After a while Michel Bouvier, one of Mrs. Kennedy's cousins, went up to see Jackie and returned to say: "She's just resting.... You know she's got to go to five goddamn balls this evening, don't you?" "But," said one of the guests disappointedly, "can't she come down even for a *minute?*" "Not even for a *second,*" said Bouvier. The party finally broke up without anyone getting to see Jackie.

Years later, Michel Bouvier revealed that when he went up to see Jackie, she was sitting in bed looking frightened. "Oh, Michel," she wailed, "I don't know what to do. Is everybody there?" "Just about everybody," he replied. "Oh, Michel, really, I can't go down, I can't go down. I really can't. I've got all those balls to go to and I've got to look good for them." One of her relatives thought an attack of shyness explained her reluctance to go down for the reception.

Jackie did attend the balls that night with her husband. But in the midst of one of them, she "just crumbled," and returned to the White House, leaving her husband to attend the last two by himself. JFK didn't get back to the White House until dawn, so Jackie spent her first night there alone.[42]

Integration (1961)

In 1961, JFK noticed there were no blacks among the Coast Guard cadets marching in the inaugural parade, so he instructed one of his aides to look into the matter. A few blacks had attended the Coast Guard Academy in the past, but to increase the number, after JFK's inquiry, the academy sent two black officers around the country to make it clear that the Coast Guard was open to any youngster who met the rigorous physical and scholastic requirements. Four years later, three young blacks marched in the six-hundred-man cadet corps as it passed LBJ's reviewing stand. "The Kennedys had the most integrated Inauguration in history," observed Washington newsman Simeon Booker, "the first time Negroes were included on more than a token basis." In 1965, however, he added, "L.B.J. is going to outdo that by double." And he did.[43]

Texas (1965)

"Whoooeee!" yelled a lanky, sun-bronzed Texan aboard a Braniff DC-8 that bucked and yawed in a downdraft on the approach to the Washington National Airport. "This buckin' don't bothuh us none. This heah's a Texas plane." After the big plane made a perfect landing, a bunch of charter-flight Texans taxied to Washington, the vanguard of some three thousand Texans heading to the nation's capital in 1965 to attend Lyndon B. Johnson's inauguration. They came by charter flight, in private aircraft, by train, bus, and private automobiles. They also came with a word of caution from Marvin Watson, the Texas State Democratic chairman, one of LBJ's friends. "All the world will be watching," he notified the inauguration-bound Texans. "It is our duty and privilege to assist our President assume this office with the dignity, love, and respect we have for him. Let the others come in their boots and 10-gallon hats, but let us explode with pride and present to the world the moderate and warm temperament of the true Texas as we share our own Lyndon B. Johnson with the world."

The Texans gathering in Washington mostly followed

Watson's advice. One Fort Worth matron, it is true, showed up in a tiara that lighted up and spelled T-E-X-A-S; and a bunch of Lone Star Staters boisterously sang "The Eyes of Texas," and gave rebel yells, at the Texas State Society reception in the Statler Hilton. "But," *Newsweek* reported, "a check after two and one-half hours of free-flowing booze revealed only two drunks, no fights, and no six-guns." Boasted State Representative Jake Johnson: "This is the new Texas. There's not a six-gun in the crowd. Of course," he added, "back home you could check their Cadillacs, and you just might find a few in the glove compartments." But from the beginning to the end of what *Newsweek* called "the breeziest, most informal inauguration week in memory," it was clear that "the only Texas brand the festivities would bear was that of LBJ himself."

Johnson kept himself posted on just about every detail of his inauguration, and he seemed intent on being every-where at once, *Time* reported. "Moving pell-mell from fete to fete, hatless and coatless, one minute out in the frigid Po-tomac wind, the next in densely packed overheated rooms." *Time* thought that with so many Texans in town, "it some-times seemed as if it had been Jack Kennedy four years ago who really assembled the Great Society and Lyndon John-son who was now opening up the New Frontier. If so, it was a prosperous, well-behaved and superbly dressed frontier—and a dazzling show."[44]

LBJ and RMN (1969)

In his memoirs, LBJ recalled that the atmosphere in the Red Room of the White House on the morning Richard M. Nixon became president was jovial and lighthearted. At one point Johnson told Nixon about a fellow in Texas he once stopped to talk with. "Let me tell you a story," LBJ told the man, and he answered: "OK, but how long will it take?" LBJ went on to say he didn't want to be like that fellow, but that he was curious: "How long will your inaugural address take?" Nixon said the speech ran just over two thousand words, and that he estimated it would take between eighteen and twenty minutes to deliver. He then turned to Vice President Hubert Humphrey, the man he defeated in the 1968 election, and said with a smile: "Hubert, why don't you deliver the address for me?" "Dick," said Humphrey, "I had planned to do that, but you sort of interfered. Since you're more familiar with the text than I am, I guess you ought to go ahead and deliver it as scheduled."[45]

Omitting Lincoln (1973)

A few weeks before Nixon's second inauguration, the inaugural committee commissioned composer Vincent Persichetti to write an orchestral piece for the January 19 inaugural concert at Kennedy Center. The committee suggested that Persichetti use Lincoln's second inaugural address as the text for a composition for orchestra and narrator, and picked actor Charlton Heston (who had campaigned for Nixon) as the narrator. But on January 9, the very day Persichetti completed an eleven-minute tone poem entitled, "A Lincoln Address," the inaugural organizers notified him they had cut his music from the program.

Persichetti was perplexed. He wondered whether his longtime opposition to the Vietnam War had something to do with the cancellation. Or, perhaps, he thought, Lincoln's searing blast against slavery and some of the passages in the address—"Fondly do we hope, fervently do we pray, that this mighty scourge of war may speedily pass away"—offended the inaugural planners, since the United States was still involved in Vietnam. All that a spokesman for the inaugural committee would say was: "We just changed our plans." Instead of Persichetti, the orchestra played Tchaikovsky's *1812 Overture* for the Nixon concert. A few days later, however, just after a cease-fire was announced, the St. Louis Symphony Orchestra gave Persichetti's tone poem its premiere.[46]

Presidential Gala (1997)

The day before Bill Clinton's second inauguration, a Presidential Gala—"a glitzy, black-tie affair," reported the *Washington Post*—was held in the USAir Arena. Twelve thousand people attended. Women in mink coats wolfed down popcorn while men in tuxedos juggled hot dogs, tacos, and champagne in plastic flutes. The best-selling souvenir that night was a gray gala T-shirt—with an inaugural seal on the front and the names of the gala's performers on the back—which went for twenty dollars. On the floor, ushers asked the ticket holders to tuck their coats under the seats. "We don't want any fur showing for the telecast," explained one usher. "You know it wouldn't be politically correct."

The two-hour show, the *Post* reported, "served up a fat helping of feel-good populism, a little Hollywood, a little country, a touch of rock-and-roll, and a lot of red, white and blue." The cast included Whoopi Goldberg, Stevie Wonder, Babyface, Gloria Estefan, Mikhail Baryshnikov, Yo-Yo Ma, and Trisha Yearwood. "The audience of 12,000 responded exactly the way inaugural crowds are supposed to," according to the *Post.* "They smiled on cue and shed patriotic tears." Seats in the back rows cost $100; down in front, $3,000. Profits went to defray the expenses of 1997's inaugural festivities. President Clinton was, of course, the guest of honor; he sat in the presidential row with his wife, Hillary, and daughter, Chelsea, along with Vice President Al Gore and his family.

The show opened with gospel singer Sandi Patti belting out what the *Post* called "perhaps the longest and most elaborate rendition ever of the national anthem." Bernadette Peters followed with a song, accompanied by three hundred college freshmen from local universities, all members of the class of 2000. Then Candice Bergen stepped onstage and announced: "You know, Mr. President, before you ever spoke of a bridge to the 21st century, there was a bridge to the 20th century.... It spanned the Atlantic and ended at Ellis Island." That served as an introduction to Kenny G and Mikhail Baryshnikov. As Kenny G played his soprano sax, Baryshnikov danced solo to a George Gershwin number.

Featured on the program was a montage of movie clips containing performers who had played the role of president of the United States, ending with Michael Douglas waltzing around the East Room of the White House in the most recent presidential film, *An American President* (1995). At the end, Douglas appeared in the audience, went over to Clinton, and declared: "Vincent Lombardi once said, 'If you're lucky enough to have a guy with a lot of head and a lot of heart, he'll never come off the field second.' And that, Mr. President, is why you're about to be inaugurated for a second term." Whoopi Goldberg also had kind words for the president. "It's amazing to be here to see your *friend,*" she cried, nodding at the Clintons. "You're three of the coolest people I know. I'm proud of you. I'm so proud to be an American."

There was more, much more, and when the program was finished, Clinton walked to the stage to thank everyone for the "celebration of the American spirit." He said the gala had not only honored America's cultural heritage; "we did something else: We honored our democracy.... Tomorrow we will not just celebrate our democracy. We must renew it." The Clintons and the Gores then joined all the performers onstage in singing Neil Diamond's "America." When the show ended, former Texas governor Ann Richards, no softie, sighed: "It's a sure sign you're getting old when you get choked up seeing young people. It was really thrilling to see them included."[47]

INAUGURAL "FIRSTS"

15

1821   The U.S. Marine Band may have made its first appearance at an inauguration (Monroe's second), playing "Hail Columbia."

1825   John Quincy Adams was the first president to take his oath in long pants.

1837   Martin Van Buren was the first president to call on his predecessor, Andrew Jackson, at the White House, and ride with him to the Capitol for the oath-taking. After that, it became customary for the outgoing President to sit on the right en route to Capitol Hill and for the new President to sit on the right when returning to the White House after the inaugural ceremony.

1837   Martin Van Buren was the first president who was born an American citizen.

1841   William Henry Harrison was the first president to arrive in Washington by train for the inauguration.

1841   John Tyler was the first vice president to become president on the death of the president.

1845   James K. Polk's inaugural address was the first to be relayed (to Baltimore) by telegraph.

1845   The Marine Band played "Hail to the Chief," probably for the first time, after Polk took his oath of office.

1853   Franklin Pierce was the first, and thus far the only president to affirm rather than swear his loyalty to the Constitution.

1853   Franklin Pierce was the first president to deliver his inaugural address from memory.

1857   Gas chandeliers, not candles, provided the illumination for James Buchanan's inaugural ball.

1865   Black soldiers participated in the inaugural parade for the first time.

1881   The Garfield ball featured a tall plaster statue of Columbia holding a torch from which a powerful electric light lit up the area.

1885   Electric lights illuminated the lavish ball for Grover Cleveland.

1897   Motion-picture cameramen filmed McKinley's first inauguration.

1909   Mrs. Taft accompanied her husband back to the White House after he took his oath.

1917   Mrs. Wilson rode to the Capitol with her husband for Wilson's second inauguration. A sizable number of women marched in the afternoon parade.

1921   The presidential party rode in automobiles, rather than carriages, to Capitol Hill for Harding's inauguration. Amplifiers made Harding's address audible to people gathered outside the Capitol.

1925   Coolidge's inaugural address was broadcast by radio.

1929   Hoover's address was recorded for "talking pictures."

1949   Harry Truman's inauguration was the first to appear on television.

1961   John F. Kennedy's inauguration appeared on color TV.

1965   Lady Bird Johnson took part in her husband's oath-taking ceremony.

1977   Jimmy Carter walked back to the White House with his family after taking his oath at the Capitol.

George Washington

"The preservation of the sacred fire of liberty and the destiny of the republican model of government are justly considered, perhaps, as *deeply,* as *finally,* staked, on the experiment entrusted to the hands of the American people." (1789)

Thomas Jefferson

"All, too, will bear in mind this sacred principle, that though the will of the majority is in all cases to prevail, that will to be rightful must be reasonable; that the minority possesses their equal rights, which equal law must protect, and to violate would be oppression." (1801)

"If there be any among us who would wish to dissolve this Union or to change its republican form, let them stand undisturbed as monuments of the safety with which error of opinion may be tolerated where reason is left free to combat it." (1801)

"Sometimes it is said that man cannot be trusted with the government of himself. Can he, then, be trusted with the government of others? Or have we found angels in the forms of kings to govern him? Let history answer this question." (1801)

James Monroe

"National honor is national property of the highest value." (1817)

Abraham Lincoln

"It is safe to assert that no government proper ever had a provision in its organic law for its own termination." (1861)

"This country, with its institutions, belongs to the people who inhabit it. Whenever they shall grow weary of the existing government, they can exercise their *constitutional* right of amending it, or their *revolutionary* right to dismember or overthrow it." (1861)

"Why should there not be a patient confidence in the ultimate justice of the people? Is there any better or equal hope in the world?" (1861)

"We are not enemies, but friends. We must not be enemies. Though passion may have strained, it must not break our bonds of affection. The mystic chords of memory, stretching from every battlefield and patriot grave to every living heart and hearthstone all over this broad land, will yet swell the chorus of the Union, when touched again, as surely they will be, by the better angels of our nature." (1861)

"Both read the same Bible and pray to the same God, and each invokes His aid against the other. It may seem strange that any men should dare to ask a just God's assistance in wringing their bread from the sweat of other men's faces, but let us judge not, that we be not judged. The prayers of both could not be answered. That of neither has been answered fully. The Almighty has His own purposes. (1865)

"Fondly we do hope, fervently do we pray, that this mighty scourge of war may speedily pass away. Yet, if God will that it continue until all the wealth piled by the bondsman's 250 years of unrequited toil shall be sunk, and until every drop of blood drawn with the lash shall be paid by another drawn with the sword, as was said three thousand years ago, so still it must be said, 'The judgments of the Lord are true and righteous altogether.'" (1865)

Ulysses S. Grant

"I know of no method to secure the repeal of bad or obnoxious laws so effective as their stringent execution." (1869)

Rutherford B. Hayes

"He serves his party best who serves his country best." (1877)

Grover Cleveland

"Your every voter, as surely as your chief magistrate . . . exercises a public trust." (1885)

Woodrow Wilson

"We have been proud of our industrial achievements, but we have not hitherto stopped thoughtfully enough to count the human cost, the cost of lives snuffed out, of energies overtaxed and broken, the fearful physical and spiritual cost to the men and women and children upon whom the dead weight and burden of it all has fallen pitilessly the years through." (1913)

"We have come now to the sober second thought. The scales of heedlessness have fallen from our eyes. We have made up our minds to square every process of our national life again with the standards we so proudly set up at the beginning and have always carried in our hearts. Our work is a work of restoration." (1913)

Franklin D. Roosevelt

"First of all, let me assert my firm belief that the only thing we have to fear is fear itself—nameless, unreasoning, unjustified terror which paralyzes needed efforts to convert retreat into advance." (1933)

"We have always known that heedless self-interest was bad morals; we know now that it is bad economics." (1937)

"We have learned that we cannot live alone, at peace; that our own well-being is dependent on the well-being of other nations, far away.... We have learned to be citizens of the world, members of the human community." (1945)

John F. Kennedy

"If a free society cannot help the many who are poor, it cannot save the few who are rich." (1961)

"Let us never negotiate out of fear, but let us never fear to negotiate." (1961)

"And so, my fellow Americans, ask not what your country can do for you; ask what you can do for your country." (1961)

Ronald Reagan

"We will not rest until every American enjoys the fullness of freedom, dignity, and opportunity as our birthright. It is our birthright as citizens of this great Republic." (1985)

Bill Clinton

"We must do what America does best: offer more opportunity to all and demand more responsibility from all." (1993)

NOTES

Preface

1. Thomas Hudson McKee, *Presidential Inaugurations: from George Washington, 1789, to Grover Cleveland, 1893* (Washington, D.C.: Statistical Publishing Co., 1893); E. Edward Hurja, *History of Presidential Inaugurations* (New York: New York Democrat, 1933); Glenn D. Kittler, *Hail to the Chief: The Inauguration Days of Our Presidents* (Philadelphia: Chilton Books, 1965); Milton Lomask, *"I Do Solemnly Swear...": The Story of the Presidential Inauguration* (New York: Ariel Books, 1966); *The Inaugural Story, 1789–1969* (New York: American Heritage Pub. Co., 1969); and Louise Durbin, *Inaugural Cavalcade* (New York: Dodd, Mead, 1971).

Introduction

1. Paul F. Boller, Jr., *Presidential Campaigns,* rev. ed. (New York: Oxford University Press, 1996), 4.

2. *Journal of William Maclay,* ed. Edgar S. Maclay (New York: D. A. Appleton, 1890), 7–9.

3. Don Oberdorfer, "No Wonder Madison Said, 'I'd Rather Be in Bed,'" *New York Times Magazine,* January 17, 1965, p. 10.

4. Earl W. Mayo, "The Growth of the Inaugural," *Harper's Weekly,* March 9, 1901, p. 256.

5. James C. Humes, *Confessions of a White House Ghostwriter: Five Presidents and Other Political Adventures* (Washington, D.C.: Regnery, 1997), 117.

6. T. R. B., *New Republic,* January 23, 1961, 2; January 30, 1961, p. 2.

1. 1789 – The First Inauguration

1. Thomas Fleming, *Liberty! The American Revolution* (New York: Viking, 1997), 343.

2. Max Farrand, ed., *The Records of the Federal Convention of 1787,* rev. ed. vol. 1 (New Haven: Yale University Press, 1937), 285, 288, 299, 103.

3. Washington to Henry Knox, April 1, 1789, *The Writings of George Washington,* ed. John C. Fitzpatrick, vol. 30 (Washington: Government Printing Office, 1931–1944), 268.

4. "Undelivered First Inaugural Address Fragments," *The Papers of George Washington,* Presidential Series 2, April–June 1789, ed. Dorothy Twohig (Charlottesville: University Press of Virginia, 1987), 162.

5. John Gabriel Hunt, ed., *The Inaugural Addresses of the Presidents* (New York, 1995), 4.

6. Thomas Hudson McKee, *Presidential Inaugurations from George Washington, 1789, to Grover Cleveland, 1893* (Washington, D.C.: Statistical Publishing Co., 1893), 2.

7. Frank Monaghan, *Notes on the Inaugural Journey and Inaugural Ceremonies of George Washington as First President of the United States* (Private distribution, typescript, 1939, Library of Congress), 5.

8. William Spohn Baker, *Washington after the Revolution, 1784–1799* (Philadelphia: J. B. Lippincott, 1898), 123.

9. *Ibid.,* 124.

10. *Ibid.,* 124.

11. *Ibid.,* 125–26; Monaghan, *Notes on the Inaugural Journey,* 30–31.

12. Monaghan, *Notes on the Inaugural Journey,* 38.

13. *Ibid.,* 36; Douglas Southall Freeman, *George Washington,* vol. 6, *Patriot and President* (New York: Scribner, 1954), 182.

14. Glenn D. Kittler, *Hail to the Chief! The Inauguration Days of Our Presidents* (Philadelphia: Chilton Books, 1965), 9; Louise Durbin, *Inaugural Cavalcade* (New York: Dodd, Mead, 1971), 8.

15. *Journal of William Maclay,* ed. Edgar S. Maclay (New York: D. A. Appleton, 1890), 4.

16. Michael Harwood, *In the Shadow of Presidents: The American Vice Presidency and Succession System* (Philadelphia: J. B. Lippincott, 1966), 14–15.

17. Gaillard Hunt, "Early Inaugurations," *Washington Post,* March 4, 1897, p. 2; Clarence Winthrop Bowen, ed., *The History of the Centennial Celebration of the Inauguration of George Washington as First President of the United States* (New York: D. Appleton, 1892), 41–58; Freeman, *Washington,* 167–98.

18. Theron Lowell Brant, "The Fourth of March," *Everybody's Magazine,* vol. 12 (March 1905), 372.

19. Hunt, *Inaugural Addresses,* 3–7.

20. *Works of Fisher Ames,* vol. 1, ed. Seth Ames (Boston: Little, Brown, 1854), 34; Lawrence Shaw Mayo, *John Langdon of New Hampshire* (Concord, N.H.: Rumford Press, 1937), 229.

21. *Journal of Maclay,* 9.

22. *Works of Ames,* vol. 1, 34; Winfred E. A. Bernhard, *Fisher Ames: Federalist and Statesman, 1758–1808* (Chapel Hill: University of North Carolina Press, 1965), 80.

23. *Works of Ames,* I, 34.

24. Monaghan, *Notes on the Inaugural Journey,* 52.

25. Edna M. Colman, *Seventy-Five Years of White House Gossip From Washington to Lincoln* (New York: Doubleday, Page, & Co., 1925), 12; Louise Durbin, *Inaugural Cavalcade* (New York: Dodd, Mead, 1971), 9.

26. Washington to Edward Rutledge, May 5, 1789, *Writings of Washington,* vol. 30, 309.

27. *Journal of Maclay,* 10.

28. Durbin, *Inaugural Cavalcade,* 8; Freeman, *Washington,* 195.

2. Picking the Day

1. *Memoirs of John Quincy Adams,* vol. 5, ed. Charles Francis Adams (Philadelphia: J. B. Lippincott, 1874–1877), 317.
2. *Ibid.*
3. Harry Barnard, *Rutherford B. Hayes and His America* (Indianapolis: Bobbs Merrill, 1954), 401–2.
4. *Diary and Letters of Rutherford Birchard Hayes,* ed. Charles R. Williams, vol. 3 (Columbus: Ohio State Archaeological and Historical Society, 1924), 426.
5. Charles R. Williams, *The Life of Rutherford Birchard Hayes: Nineteenth President of the United States,* vol. 2 (Columbus: Ohio State Archaeological and Historical Society, 1928), 5n.
6. Edith Bolling Wilson, *My Memoir* (Indianapolis: Bobbs Merrill, 1939), 130; Glenn D. Kittler, *Hail to the Chief: The Inauguration Days of Our Presidents* (Philadelphia: Chilton Books, 1965), 157.
7. *Ibid.*
8. Edmund W. Starling, *Starling of the White House: The Story of the Man Whose Secret Service Detail Guarded Five Presidents* (Chicago: People's Book Club, 1946), 85.
9. *New York Times,* March 5, 1917, p. 1.
10. "As a New Term Begins . . . ," *Newsweek,* January 28, 1957, p. 23.
11. "Second Inaugural," *Time,* January 28, 1957, p. 17.
12. *Ibid.;* Ezra Taft Benson, *Cross Fire: The Eight Years with Eisenhower* (Garden City, N.Y.: Doubleday, 1962), 348.
13. *New York Times,* January 21, 1985, p. 15.

3. Getting to Washington

1. Robert V. Remini, *Andrew Jackson and the Course of American Freedom: 1822–1833* (New York: Harper & Row, 1981), 157, 158.
2. Frances Trollope, *Domestic Manners of the Americans* (London: Whittaker, Treacher, & Co., 1832), 122–24.
3. John F. Marszalek, *The Petticoat Affair: Manners, Mutiny, and Sex in Andrew Jackson's White House* (New York: Free Press, 1997), 52.
4. Remini, *Jackson,* 159.

5. "Inauguration of Gen. Henry Harrison Colorful Affair," *Washington Post,* March 4, 1933, p. 7.

6. Freeman Cleaves, *Old Tippecanoe: William Henry Harrison and His Times* (New York: Charles Scribner's Sons, 1939), 331.

7. *Washington Post,* March 4, 1933, p. 7

8. *Ibid.*

9. John S. Jenkins, *James Knox Polk* (New Orleans: Burnett & Bostwick, 1854), 144.

10. Anson and Fanny Nelson, *Memorials of Sarah Childress Polk* (New York: A. D. F. Randolph & Co., 1892), 81.

11. *Ibid.,* 81–82.

12. Jenkins, *Polk,* 144–45.

13. Laura Carter Holloway, *Ladies of the White House* (New York: United States Publishing Co., 1870), 492.

14. Brainerd Dyer, *Zachary Taylor* (Baton Rouge: Louisiana State University Press, 1946), 302.

15. Silas Bent McKinley and Silas Bent, *Old Rough and Ready: The Life and Times of Zachary Taylor* (New York: Vanguard Press, 1946), 222–23.

16. *Ibid.,* 222.

17. Holman Hamilton, *Zachary Taylor: Soldier in the White House* (Indianapolis: Bobbs-Merrill, 1951), 147.

18. McKinley and Bent, *Old Rough and Ready,* 224; Dyer, *Taylor,* 305.

19. Dyer, *Taylor,* 305.

20. Hamilton, *Taylor,* 147.

21. Joseph B. Bishop, *Presidential Nominations and Elections* (New York: C. Scribner's Sons, 1916), 205–6.

22. February 11, 1861, *The Collected Works of Abraham Lincoln,* vol. 4, ed. Roy P. Basler (New Brunswick, N.J.: Rutgers University Press, 1953), 190.

23. February 15, 1861, *Ibid.,* 193, 211.

24. T. C. Evans, *Of Many Men* (New York: The American News Co., 1888), 95.

25. February 16, 1861, *Collected Works of Lincoln,* vol. 4, 219.

26. February 22, 1861, *Ibid.,* 242.

27. Glenn D. Kittler, *Hail to the Chief!* (Philadelphia: Chilton Books, 1965), 79.

28. February 22, 1861, *Collected Works of Lincoln,* vol. 4, 240.

29. *Ibid.,* 245.

30. Kittler, *Hail to Chief,* 79.

31. John G. Nicolay and John Hay, "Lincoln's Inauguration," *Century Magazine,* vol. 35 (November 1887), 271.

32. *Ibid.,* 272; John G. Randall, *Lincoln the President: Springfield to Gettysburg,* vol. 1 (New York: Dodd, Mead, 1945), 290–91.

33. Malcolm R. Eiselen, "Preserve, Protect, and Defend," *North American Review,* December 1936, p. 344.

34. Frederick Seward, *Seward at Washington* (New York: Derby and Miller, 1891), 511.

35. *Washington Post,* March 2, 1897, p. 1.

36. *New York Times,* March 2, 1897, p. 1.

37. *Washington Post,* March 3, 1897, p. 1.

38. Arthur Walworth, *Woodrow Wilson,* vol. 1 (New York: Longman's Green, 1958), 260–61.

39. Arthur S. Link, *Wilson: The New Freedom* (Princeton: Princeton University Press, 1956), 56; Eleanor W. McAdoo, *The Woodrow Wilsons* (New York: Macmillan, 1937), 199.

40. Walworth, *Wilson,* 261; Ray Stannard Baker, *Woodrow Wilson: Life and Letters,* vol. 4 (Garden City, N.Y.: Doubleday, Doran and Company, 1931), 4.

41. Link, *Wilson,* 56; McAdoo, *The Woodrow Wilsons,* 199.

42. *New York Times,* March 4, 1913, pp. 1, 2.

43. "Reagan's Vision: Era of Renewal," *Newsweek,* January 26, 1981, p. 30.

44. Richard L. Berke, "The New Presidency: His Long Goodbye," *New York Times,* January 17, 1993.

45. Maureen Dowd and Frank Rich, "The Inauguration: The Boomers' Ball: A Lowly Advance Man Shows a Golden Touch," *New York Times,* January 18, 1993.

46. *Washington Post,* January 18, 1993, sec. A, p. 10; *New York Times,* January 18, 1993, sec. A, p. 7.

47. *New York Times,* January 18, 1993; *Washington Post,* January 18, 1993, sec. A, p. 10.

48. *Washington Post,* January 18, 1993, sec. A, p. 10; *New York Times,* January 18, 1993, sec. A, p. 8.

49. *Washington Post,* January 18, 1993, sec. A, p. 10.

50. *Ibid.,* sec. A, p. 11.

4. Coping with the Weather

1. Charles Warren, *Odd Byways in History* (Cambridge, Mass.: Harvard University Press, 1942), 92–101.

2. Harry J. Sievers, *Benjamin Harrison: Hoosier President,* vol. 3 of *Benjamin Harrison* (Indianapolis: Bobbs-Merrill, 1968), 35.

3. *Life,* February 1, 1937, 11.

4. Thomas Hudson McKee, *Presidential Inaugurations from George Washington, 1789, to Grover Cleveland, 1893* (Washington, D.C.: Statistical Publishing Co., 1893), 29.

5. *Niles' Weekly Register* (Baltimore), March 8, 1817, p. 2; James Schouler, *History of the United States under the Constitution,* vol. 3 (New York: Dodd, Mead, 1885), 1.

6. *Washington Post,* March 4, 1929, p. 16.

7. Thomas Hart Benton, *Thirty Years' View,* vol. 2 (New York: D. Appleton & Co., 1854–56), 114.

8. Nathan Sargent, *Public Men and Events,* vol. 2 (Philadelphia: J. B. Lippincott, 1875), 114.

9. W. H. Crook, *Memories of the White House: The Home Life of Our Presidents from Lincoln to Roosevelt* (Boston: Little, Brown, 1911), 169; Bascom N. Timmons, *Portrait of an American: Charles G. Dawes* (New York: Holt, 1953), 240; Ezra Taft Benson, *Cross Fire: The Eight Years with Eisenhower* (Garden City, N.Y.: Doubleday, 1962), 348.

10. *New York Times,* March 4, 1897, p. 1; *Ibid.,* March 5, 1897, p. 2.

11. James G. Blaine, *Twenty Years of Congress: From Lincoln to Garfield,* vol. 2 (Norwich, Conn.: Henry Bill, 1886), 537.

12. Mary Clemmer Ames, *Ten Years in Washington* (Hartford, Conn.: Hartford Publishing Co., 1882), 271.

13. *Ibid.,* 272.

14. Nicholas Murray Butler, *Across the Busy Years,* vol. 1 (New York: C. Scribner's Sons, 1939), 293.

15. Harry Thurston Peck, *Twenty Years of the Republic* (New York: Dodd, Mead & Co., 1926), 166; Julia B. Foraker, *I Would Live It Again* (New York: Harper & Bros., 1932), 135.

16. Champ Clark, *My Quarter Century of American Politics,* vol. 1 (New York: Harper & Bros., 1920), 229.

17. *New York Times,* March 5, 1893, p. 1.

18. *Ibid.,* pp. 2, 3.

19. *As I Knew Them: Memoirs of James E. Watson* (Indianapolis: Bobbs-Merrill, 1936), 44.

20. *New York Times,* March 3, 1909, p. 2; March 4, 1909, p. 1; March 5, 1909, p. 1.

21. *Ibid.,* March 5, 1909; Paolo E. Coletta, *The Presidency of William Howard Taft* (Lawrence: University of Kansas Press, 1973), 47.

22. Gene Smith, *The Shattered Dream: Herbert Hoover and the Great Depression* (New York: Morrow, 1970), 10.

23. *Life,* February 1, 1937, p. 11; *Time,* February 1, 1937, p. 9; *Newsweek,* January 30, 1937, p. 11.

24. *Time,* February 4, 1985, pp. 14–15.

25. *New York Times,* January 21, 1985, pp. 1, 15; *Newsweek,* January 28, 1985, p. 21.

26. *Time,* February 4, 1985, p. 14.

27. *Ibid.,* p. 16.

5. On the Eve of Their Inaugurations

1. James A. Farley, *Jim Farley's Story: The Roosevelt Years* (New York: Whittlesey House, 1948), 36.

2. Charles Francis Adams, *The Life of John Adams,* vol. 2 (Philadelphia: J. B. Lippincott, 1874), 221.

3. Samuel Flagg Bemis, *John Quincy Adams and the Union* (New York: Knopf, 1956), 51; *Memoirs of John Quincy Adams,* vol. 6 (Philadelphia: J. B. Lippincott, 1874–1877), 518; John Gabriel Hunt, ed., *The Inaugural Addresses of the Presidents* (New York: 1995), 83.

4. Freeman Cleaves, *Old Tippecanoe: William Henry Harrison and His*

Time (New York: Charles Scribner's Sons, 1939), 334; Glenn D. Kittler, *Hail to the Chief: The Inauguration Days of Our Presidents* (Philadelphia: Chilton Books, 1965), 48.

5. Roy F. Nichols, *Franklin Pierce: Young Hickory of the Granite Hills,* rev. ed. (Philadelphia: University of Pennsylvania Press, 1958), 234.

6. Adam Badeau, *Grant in Peace: From Appomattox to Mount McGregor* (Freeport, N.Y.: Books for Libraries Press, 1971), 159–60.

7. Irwin Hood Hoover, *Forty-Two Years in the White House* (Boston: Houghton Mifflin, 1934), 139, 143.

8. John D. Long, *The Life, Speeches, and Public Services of General James A. Garfield* (Portland, Maine: Stinson & Co., 1881), 336; Chelsea House Publishers, ed., *The Chief Executive: Inaugural Addresses of the Presidents of the United States,* with commentary by Fred L. Israel (New York: Crown, 1965), 157.

9. John M. Taylor, *Garfield of Ohio: The Available Man* (New York: Norton, 1970), 235.

10. Margaret Leech and Harry J. Brown, *The Garfield Orbit* (New York: Harper & Row, 1978), 222–23.

11. Allan Nevins, ed., *Letters of Grover Cleveland, 1850–1908* (Boston: Houghton Mifflin, 1933), 48, 51; Robert McElroy, *Grover Cleveland: The Man and the Statesman,* vol. 2 (New York: Harper & Bros., 1923), 7.

12. Nathan Miller, *Theodore Roosevelt: A Life* (New York: Morrow, 1922), 18; Francis Russell, *The Shadow of Blooming Grove: Warren G. Harding in His Times* (New York: McGraw-Hill, 1968), 436; *Newsweek,* January 27, 1969, p. 18.

13. *Newsweek,* January 22, 1973, p. 19.

14. *Newsweek,* January 26, 1981, p. 30; Lou Cannon, *Reagan* (New York: Putnam, 1982), 17.

15. Michael Deaver, *Behind the Scenes* (New York: Morrow, 1987), 98–99.

6. The Morning Procession

1. Louise Durbin, *Inaugural Cavalcade* (New York: Dodd, Mead, 1971), 12; Page Smith, *John Adams,* vol. 2 (Garden City, N.Y.: Doubleday, 1962), 916.

2. Margaret Bayard Smith, *The First Forty Years of American Society* (New York: C. Scribner's Sons, 1906), 410; Willard Sterne Randall, *Thomas Jefferson: A Life* (New York: Holt, 1993), 5.

3. Durbin, *Inaugural Cavalcade,* 46; *Washington Post,* March 3, 1901, p. 23.

4. Carl Sandburg, *Abraham Lincoln: The War Years,* vol. 1 (New York: Harcourt, Brace & Co., 1939), 121.

5. *Polk: The Diary of a President, 1845–1849,* ed. Allan Nevins (New York: Longmans, Green, 1952), 389.

6. Joseph B. Bishop, *Presidential Nominations and Elections* (New York: C. Scribner's Sons, 1916), 207; Philip Shriver Klein, *President James Buchanan: A Biography* (University Park: Pennsylvania State University Press, 1962), 402; Asa E. Martin, *After the White House* (State College, Pa.: Penns Valley Publishers, 1951), 235; James Buchanan, *Mr. Buchanan's Administration on the Eve of the Rebellion* (Freeport, N.Y.: Books for Libraries Press, 1970), 170.

7. Charles Winslow Elliott, *Winfield Scott: The Soldier and the Man* (New York: Macmillan, 1937), 695, 696.

8. *New York Times,* January 21, 1953, p. 30.

9. Festus P. Summers, ed., *The Cabinet Diary of William L. Wilson, 1896–1897* (Chapel Hill: University of North Carolina Press, 1957), 248.

10. Drew Pearson and Robert S. Allen, "Inaugurating the Presidents," *Redbook,* February 1937, pp. 79–80.

11. Irwin H. Hoover, *Forty-Two Years in the White House* (Boston: Houghton Mifflin, 1934), 227; Grace Tully, *F.D.R.: My Boss* (New York: Scribner, 1949), 64; James Roosevelt and Sidney Shalett, *Affectionately, F.D.R: A Son's Story of a Lonely Man* (New York: Harcourt Brace, 1959), 226–27.

12. Roosevelt, *Affectionately, F.D.R.,* 227; Tully, *F.D.R.,* 68; Ted Morgan, *F.D.R.: A Biography* (New York: Simon & Schuster, 1985), 374.

13. Robert H. Ferrell, *Harry S. Truman: A Life* (Columbia: University of Missouri Press, 1994), 379.

14. *Washington Post,* January 21, 1953, p. 2; Harry S. Truman, "The Day Ike Snubbed Me," *Look,* May 24, 1960, p. 26.

15. Robert H. Ferrell, *Off the Record: The Private Papers of Harry S. Truman, 1953–1971* (New York: Harper & Row, 1980), 287; Piers Brendon, *Ike: His Life and Times* (New York: Harper & Row, 1986), 237.

16. Ferrell, *Truman,* 379–80; *Look,* p. 26; Dwight D. Eisenhower, *Mandate for Change, 1953–1956: The White House Years* (Garden City, N.Y.: Doubleday, 1963), 101.

17. Ishbel Ross, *An American Family: The Tafts, 1678–1964* (Cleveland: World Publishing Co., 1964), 211.

18. Mrs. William Howard Taft, *Recollections of Full Years* (New York: Dodd, Mead, 1914), 331–32.

19. Edith Bolling Wilson, *My Memoir* (Indianapolis: Bobbs-Merrill, 1939), 130.

20. Jimmy Carter, *Keeping Faith: Memoirs of a President* (New York: Bantam Books, 1982), 17; James M. Naughton, "Crowd Delighted as Carters Shun Limousine and Walk to New Home," *New York Times,* January 21, 1977, p. 1, B3; *Newsweek,* January 31, 1977.

21. James M. Naughton, "Crowd Delighted," *New York Times,* January 21, 1977, p. 1; Haynes Johnson, "President Leads Walk up Avenue," *Washington Post,* January 21, 1977, p. A1; Cynthia Gorney, "Carters Stun Nearly All By Walking Parade Route," *Washington Post,* January 21, 1977, p. A16.

7. Installing the Vice President

1. John Ferling, *John Adams: A Life* (Knoxville: University of Tennessee Press, 1992), 299; *Journal of William Maclay,* ed. Edgar S. Maclay (New York: D. A. Appleton, 1890), 3; L. Edward Purcell, ed., *The Vice Presidents: A Biographical Dictionary* (New York: Facts on File, 1998), 5.

2. Letter to wife, December 19, 1793. *The Works of John Adams,* vol. 1 (Boston: Little, Brown, 1856), 460.

3. *The Writings of Thomas Jefferson,* vol. 11 (Washington: Jefferson Memorial Association, 1904), 381; George H. Haynes, *The Senate of the United States,* vol. 1 (Boston: Houghton Mifflin, 1938), 211–12; Diana Dixon Healy, *America's Vice-Presidents* (New York:

Atheneum, 1984), 151–52; Claude M. Fuess, *Calvin Coolidge: The Man from Vermont* (Boston: Little, Brown, 1940), 283; Carol Felsenthal, *Alice Roosevelt Longworth* (New York: Putnam, 1988), 170; Bascom N. Timmons, *Garner of Texas: A Personal History* (New York: Harper, 1948), 176; *Time,* January 29, 1965, p. 19.

4. Benjamin Perley Poore, *Perley's Reminiscences of Sixty Years in the National Metropolis,* vol. 1 (New York: W. A. Houghton, 1886), 427.

5. *Ibid.,* vol. 2, 159–60; Carl Sandburg, *Abraham Lincoln: The War Years,* vol. 4 (New York: Harcourt, Brace, 1939), 89.

6. Sandburg, *Lincoln,* 90.

7. *Ibid.,* 91.

8. *New York Times,* March 5, 1901, p. 2.

9. *Ibid.*; Francis E. Leupp, "The Inauguration," *Harper's Weekly,* March 9, 1901, p. 246.

10. *Literary Digest,* March 14, 1925, p. 9; *Time,* March 16, 1925, pp. 3, 5–6; *New York Times,* March 5, 1925, pp. 1, 4; Charles G. Dawes, *Notes as Vice President* (Boston: Little, Brown, 1935), 58–60; Bascom N. Timmons, *Portrait of an American: Charles G. Dawes* (New York: Holt, 1953), 243–46.

11. Frances Parkinson Keyes, "A Story of Friendly Flags," *Good Housekeeping,* May 1925, p. 171; *Time,* March 11, 1929, p. 11; *ibid.,* March 16, 1925, p. 6.

12. Lyon G. Tyler, *The Letters and Times of the Tylers,* vol. 2 (Richmond, Va.: Whittet & Shepperson, 1885), 361.

13. Thomas Hudson McKee, *Presidential Inaugurations from George Washington, 1789, to Grover Cleveland, 1893* (Washington, D.C.: Statistical Publishing Co., 1893), 95; Louise Durbin, *Inaugural Cavalcade* (New York: Dodd, Mead, 1971), 70.

14. McKee, *Inaugurations,* 122–23.

15. *Ibid.,* 145–47; George Frederick Howe, *Chester A. Arthur: A Quarter Century of Machine Politics* (New York: Dodd, Mead, 1934), 150–57.

16. Harry Thurston Peck, *Twenty Years of the Republic* (New York: Dodd, Mead, 1907), 666–68.

17. Robert Sobel, *Coolidge: An American Enigma* (Washington, D.C.: Regnery Pub., 1998), 232.

18. Robert J. Donovan, *Conflict and Crisis: The Presidency of Harry S. Tru-*

man, 1945–1948 (New York: Norton, 1977), 8–9; Alfred Steinberg, *The Man from Missouri: The Life and Times of Harry S. Truman* (New York: Putnam, 1962), 232–33.

19. Robert H. Ferrell, *Harry S. Truman: A Life* (Columbia: University of Missouri Press, 1994), 294.
20. Lyndon Baines Johnson, *The Vantage Point: Perspectives of the Presidency, 1908–1973* (New York: Holt, Rinehart & Winston, 1971), 8–14.
21. *Ibid.,* 17; "Achilles in the White House," *Wilson Quarterly,* Spring 2000, p. 89.
22. Gerald R. Ford, *A Time to Heal* (New York: Harper & Row, 1979), 40.
23. *Ibid.,* 41.

8. Swearing in the President

1. Richard Harding Davis, *A Year from a Reporter's Note-Book* (New York: Harper & Bros., 1898), 155–56, 160.
2. *Washington Post,* March 5, 1917, p. 8.
3. Alberta Powell Graham and Muriel Fuller, "Inaugural 'Firsts,'" *American Mercury,* February 1925, p. 10; Glyndon G. Van Deusen, *The Life of Henry Clay* (Boston: Little, Brown, 1937), 116; *The Papers of Henry Clay,* ed. James F. Hopkins, vol. 2 (Lexington: University of Kentucky Press, 1959–1992), 320; Harry Ammon, *James Monroe: The Quest for National Identity* (New York: McGraw-Hill, 1971), 367–68.
4. *Washington Post,* January 21, 1981, pp. A13, B4.
5. William Allen White, *A Puritan in Babylon: The Story of Calvin Coolidge* (New York: Macmillan, 1938), 314; Louise Durbin, *Inaugural Cavalcade* (New York: Dodd, Mead, 1971), 83, 155; Carl Sandburg, *Abraham Lincoln: The War Years,* vol. 1 (New York: Harcourt, Brace & Co., 1939), 122.
6. *New York Times,* March 5, 1905, p. 2.
7. F. Raymond Daniell, "Crowd Undaunted by Street Floods," *New York Times,* January 21, 1937, pp. 1, 15.
8. Samuel I. Rosenman, *Working with Roosevelt* (New York: Harper, 1952), 144; Merlo J. Pusey, *Charles Evans Hughes,* vol. 2 (New York: Macmillan, 1951), 786.

9. *Time,* January 27, 1941, p. 11.

10. Ishbel Ross, *The General's Wife: The Life of Mrs. Ulysses S. Grant* (New York: Dodd, Mead, 1959), 204; *Washington Post,* March 5, 1921, p. 3.

11. Nancy Reagan, *My Turn* (New York: Random House, 1989), 233.

12. *New York Times,* January 21, 1997, p. A10.

13. *New York Times,* January 21, 1989, p. A1.

14. Samuel Shaffer, *On and Off the Floor: Thirty Years as a Correspondent on Capitol Hill* (New York: Newsweek Books, 1980), 125; U. E. Baughman, *Secret Service Chief* (New York: Harper, 1962), 4.

15. Baughman, *Secret Service Chief,* 3–4; *Newsweek,* January 30, 1961, p. 18; Shaffer, *On and Off the Floor,* 125.

16. *Newsweek,* January 30, 1961, p. 18; *Time,* January 27, 1961, p. 12.

17. *Newsweek,* January 30, 1961, p. 18.

9. The Inaugural Addresses

1. John Gabriel Hunt, ed., *The Inaugural Addresses of the Presidents* (New York: Gramercy Books, 1995), 9–10.

2. Allan L. Benson, *Daniel Webster* (New York: Cosmopolitan Book Corp., 1929), 257–58; Peter Harvey, *Reminiscences and Anecdotes of Daniel Webster* (Boston, 1877), 161–63.

3. *The Diary of James A. Garfield,* eds. Harry James Brown and Frederick D. Williams, vol. 4 (East Lansing: Michigan State University, 1967–1981), 511, 529, 542–43, 554.

4. Benjamin Perley Poore, *Perley's Reminiscences,* vol. 2 (New York: W. A. Houghton, 1886), 65–67.

5. Frederick Seward, *Seward at Washington* (New York, 1891), 512–13.

6. Milton Lomask, *"I Do Solemnly Swear...": The Story of Presidential Inaugurations* (New York: Ariel Books, 1966), 92–93.

7. L. A. Gobright, *Recollection of Men and Things at Washington* (Philadelphia: Claxton, Remson, & Haffelfinger, 1869), 289.

8. *Memoirs of John Quincy Adams,* vol. 1, ed. Charles Francis Adams (Philadelphia: J. B. Lippincott, 1874), 373; Josephine Seaton, *William Winston Seaton of the "National Intelligencer"* (Boston: J. R. Osgood & Co., 1871), 99.

9. *New York Times,* March 5, 1909, p. 2.

10. *Ibid.,* March 6, 1917, p. 3.

11. Claude M. Fuess, *Calvin Coolidge: The Man from Vermont* (Boston: Little, Brown, 1940), 283.

12. *Newsweek,* January 26, 1981, p. 30.

13. Hunt, *Inaugural Addresses of the Presidents,* 70, 106, 143, 179.

14. Halford Ryan, ed., *The Inaugural Addresses of Twentieth-Century American Presidents* (Westport, Conn.: Praeger, 1993), 53.

15. Hunt, *Inaugural Addresses of the Presidents,* 98.

16. *Ibid.,* 490.

17. *Ibid.,* 35, 320.

18. *Ibid.,* 133, 182, 197.

19. Carl Sandburg, *Abraham Lincoln: The War Years,* vol. 1 (New York: Harcourt, Brace, 1939), 86.

20. Hunt, *Inaugural Addresses of the Presidents,* 199–201.

21. Paul Berman, reviewing Alfred Kazin, *God and the American Writer, New York Times Book Review,* October 12, 1997, p. 7.

22. Noah Brooks, *Washington in Lincoln's Time,* ed. Herbert Mitgang (New York: Rinehart, 1958), 213.

23. *Collected Works of Abraham Lincoln,* vol. 8, ed. Roy P. Basler (New Brunswick, N.J.: Rutgers University Press, 1953–1955), 356.

24. *New York Times,* March 6, 1865, p. 4; J. G. Randall and Richard Current, *Lincoln the President: Last Full Measure* (New York: 1955), 342–43.

25. Sandburg, *Lincoln,* 96.

10. Receptions

1. Margaret Bayard Smith, *Forty Years of Washington Society,* ed. Gaillard Hunt (London: T. Fisher Unwin, 1906), 294.

2. *Ibid.,* 295–96; James Parton, *Life of Andrew Jackson,* vol. 3 (New York: Mason Bros., 1861), 170–71; Bessie Rowland James, *Anne Royall's USA* (New Brunswick, N.J.: Rutgers University Press, 1972), 249.

3. Parton, *Jackson,* 170; *Washington City Chronicle,* quoted in *New York Times,* January 22, 1993, p. A8.

4. John Spencer Bassett, *The Life of Andrew Jackson* (New York: Macmillan, 1916), 424–25; *National Intelligencer,* March 6, 1829, quoted in *New York Times,* January 22, 1993, A8; Smith, *Forty Years,* 296.

5. Ben Perley Poore, *Perley's Reminiscences,* vol. 1 (New York: W. A. Houghton, 1885), 201; Thomas Hudson McKee, *Presidential Inaugurations from George Washington to Grover Cleveland* (New York: Statistical Publishing Co., 1893), 105.

6. Carl Sandburg, *Abraham Lincoln: The War Years,* vol. 4 (New York: Harcourt, Brace, 1939), 97.

7. Walt Whitman, *Specimen Days, Democratic Vistas, and Other Prose,* ed. Louise Pound (Garden City, N.Y.: Doubleday, Doran, 1935), 78–79; Sandburg, *Lincoln,* vol. 4, 98.

8. Frederick Douglass, *Life and Times of Frederick Douglass* (New York: Collier Books, 1962), 359, 365–66.

9. *Ibid.,* 366.

10. *Ibid.*

11. Mary Clemmer Ames, *Ten Years in Washington* (Hartford, Conn.: A. D. Worthington, 1880), 278–79.

12. Louise Durbin, *Inaugural Cavalcade* (New York: Dodd, Mead, 1971), 97.

13. Ames, *Ten Years in Washington,* 279–80.

14. Ona Griffin Jeffries, *In and Out of the White House: From Washington to the Eisenhowers* (New York: W. Funk, 1960), 193–94.

15. Lillian Rogers Parks, *My Thirty Years Backstairs at the White House* (New York: Fleet Publishing Corporation, 1961), 238.

16. Bess Furman, *Washington By-line: The Personal History of a Newspaperwoman* (New York: A. A. Knopf, 1949), 151.

17. James Roosevelt and Sidney Shalett, *Affectionately, F.D.R.* (New York: Harcourt, Brace, 1959), 317–18; James Roosevelt, *My Parents: A Differing View* (Chicago: Playboy Press, 1976), 281–83.

18. Glenn D. Kittler, *Hail to the Chief* (Philadelphia: Chilton, 1965), 194.

19. *Washington Post,* January 21, 1993, p. A28.

20. *Fort Worth Star-Telegram,* January 21, 1997, p. 11.

11. The Inaugural Parades

1. Don Oberdorfer, "No Wonder Madison Said, 'I'd Rather Be in Bed,'" *New York Times Magazine,* January 17, 1965, p. 33.

2. Mary Clemmer Ames, *Ten Years in Washington* (Hartford, Conn.: A. D. Worthington, 1880), 277.

3. Harry Loomis Nelson, *Harper's Weekly,* March 13, 1897, p. 259; *Washington Post,* March 5, 1897, p. 6.

4. Harry J. Sievers, *Benjamin Harrison: Hoosier President* (Indianapolis: Bobbs-Merrill, 1968), 37; Alice Roosevelt Longworth, *Crowded Hours: Reminiscences of Alice Roosevelt Longworth* (New York: C. Scribner's Sons, 1933), 66; Margaret Truman, *Souvenir* (New York: McGraw-Hill, 1956), 255; *New York Times,* January 21, 1953, p. 21.

5. *Washington Post,* January 19, 1961, p. B2.

6. Peter Lyon, *Eisenhower: Portrait of a Hero* (Boston: Little, Brown, 1974), 477; *New York Times,* January 21, 1953, p. 30.

7. *New York Times,* March 4, 1905, p. 2, March 4, 1913, p. 2, January 9, 1997, p. A1.

8. Dorothy Brandon, *Mamie Doud Eisenhower: A Portrait of a First Lady* (New York: Scribner, 1954), 3.

9. Dwight D. Eisenhower, *Mandate for Change, 1953–1956: The White House Years* (Garden City, N.Y.: Doubleday, 1963), 102.

10. Margaret Truman, *Bess W. Truman* (New York: Macmillan, 1986), 309; *Life,* January 31, 1949, p. 22.

11. Richard Nixon, *RN: The Memoirs of Richard Nixon* (New York: Grosset & Dunlap, 1978), 366; Julie Eisenhower, *Pat Nixon: The Untold Story* (New York: Simon & Schuster, 1986), 252.

12. *Washington Post,* January 21, 1969, p. A10, B13; *New York Times,* January 21, 1969, p. 24.

13. *Time,* January 24, 1969, p. 10.

14. *New York Times,* March 5, 1925, p. 3; Irwin Hood Hoover, *Forty-Two Years in the White House* (Boston: Houghton Mifflin, 1934), 139, 141–42, 143; William Allen White, *A Puritan in Babylon: The Story of Calvin Coolidge* (New York: Macmillan, 1938), 316.

15. Nathan Miller, *Theodore Roosevelt: A Life* (New York: Morrow, 1992), 20–21.

16. *Washington Post,* March 5, 1905, p. 2.

17. *New York Times,* March 3, 1905, p. 1; Miller, *Roosevelt,* 21.

18. *Washington Post,* March 5, 1905, p. 2.

19. *New York Times,* March 5, 1905, p. 2; *Washington Post,* March 5, 1905, p. 1.

20. *New York Times,* March 5, 1905, p. 2.

21. Mary Van Rensselaer Thayer, *Jacqueline Kennedy: The White House Years* (Boston: Little, Brown, 1971), 83–84.

22. Michael Deaver, *Behind the Scenes* (New York: Morrow, 1987), 154.

23. Maureen Dowd and Frank Rich, "Picking Up the Perks of Presidential Power," *New York Times,* January 21, 1993, p. A7.

24. Peter Finn and Victoria Benning, "Paraders, Viewers Bask in Journey Down the Avenue," *Washington Post,* January 21, 1997, pp. A13, A18; Dan Barry, "Inaugural Parade Mixes Patriotism and Silliness," *New York Times,* January 19, 1997, pp. 12–13.

25. Barry, "Inaugural Parade," *New York Times,* January 21, 1997, p. 13.

12. The Inaugural Balls

1. Francis E. Leupp, "The Inauguration," *Harper's Weekly,* March 9, 1901, 246–47.

2. *Washington Post,* March 5, 1897, p. 1.

3. Curt Smith, "Waltzing into the White House," *Saturday Evening Post,* January–February 1981, p. 6.

4. *Harper's Weekly,* March 6, 1909, p. 29.

5. Henry J. Kintz, *The Inauguration of Grover Cleveland* (Philadelphia: W. F. Fell & Co., Printers, 1885), 74.

6. Pete Axthelm, "A Voice of the South," *Newsweek,* January 31, 1977, p. 25.

7. Irving Brant, *James Madison: The President, 1809–1812* (Indianapolis: Bobbs-Merrill, 1956), 13; Margaret Bayard Smith, *Forty Years of American Society,* ed. Gaillard Hunt (London: T. Fisher Unwin, 1906), 62.

8. Smith, *Forty Years,* 63.

9. *Ibid.,* 62.

10. *Ibid.*

11. *Memoirs of John Quincy Adams,* ed. Charles Francis Adams, vol. 1 (Philadelphia: J. B. Lippincott, 1874–77), 544.

12. Irving Brant, *James Madison: Commander in Chief, 1812–1836* (Indianapolis: Bobbs-Merrill, 1961), 150.

13. L. A. Gobright, *Recollection of Men and Things at Washington* (Philadelphia: Claxton, Remson, & Haffelfinger, 1869), 27; Edna M.

Colman, *Seventy-Five Years of White House Gossip* (New York: Doubleday, Page, & Co., 1925), 269.

14. Carl S. Anthony, *First Ladies: The Saga of the Presidents' Wives and Their Power, 1789–1961* (New York: W. Morrow, 1990), 310.

15. Anthony, *First Ladies,* 332.

16. *Newsweek,* January 27, 1969, p. 18; *Time,* January 17, 1969, p. 14, and January 29, 1973, p. 16; *Time,* January 31, 1977, p. 17; *Ibid.,* February 4, 1985, p. 16.

17. Holman Hamilton, *Zachary Taylor: Soldier in the White House* (Indianapolis: Bobbs-Merrill, 1951), 159–61; Esther Singleton, *The Story of the White House,* vol. 2 (New York: McClure Co., 1907), 4–6.

18. Philip S. Klein, *President James Buchanan* (University Park: Pennsylvania State University Press, 1962), 272; *New York Times,* March 7, 1857, p. 1; Louise Durbin, *Inaugural Cavalcade* (New York: Dodd, Mead, 1971), 77–79.

19. *Washington Post,* March 4, 1933, p. 15; Ben Perley Poore, *Perley's Reminiscences,* vol. 2 (New York: W. A. Houghton, 1885), 162–63; Noah Brooks, *Washington in Lincoln's Time,* ed. Herbert Mitgang (New York: Rinehart, 1958), 215.

20. Margaret Truman, *Souvenir* (New York: McGraw-Hill, 1956), 255; *New Yorker,* February 2, 1957, p. 27.

21. *Washington Post,* January 21, 1961, pp. B9, B12; *Time,* January 27, 1961, p. 12; Paul B. Fay, *The Pleasure of His Company* (New York: Harper & Row, 1966), 94; Thomas C. Reeves, *A Question of Character: A Life of John F. Kennedy* (New York: Free Press, 1991), 236.

22. *New York Times,* January 21, 1965, p. 18; *Time,* January 29, 1965, p. 20.

23. *Newsweek,* February 1, 1965, p. 17; *Time,* January 29, 1965, p. 20.

24. *New York Times,* January 21, 1969, pp. 25, 26; *Washington Post,* January 21, 1969, p. D1.

25. *Washington Post,* January 21, 1981, p. A33; *Newsweek,* February 2, 1981, p. 55.

26. *Washington Post,* January 21, 1981, p. E1.

27. *Newsweek,* January 29, 1989, p. 27; *New York Times,* January 21, 1989, pp. 6, 8.

28. *Washington Post,* January 21, 1993, p. D1.
29. *Ibid.*

13. 2001—Into the Twenty-First Century

1. Mike Peters, editorial cartoonist for the *Dayton* (Ohio) *Daily News,* reprinted in the *Fort Worth Star-Telegram,* December 20, 2000.
2. Stanley Wainapel, "Inaugural Menu," *New York Times,* November 26, 2000.
3. Marian Burros, "Pity the Vote Counters? What about the Caterers?" *New York Times,* January 17, 2001. Carolyn Barta and Victoria Loe Hicks, "Standing Room Only," *Dallas Morning News,* January 18, 2001.
4. Bud Kennedy, "Bush Inaugural," *Fort Worth Star-Telegram.* January 11, 2001. Maria Recio, "Fort Worth Zoo to Exhibit Texas Animals at Inaugural Ball," *Ibid.*
5. Bud Kennedy, "Midland Sends Bush Off to Washington," *Fort Worth Star-Telegram,* January 18, 2001.
6. Melinda Henneberger, "Texans Coming to Town," *New York Times,* January 19, 2001.
7. Olivia Barker, "Grand Old Party Parties Down," *USA Today,* January 22, 2001.

14. Inaugural Vignettes

1. Joseph B. Bishop, *Presidential Nominations and Elections* (New York: C. Scribner's Sons, 1916), 178–79.
2. Dumas Malone, *Jefferson and His Time,* vol. 4 (Boston: Little, Brown, 1948–1981), 4, 16.
3. Jean Edward Smith, *John Marshall: Definer of a Nation* (New York: H. Holt, 1996), 17–19.
4. Bishop, *Presidential Nominations,* 192.
5. Louise Durbin, *Inaugural Cavalcade* (New York: Dodd, Mead, 1971), 34.
6. Holman Hamilton, *Zachary Taylor: Soldier in the White House* (Indianapolis: Bobbs-Merrill, 1951), 149–50.
7. Philip S. Klein, *President James Buchanan* (University Park: Pennsylvania State University, 1962), 268–69.

8. Ona Griffin Jeffries, *In and Out of the White House: From Washington to the Eisenhowers* (New York: W. Funk, 1960), 147; Klein, *Buchanan*, 272.

9. Edna M. Colman, *Seventy-Five Years of White House Gossip* (Garden City, N.Y.: Doubleday, Page, & Co., 1925), 269–70.

10. Carl Sandburg, *Abraham Lincoln: The War Years,* vol. 1 (New York: Harcourt, Brace, & Co., 1939), 139.

11. *New York Times,* March 4, 1905, p. 2.

12. William H. Crook, *Memories of the White House* (Boston: Little, Brown, 1911), 197–98.

13. *Washington Post,* March 3, 1901, p. 20.

14. Allan Nevins, *Grover Cleveland: A Study in Courage* (New York: Dodd, Mead, 1932), 510; Robert McElroy, *Grover Cleveland,* vol. 2 (New York: Harper & Bros., 1923), 8.

15. O. O. Stealey, *Twenty Years in the Press Gallery* (New York: Publishers Printing Company, 1906), 253–54.

16. Festus P. Summers, ed., *Cabinet Diary of William L. Wilson, 1896–1897* (Chapel Hill: University of North Carolina Press, 1957), 247–48.

17. *Harper's Weekly,* March 9, 1901, p. 254.

18. Henry F. Pringle, *The Life and Times of William Howard Taft,* vol. 1 (New York: Farrar & Rinehart, 1939), 392–93; Judith Icke Anderson, *William Howard Taft: An Intimate History* (New York: Norton, 1981), 118–19; Carol Felsenthal, *Alice Roosevelt Longworth* (New York: Putnam, 1988), 119.

19. *New York Times,* March 4, 1913, p. 2.

20. *Washington Post,* March 5, 1913, pp. 2, 5.

21. Ray Stannard Baker, *Woodrow Wilson: Life and Letters,* vol. 4 (Garden City, N.Y.: Doubleday, 1931), 9–10.

22. *Washington Post,* March 5, 1913, p. 2.

23. William Irwin Hoover, *Forty-Two Years in the White House* (New York: Houghton Mifflin, 1934), 55–57.

24. *Washington Post,* March 5, 1917, p. 1, 9; *New York Times,* March 5, 1917, p. 3.

25. Edith Bolling Wilson, *My Memoir* (Indianapolis: Bobbs-Merrill, 1939), 316.

26. William Allen White, *A Puritan in Babylon: The Story of Calvin Coolidge* (New York: Macmillan, 1938), 313–14.

27. *New York Times,* March 5, 1929, p. 3.

28. *Ibid.,* March 5, 1929, p. 8.

29. Bernard Asbell, *The F.D.R. Memoirs* (Garden City, N.Y.: Doubleday, 1973), 36; Joseph P. Lash, *Eleanor and Franklin* (New York: Norton, 1971), 359; Milton Lomask, *"I Do Solemnly Swear...": The Story of Presidential Inaugurations* (New York: Ariel Books, 1966), 146.

30. Lillian Rogers Parks, *My Thirty Years Backstairs at the White House* (New York: Fleet Publishing Corporation, 1961), 238; James A. Farley, *Jim Farley's Story: The Roosevelt Years* (New York: Whittlesey House, 1948), 37; Hoover, *Forty-Two Years in White House,* 225–27; Lash, *Eleanor and Franklin,* 356.

31. Ted Morgan, *FDR: A Biography* (New York: Simon & Schuster, 1995), 376.

32. *Time,* January 25, 1937, p. 9; *Literary Digest,* January 23, 1937, p. 4; Paul F. Boller, Jr., *Presidential Wives* (New York: Oxford University Press, 1988), 350.

33. *Newsweek,* January 30, 1937, p. 14.

34. Samuel I. Rosenman, *Working with Roosevelt* (New York: Harper, 1952), 270–71.

35. *Washington Post,* January 21, 1941, p. 4.

36. Hugh Gallagher, *FDR's Splendid Deception* (New York: Dodd, Mead, 1985), 200; Rosenman, *Working with Roosevelt,* 517.

37. Alben Barkley, *That Reminds Me* (Garden City, N.Y.: Doubleday, 1954), 205; *Newsweek,* January 24, 1949, p. 15; *Time,* January 24, 1949, p. 13.

38. Margaret Truman, *Bess W. Truman* (New York: Macmillan, 1986), 339–40; Eric Goldman, *The Crucial Decade—and After: America, 1945–1960* (New York: Vintage Books, 1960), 92; "The March of the Little Fellows," *Newsweek,* January 31, 1949, p. 15.

39. *Washington Post,* January 20, 1953, p. 39.

40. E. Frederick Morrow, *Black Man in the White House* (New York: Coward-McCann, 1963), 118–21.

41. Anthony Lewis, *New York Times,* January 20, 1977, p. 37; *New York Times,* January 21, 1961, p. 11; *Life,* January 27, 1961, p. 29; Carl Sferazza Anthony, "First Ladies' Day of Destiny," *Washington Post,* January 20, 1985, p. B1.

42. Boller, *Presidential Wives,* 374.

43. Don Oberdorfer, "No Wonder Madison Said...," *New York Times Magazine,* January 17, 1965, p. 38.

44. *Newsweek,* February 1, 1965, p. 12; *Time,* January 29, 1965, p. 10.

45. Lyndon Baines Johnson, *The Vantage Point: Perspectives of the Presidency, 1963–1969* (New York: Holt, Rinehart, & Winston, 1971), 564.

46. *Christian Century,* February 7, 1973, p. 144; Tom Braden, "Why Lincoln's Second Inaugural Might Embarrass Mr. Nixon," *Washington Post,* January 20, 1973, p. A15.

47. *Washington Post,* January 20, 1997, pp. A1, C1, C4.

INDEX